The Mystical Gesture:
Essays on Medieval and Early Modern Spiritual Culture in Honor of Mary E. Giles

The Mystical Gesture

Essays on Medieval and Early Modern Spiritual Culture in Honor of Mary E. Giles

Edited by

ROBERT BOENIG

LONDON AND NEW YORK

First published 2000 by Ashgate Publishing

Reissued 2018 by Routledge
2 Park Square, Milton Park, Abingdon, Oxon OX14 4RN
711 Third Avenue, New York, NY 10017, USA

Routledge is an imprint of the Taylor & Francis Group, an informa business

Copyright © Robert Boenig, 2000

The editor has asserted his right under the Copyright, Designs and Patents Act, 1988, to be identified as the editor of this work.

All rights reserved. No part of this book may be reprinted or reproduced or utilised in any form or by any electronic, mechanical, or other means, now known or hereafter invented, including photocopying and recording, or in any information storage or retrieval system, without permission in writing from the publishers.

Notice:
Product or corporate names may be trademarks or registered trademarks, and are used only for identification and explanation without intent to infringe.

Publisher's Note
The publisher has gone to great lengths to ensure the quality of this reprint but points out that some imperfections in the original copies may be apparent.

Disclaimer
The publisher has made every effort to trace copyright holders and welcomes correspondence from those they have been unable to contact.

A Library of Congress record exists under LC control number: 99054068

ISBN 13: 978-1-138-70394-0 (hbk)
ISBN 13: 978-1-138-70392-6 (pbk)
ISBN 13: 978-1-315-20293-8 (ebk)

Contents

Mary E. Giles: Publications	vii
Introduction *Robert Boenig*	1
Tribute to Mary E. Giles *Kathryn Hohlwein*	7
1 Mechthild von Magdeburg, the Devil, and Antichrist *Frank Tobin*	9
2 The Spirituality of *Piers Plowman* *M. Clemente Davlin, O.P.*	23
3 Doubled Truth: Skeptical Fideism, Pseudo-Dionysius, and *The Second Shepherds' Play* *Robert Boenig*	41
4 Ecstasy, Prophecy, and Reform: Catherine of Siena as a Model for Holy Women of Sixteenth-Century Spain *Gillian T. W. Ahlgren*	53
5 Bernadino de Laredo's *Treatise on the Mysteries of St. Joseph* and the Evangelization of Mexico *Joseph F. Chorpenning*	67
6 What's in a Name: On Teresa of Ávila's *Book* *Elizabeth Rhodes*	79
7 Teresa and Her Sisters *Jane Ackerman*	107

CONTENTS

8 Demonizing Ecstasy: Alonso de la Fuente and the *Alumbrados* of
     Extremadura   141
            Alison Weber

9 The Beautiful Dove, the Body Divine: Luisa de Carvajal y Mendoza's
     Mystical Poetics   159
            Michael Bradburn-Ruster

10 Cecilia de Nacimiento: Mystic in the Tradition of John of the Cross   169
            Evelyn Toft

11 Inside My Body Is the Body of God: Margaret Mary Alacoque
     and the Tradition of Embodied Mysticism   185
            Wendy M. Wright

12 Making Use of the Holy Office: Exploring the Contexts and
     Concepts of Sor Juana's References to the Inquisition in the
     Respuesta a Sor Filotea   193
            Amanda Powell

List of Contributors   217

Index   219

Mary E. Giles: Publications

Books:

Translation with introduction. *Third Spiritual Alphabet* by Francisco de Osuna. New York: Paulist Press, 1981.
Co-editor. *Enter the Heart of the Fire: A Collection of Mystical Poems.* Sacramento: Studia Mystica, 1981.
The Feminist Mystic. New York: Crossroad Publishing Company, 1982.
When Each Life Shines: Voices of Women's Ministry. Denville, New Jersey: Dimension Books, 1986.
The Poetics of Love: Meditations with John of the Cross. New York: Peter Lang Publishing, 1986.
The Book of Prayer of Sor María of Santo Domingo: A Study and Translation. Albany, New York: State University of New York Press, 1990.
Translator and editor. *Prison of Women: Testimonies of War and Resistance in Spain, 1931-1975.* Albany, New York: State University of New York Press, 1998.
Editor. *Women in the Inquisition: Spain and the New World.* Baltimore: The Johns Hopkins University Press, 1999.

Articles:

"Impressionist Techniques in Descriptions by Emilia Pardo Bazán," *Hispanic Review* 30 (1962): 304-16.
"Pardo Bazán's Two Styles," *Hispania* 48 (1965): 456-62.
"Descriptive Conventions in Pereda, Pardo Bazán, and Palacio Valdés," *Hispania* 50 (1968): 285-91.
"Color Adjectives in Pardo Bazán's Novels," *Romance Notes* 10 (1968): 1-5.
"Symbolic Imagery in *La sirena negra*," *Papers on Language and Literature* 4 (1968): 182-91.
"Juan Goytisolo's *Juegos de manos*: An Archetypal Interpretation," *Hispania* 55 (1973): 1021-9.

"Poetic Expressiveness and Mystical Consciousness: A Reading of St. John's 'Dark Night of the Soul'," *Studia Mystica* 2 (1979): 3-15.
"Feminism and the Feminine in Emilia Pardo Bazán's Novels," *Hispania* 63 (1980): 356-67.
"Meditations on Teresa," *Studia Mystica* 5 (1982): 3-24.
"Beyond Frenzy," *Religion and Intellectual Life* 4 (1986): 95-108.
"From Careerism to Caritas: Toward a Spiritual Vision of the University," *Studies in Formative Spirituality* 9 (1988): 283-97.
"The Ecstatic Scholar," *Studia Mystica* 12 (1989): 178-81.
"Christian Scholarship on the Edge: Marginality and Creativity," *Studia Mystica* 13 (1990): 4-20.
"Thoughts in Time of War," *Spiritual Life* 37 (1991): 178-81.
"Reflections on Suffering in a Mystical-Feminist Key," *Journal of Spiritual Formation* 15 (1994): 137-46.

Chapters in Books:

"Prayer and Spirituality: The Language of Love." Pp. 240-56 in Theresa King, ed. *The Spiral Path: Explorations in Women's Spirituality*. Saint Paul, Minnesota: Yes International Publishers, 1992.
"Holy Theatre/ Ecstatic Theatre." Pp. 117-28 in Anne Clark Bartlett, Thomas H. Bestul, Janet Goebel, and William F. Pollard, eds *Vox Mystica: Essays on Medieval Mysticism*. Woodbridge, Suffolk: D. S. Brewer, 1995.
"The Discourse of Ecstasy: Late Medieval Spanish Women and their Texts." Pp. 306-30 in Jane Chance, ed. *Gender and Text in the Later Middle Ages*. Gainesville, Florida: University Press of Florida, 1996.
"Creativity and Feminism: Clare and Teresa of Avila." Pp. 115-21 in Ingrid Peterson, O.S.F., ed. *Clare of Assisi: A Medieval and Modern Woman*. Clare Centenary Series, ed. Mary Francis Hone, O.S.C., vol. 8. St. Bonaventure, New York: St. Bonaventure University, The Franciscan Institute, 1996.
"Spanish Visionary Women and the Paradox of Performance." Pp. 273-97 in Mary A. Suydam and Joanna E. Zeigler, eds *Performance and Transformation: New Approaches to Late Medieval Spirituality*. New York: St. Martin's Press, 1999.

Entries in Collections:

Entries on Teresa of Avila, John of the Cross, and Francisco de Osuna in Frank N. Magill and Ian P. McGreal, eds *Classics of Christian Spirituality*. San Francisco: Harper and Row Publishers, 1988.

Entries on ten poets in *Biographical Dictionary of Contemporary Catholic American Writing*. New York: Greenwood Press, 1989.

Entries on Emilia Pardo Bazán, Rosalía de Castro, and Dolores Medio in Katharina M. Wilson, ed. *An Encyclopedia of Continental Women Writers*. New York: Garland Publishing, 1991.

Entries on Dante, Teresa of Avila, John of the Cross, Maimonides, Erasmus, Ortega y Gasset, Unamuno, and Teilhard de Chardin in Ian P. McGreal, ed. *Great Thinkers of the World*. San Francisco: Harper and Row Publishers, 1992.

Entries on Emilia Pardo Bazán and John of the Cross in Laura Standley Berger, ed. *Reference Guide to World Literature*. Detroit: St. James Press, 1995.

Entries on Teresa of Avila and Emilia Pardo Bazán in Mary R. Reichardt, ed. *Catholic Women Writers: A Bio-Bibliographical Sourcebook*. New York: Greenwood Press, forthcoming.

Reviews:

Dozens of reviews in: *Hispanic Review, Romance Philology, Hispania, Studia Mystica, Christianity and Literature, Mystics Quarterly, Theological Studies, Cross Currents, Medieval Feminist Newsletter*, and *The Women's Review of Books*.

Introduction

Robert Boenig

The articles of *The Mystical Gesture: Essays on Medieval and Early Modern Spiritual Culture* are assembled in honor of Mary E. Giles, who has retired after a distinguished teaching career at California State University, Sacramento and in anticipation of her continued ground-breaking scholarship in the areas of sixteenth-century Spanish spiritual culture and the feminist aspects of mysticism. Giles is the Founding Editor of *Studia Mystica*, a journal devoted to the interdisciplinary connections among mysticism and the arts. The contributors to this volume are her friends, colleagues, and former students (both official and unofficial).

The topics range chronologically from the late thirteenth to late seventeenth centuries and geographically from Germany, England, Italy, France, Spain, and New Spain (Mexico), though the volume's center of gravity is the spiritual culture of sixteenth-century Spain—as is fitting, given the profile of Giles's scholarly career. But the common concerns of each are the exploration of spiritual culture—how texts and writers shape expectations attending the life of the spirit and how they are in turn shaped by them. The important sub-themes many of the essays share are the gendering of spiritual culture and the relationship between traditional literary genres like poetry and drama and spiritual discourse. Each text or spiritual figure covered here has a distinctive spiritual voice—a mystical gesture, if you will—that contributes an individual mysticism to the common spiritual culture they all share. Each scholar in her or his own way defines this mystical gesture.

In "Mechthild von Magdeburg, the Devil and Antichrist," Frank Tobin focuses on the thirteenth-century beguine visionary's imaginative treatment of evil in her *Flowing Light of the Godhead*. Mechthild depicts her confrontations with tempting devils in lively and vivid terms, taking particular delight in her verbal sparring with them. She emerges the victor in a contest of words in scenes that draw from folklore and, most importantly, medieval drama. In her two descants on the Antichrist tradition—which oddly break off without reaching any sense of conclusion—she adds her own imaginative details to the tradition of Antichrist and the end times. To the tradition delineated by such writers as Adso and Joachim of Fiore and such texts as the late-twelfth-century *Play of Antichrist*, she appends details like the care the eschatological brothers give to grooming their beards. For Tobin, Mechthild is essentially a creative writer rather than composer of theological treatises whose vision of the nature of evil is tempered by her imagination and sense of drama.

William Langland's great fourteenth-century English poem, *Piers Plowman*, has been looked at primarily as a work of literature. Along with works like Chaucer's *Canterbury Tales* and the anonymous *Sir Gawain and the Green Knight*, it occupies the pinnacle of literary excellence in an age of great poems. Scholars and critics who contextualize it tend to speak of its social or theological nature. If Tobin invests a spiritual writer with attributes usually associated with poets and playwrights, M. Clemente Davlin in "The Spirituality of *Piers Plowman*," invests Langland with a spirituality usually associated with his close contemporaries Richard Rolle and Julian of Norwich. For Davlin the spirituality of *Piers Plowman* is biblical and liturgical, social and personal, God-centered yet oriented towards the laity. Davlin's objective is to encourage reading *Piers Plowman* as a devotional work in the tradition of Rolle, Julian, and other mystics like Hildegard of Bingen and Meister Eckhardt.

Robert Boenig likewise looks at a primarily "literary" text in light of its mysticism and spirituality. In "Doubled Truth: Skeptical Fideism, Pseudo-Dionysius, and the *Second Shepherds' Play*, he contextualizes the great Wakefield Master's Christmas play in terms of both the late thirteenth-century philosophical trend known as "skeptical fideism" and also the Dionysian mystical theology so influential in late medieval England. The skeptical fideists posited the existence of contradictory truths, particularly between observed nature and God's revelation, with the Church's dogma taking precedence through a motion of faith. Pseudo-Dionysius posited the simultaneous affirmation and denial of attributes of God as the basis of mystical knowledge of God, and writers like the author of *The Cloud of Unknowing* and Julian of Norwich reflect and adapt his ideas. The *Second Shepherds' Play*, by presenting two contradictory manger scenes—one earthly and comic, the other heavenly and devout—participates in this doubling, which can likewise be traced on the level of the play's vocabulary and imagery.

In her "Ecstasy, Prophecy, and Reform: Catherine of Siena as a Model for Holy Women of Sixteenth-Century Spain," Gillian T. W. Ahlgren bridges the gap between medieval and early modern spiritual culture by charting the influence the fourteenth-century Italian mystic Catherine of Siena had on several women in sixteenth-century Spain—Maria de Santo Domingo, Francisca de los Apostoles, and especially Teresa of Avila. Catherine was a Dominican tertiary who died at age 33 in 1380 after a life of penance and extreme asceticism. She wielded tremendous influence, particularly over Popes Gregory XI and Urban VI in their efforts to reestablish papal presence at Rome after decades of the pontiffs' residence at Avignon. Catherine conceived of her life as a humble martyrdom offered to God for the Church. Raymond of Capua's *Life* of

INTRODUCTION

Catherine was one of the texts Cardinal Francicso Jimenez de Cisneros promoted in his efforts at a reforming spiritual renewal in early sixteenth-century Spain. Ahlgren describes how Marie de Santo Domingo, Francisca de los Apóstoles, and Teresa of Ávila consciously modeled their lives after that of Catherine, seeing in her ways of understanding their own conversions, sufferings, and roles in the Church's spiritual culture. As Ahlgren points out, Catherine's example was a formative one in the construction of a gendered spirituality in sixteenth-century Spain.

Joseph F. Chorpenning likewise takes up the issue of influence in his "Bernadino de Laredo's *Treatise on the Mysteries of St. Joseph* and the Evangelization of Mexico." Bernadino de Laredo was an early sixteenth-century Observant Franciscan friar whose treatise, also known as the *Josephina*, is an important text in the development of devotion to St. Joseph. Bernadino was an advocate of St. Joseph who strongly argued for the saint to be depicted as a young and vigorous protector of the Virgin and Jesus against the prevailing older assessment of him as an old man and the relative neglect shown to him in the Middle Ages. Bernadino cites the fifteenth-century French theologian Jean Gerson as well as scripture to support his thesis. Chorpenning notes the ubiquity of the *Josephina* in early Observant Franciscans' attempts in the early sixteenth century to convert the Amerindians in the regions recently conquered by the Spanish. He notes the social circumstances which contributed to early Mexican devotion to St. Joseph, especially the prevalence of mixed-race Spanish/Amerindian illegitimacy: in a demographic group where fathers were often absent, St. Joseph became a protecting father that the Amerindians could call their own in their emerging spiritual culture.

The relationship between gender and genre is important for Elizabeth Rhodes in her "What's in a Name: On Teresa of Ávila's *Book*." Rhodes points out that St. Teresa's first book, since Luis de Leon entitled it her *Vida (Life)* in the sixteenth century, has occasioned certain expectations about its genre that the book itself eludes. Teresa wrote it at age 47 at the behest of her confessor as a means of allaying fears that her experiences were not within the bounds of orthodoxy. She had yet to accomplish the major work of founding the Discalced Carmelites, so in no sense is this a completed "Life." The experiences she chooses to recount are more about her relationship with God than an orderly setting forth of the events of her life. The expectations that St. Augustine's *Confessions* engendered in her contemporary readership—and those that it still engenders in us today—are for a narrative of a dissolute early life interrupted by a radical conversion. Teresa rejects this model of autobiography, which male spiritual writers tend to follow, in favor of one Rhodes terms the "tradition of the virgin bride of Christ," one associated with medieval women like Catherine of Siena, Angela of Foligno, Clare of Assisi, and Birgitta of Sweden. In this woman's tradition a dissolute life and radical conversion are replaced by a quiet struggle to find God's will. Thus the male-model does not fit Teresa's text. Rhodes notes that Teresa's own term for it was her "Book"—a name that makes all the difference for a gendered reading of it.

Jane Ackerman's "Teresa and her Sisters" is also a gendered reading of St. Teresa but from a biographical rather than generic point of view. Ackerman notes that most scholars who identify influences on Teresa concentrate on men, but as Mary Giles and Jodi Bilinkoff have maintained, individuals learn most from those who surround them—and in Teresa's case this was largely women. After an excursus about the role of the Virgin Mary in Carmelite spiritual culture, Ackerman gives brief biographical sketches of the women—most of the Carmelite nuns—who helped shape Teresa's spirituality and who were in turn shaped by her: Dona Guiomar de Ulloa, Antonia del Espiritu Santo, Maria Bautista, Isabel de Santo Domingo, and Ana de San Bartolome. Ackerman traces the twin themes of humility and obedience in the relationships among Teresa and her sisters and suggests they bound these women together rather than separated them in a hierarchical structure.

Alison Weber in her "Demonizing Ecstasy: Alonso de la Fuente and the *Alumbrados* of Extremadura" looks at the disturbing aspects of sixteenth-century Spanish spiritual culture by charting and then analyzing the career of a persecutor of heretics, Alonso de la Fuente. This Dominican Friar became alarmed at reports of how a secular priest, Gaspar Sanchez, was fostering contemplative prayer among a group of pious women in the town of Llerena, Extremadura, since such prayer, he thought, was the reserve of the spiritual elite, not ignorant women. He gradually convinced the authorities that there was demonic heresy and, more important, sexual license among these people, termed *alumbrados*. Confessions extracted by torture led to public floggings of the women and the defrocking of condemned priests. Soon Alonso began to see this eroto-demonic heresy everywhere, even among the Jesuit Order. His efforts to implicate the Jesuits, however, led to his discrediting. Weber sees in his career the mixing of the categories of the demonic with the erotic—a mixture that the Inquisition as a whole was not prepared to make. For Weber the story of the *alumbrados* of Extremadura is an important one for understanding the hermeneutics attending inquisitorial documents, for the incident, as she writes, is not "a story of sexual deviance, but . . . a story of how narratives of deviance are engendered."

Michael Bradburn-Ruster's "The Beautiful Dove, The Body Divine: Luisa de Carvajal y Mendoza's Mystical Poetics" brings the volume back to the theme of the relationship between mysticism and creative writing while sustaining the attention to gender. Luisa de Carvajal y Mendoza was a late sixteenth-early seventeenth-century poet who, though never a nun, lived inside the orbit of the Spanish Jesuits, residing for a time with them in Elizabethan

INTRODUCTION

England, whose religious allegiance was hotly contested by Catholics and Protestants. Bradburn-Ruster notes her reliance in her poetry on Jesuit meditative techniques, particularly the appeal to each of the senses. Through an analysis of her image of her soul as a beautiful dove finding shelter in Christ's wounded side, Bradburn-Ruster defines in her poetry a body-oriented poetic, one which he shows has affinities with mystical themes in Hindu, Buddhist, and Jewish/Kabbalistic mysticism.

Like Bradburn-Ruster, Evelyn Toft explores the work of an early modern woman poet. Her "Cecilia de Nacimiento: Mystic in the Tradition of John of the Cross" introduces that early seventeenth-century mystical poet and argues that her work is worth more than the relative neglect it has hitherto had among scholars and critics. Cecilia de Nacimient, a second-generation Discalced Carmelite nun, was a skillful poet whose work, as Toft claims, "Demonstrates an intellectual clarity and fullness of heart reminiscent of Juan de la Cruz [John of the Cross]." Through close readings of Cecilia de Nacimiento's poetry and her own prose commentaries upon it (a dual-genre approach she shares with John of the Cross) Toft demonstrates how well-aligned her poetics and her mystical theology are with John's. Cecilia de Nacimiento's work demonstrates that the spiritual culture of the early Discalced Carmelites was still operative among their younger followers.

Wendy M. Wright picks up a theme treated in Michael Bradburn-Ruster's essay: entering into Christ's body through the wounded side. In her "Inside My Body is the Body of God: Margaret Mary Alacoque and the Tradition of Embodied Mysticism," Wright recounts a vision Alacoque had in 1673 in which through the medium of erotic-mystical imagery the visionary exchanges hearts with Christ. Alacoque was at the time a young nun of the Visitation convent in Paray-le-Monial, France, the Visitaitonists being an order of religious founded at the beginning of the seventeenth century by Francis de Sales and Jane de Chantal. Wright contextualizes Alacoque's vision in the tradition of what she terms "embodied mysticism," whose roots go back to the Middle Ages. This type of spirituality involves profound emphasis on the body—Christ's wounded and suffering body and the bodily manifestations it has on the mystics who follow this way. St. Francis's stigmata comprise, of course, one famous example of embodied mysticism. Wright establishes the specific exchange of hearts with Jesus as an important component of this mysticism and mentions analogues among the medieval women mystics Gertrude the Great, Mechthild of Hakeborn (both members of the same community as Mechthild of Magdeburg), Dorothy of Montau, Lutgard of Trond, Catherine of Siena, and others. Wright uses Alacoque's experience as an occasion for claiming that embodied mysticism "takes seriously the divine disclosure of the cross, a disclosure which is an invitation into unknowing, paradox, abandonment, and, ultimately, absence."

THE MYSTICAL GESTURE

The final essay in this collection, Amanda Powell's "Making Use of the Holy Office: Exploring the Contexts and Concepts of Sor Juana's References to the Inquisition in the *Respuesta a Sor Filotea*," is a rhetorical analysis of the New Spanish (Mexican) Jeronymite nun's efforts near the end of her life to avoid the accusations her detractors were leveling at her as a secular writer who had recently turned to theological polemic. Though her efforts were not successful and she was accused of disobedience and banned from such writing and her private library removed, her *Respuesta* (*Answer*) reveals a bold rhetorical strategy: referring to the looming power of the Inquisition as a means of staving off her detractors, who were ecclesiastical and political figures not associated with the Inquisition. If the Inquisition has found no fault with me, so her rhetorical gesture goes, why do you? Powell demonstrates Sor Juana's reliance on the earlier rhetorical gestures of Teresa of Ávila in her own efforts to avoid condemnation of her writing, particularly the earlier saint's recourse to describing herself as a poor little woman (*mujercilla*).

The studies assembled in *The Mystical Gesture: Essays in Medieval and Early Modern Spiritual Culture in Honor of Mary E. Giles* thus converse with one another. The spiritual culture shared by the texts and writers covered in this volume was that of visionaries, mystics, nuns who were poets or scholars, or creative writers who drew on spiritual themes. How poetry or drama intersected with devotion and mysticism, how rhetoric served spirituality, and how conceptions of gender were shaped by and in turn helped shape spiritual culture are themes that these essays explore and to a certain measure illuminate. They are, of course, concerns that animate a spiritual culture facing a new millennium as much as they did for our medieval and early modern sisters and brothers.

Tribute to Mary E. Giles

Kathryn Hohlwein

Among the many of us writing to celebrate and honor Mary Giles, I may be the only one of her direct colleagues on the campus of California State University at Sacramento where she has spent her teaching life. So, rather than join the rest who write to honor her scholarship, her huge contributions to studies of mysticism, Spanish literature and religious thought, women's spirituality and expression, I will write of her as the inspired teacher I have known.

The Humanities Department of our University will find it impossible to replace Mary Giles, and they know it. For over thirty years she has brought an aesthetic and intellectual range, depth, discipline, integrity, and concern for the well-being of students and for collegial responsibility that very few of my other colleagues have consistently maintained. Nothing deflected her commitment. Where others of us have become dispirited by the ever-increasing emphasis upon administration and cost-effectiveness, Mary only required more of herself, of her students. She gave to them with a rectitude and lack of sloppiness which I always found invigorating. These attitudes prevailed in all domains of campus life—in her office consultations, in committee work, in attention to the fine detail and demanding nature of what we labeled Advanced Study Courses. No faculty I know adhered so strenuously to the concept behind those courses—that students from all disciplines needed to be able to analyze well and then to express their ideas well. I know that I found myself unable to promote the high quality of writing that Mary strove for from often poorly prepared students. She offered extra writing classes voluntarily so they might witness their own improvement. I remain humbled by her efforts.

As a lecturer, Mary was and remains the embodiment of the dignity, beauty, and grace of her subject matter. Always minutely prepared, she exulted in being the messenger of spiritual depth, both intellectual and emotional, of her busy, fragmented students. They acknowledged her commitment—first to the material itself, second to the potentiality of each person, and finally to her mission between the two.

Someone in these pages will mention Mary's editorship of *Studia Mystica* during the years when she was a full-time Professor. I want only to add that as her partner in this wonderful project, I saw how she handled the many extra demands such stewardship required. I was and remain flattered that she asked me to be her Poetry and Art Editor, and I accepted readily. Now I can take this opportunity to thank you, Mary, for allowing me to participate, with you, in something so close to my interests and my heart.

Despite the fact that our University never really supported or rewarded us with financial aid or released time, we carried on and we loved it. Mary was a marvel of precision and vision, of punctuality and sensitivity. She was as attentive to the authors as she was to their submissions and vice versa. To her, they were one thing.

I followed her lead always, though she gave me full discretionary powers. We consulted and, if we disagreed on the poems or the art, she was generously trusting enough to let my choice stand. The twelve-year experience was one of the finest parts of my own professional life. Through *Studia Mystica* we met spectacular people, with many of whom we sustained private correspondences and several of whom we met in person.

In Taos and Santa Fe one winter we spent time with some unique, unforgettable contributors to the journal. An image remains with me. After pancakes at the truckstop somewhere in the high, snowy desert, we drove in companionable silence, gratified each by the work we were doing and respecting the conversations we had recently had, on higher into the empty spaces, attuned to our inner natures but loving one another. Perhaps, I believe, in prayer.

1 Mechthild von Magdeburg, the Devil, and Antichrist

Frank Tobin

Among the kinds of scenes Mechthild describes in her *Flowing Light of the Godhead*, two of the most striking are her depictions of the devil (or devils) and of the time of Antichrist. What follows is an attempt to characterize Mechthild's own literary talent and creativity in presenting this material and to say what can be said about the relationships of what she wrote to the medieval culture around her, as manifested in such areas as religious thought, drama, and art. What justifies joining the topics of the devil and Antichrist is that, in the case of both, Mechthild sets herself the task of impressing upon the minds of her readers an evil that transcends the merely human. As to form, they share most particularly Mechthild's use of material found also in medieval drama, art, and folklore. In maintaining that Mechthild, also in the case of Antichrist, describes an evil that is greater than human, I do not wish to imply that she breaks with the tradition, say, of an Adso.[1] Indeed, she refers to Antichrist at one point as a human being.[2] I simply mean that she portrays him, his reign, and its evil as so inhuman and so utterly opposed to God's salvific will for humanity, that she would have approved of Jerome's assertion that the devil is the parent of Antichrist,[3] at least figuratively, and also with Adso's description of the prenatal association of the devil with Antichrist. Any attempts to show connections between Mechthild and medieval culture are, given the state of our knowledge, fraught with problems, and seldom can one rise above showing them to be probable or even plausible. More will be said about this below in regard to specific relationships. At the outset, however, it will be well to state general difficulties affecting our investigation. First, in the case of the Antichrist material, it is generally recognized that the various strains had

---

[1] Adso maintains that Antichrist will be born of a human mother and father but that, at the beginning of his conception, the devil will enter with him into his mother's womb. Migne, *Patrologia Latina* 101, 1292.

[2] That is, *mensche*. All quotations from and references to Mechthild's writing are taken from Vol. I, *Text*, of *Mechthild von Magdeburg: Das fließende Licht der Gottheit*, ed. Hans Neumann (Munich: Artemis, 1990). References are given according to book, chapter and line number, followed by the page in the Neumann edition. Here: IV 15, 45; 223.

[3] *Commentarii in Esaiam, Corpus Christianorum*, series Latina 73, 261.

become so intermingled by her time that it is impossible to determine what her specific sources might have been.

In any case, her sources are most likely material she became familiar with through sermons and religious instruction and not actual theological writings. Second, as Petrus Tax has pointed out in his valuable study on Mechthild's visions of heaven and hell, when one looks for sources for her visual images in medieval iconography, most representations that one finds corresponding to something in one of her visions can be documented as occurring only *after* 1300, so that one can only speak of a possible *parallelism* and not of a *source* for Mechthild's depicitons.[4] As we shall see below, one is faced with similar difficulties when one explores Mechthild's possible use of medieval drama.

Finally, when attempting to establish relationships between Mechthild and her sources, one has to take into account her practice of infusing tradition with original elements—a practice evident, for example, in her appropriation of vernacular lyric poetry. Mechthild frequently draws on her obvious familiarity with various genres of courtly lyric poetry of the generations preceding her. Yet, though the influence is unmistakable, Mechthild's poetry cannot simply be reduced to courtly lyric, either as to verse form or as to content. The assonance rhyme she often employs is—to the best of our knowledge—her own creation; and, in exploiting the poetry of human love to describe a love that is both human and divine, she must reformulate according to the different nature of this love.[5] Thus her own creativity often causes an additional blurring of her relationship to sources and traditions.

The Devil

Fortunately, in treating the two most detailed occurrences of devils in Mechthild's book, the principle source is hardly in question. In describing these personal confrontations with the evil ones, she draws on the portrayal of the temptation of Christ in the wilderness as described in the synoptic gospels (Mt 4:1-11; Mk 1:12-13; and Lk 4:1-13). Twice she avails herself of this format (II 24, 47-62; 60-61; and IV 2, 40-70; 111-12), though she modifies it and adds

---

[4] Tax, "Die große Himmelsschau Mechthilds von Magdeburg und ihre Höllenvision," *Zeitschrift für deutsches Altertum und deutsche Literatur* 108 (1979), 113.

[5] For examples of Mechthild's verse, see III 1, 174-8; 79; and VI 1, pp. 104-13; 204-5. See also, Frank Tobin, "Introduction," in *Mechthild of Magdeburg: The Flowing Light of the Godhead*, translated and introduced by Tobin, Preface by Margot Schmidt (New York: Paulist Press, 1997), pp. 20-23. All translations of *The Flowing Light of the Godhead* are from this volume. For examples of Mechthild's borrowing from courtly lyric poetry, see I, pp. 12-21; 14-16; and III, pp. 23; 105-6.

touches from other sources. In both instances, she, or "the soul," replaces Christ as the one being tempted.

In his first appearance in the *Flowing Light of the Godhead*, the devil avails himself of two disguises. First, he comes as an angel of light who brings her a radiant book as a kiss of peace.[6] Mechthild's wit and verbal acuity rise to the occasion. She bests him by remarking: "He who has no peace himself, cannot bestow peace on me."[7] Thus confounded the devil returns as a sickly wretch with his guts falling out who begs her to heal him, implying that her holiness gives her such power. There follows a stichomythic exchange of several lines centering on the word *sick* in which Mechthild demonstrates her unshakable humility in language that would do anyone proud. She concludes by telling him that he is eternally sick and, like the lepers in the gospel, should show himself to a priest, or—she throws in for good measure—to a bishop, an archbishop, or the pope. "Never!" he retorts. Then, turning into black smoke and with an obscene gesture, he departs.

In Mechthild's next detailed mention of devils (IV 2, 40-98; 111-13), she is confronted by two of them who provide a counterweight to the two guardian angels whom, she confides, she has been given. The encounters with these two devils are described consecutively, each being a separate tale. Only the encounter with the first devil follows the temptation format of the gospels. This infernal creature, too, appears in beautiful angelic garb and exploits his appearance by tempting her with one of the three temptations of the gospels, namely, that she should adore him.[8] She echoes the words of Jesus in her initial response—that one should worship God alone; but rather than immediately adding a "Begone, Satan," as happens in Matthew, she lets her hellish visitor engage her in further verbal dueling: You shall be a virgin sitting on the highest throne and I shall adore you, he cajoles; and he shows her his five wounds to prove his divine identity. She responds to all his flatteries with a self-possessed cleverness which culminates in her retort that, if he is God, then who is that in the priest's hands at the altar. Like some Hollywood vampire with a cross thrust in his face, the devil seeks to retreat. Mechthild, however, goes on the offensive. Confident that she has seen through his attempt to bring her down, she commands him to listen and subjects him to a thorough tongue-lashing. Like the demons dwelling in the Gerasene man (Mt 8:28-34; Mk 5:1-20; and Lk 8:26-39), this devil wishes only to escape and promises never to trouble her again.

---

[6] The sudden appearance of the devil holding a book is strikingly similar to God's appearance two chapters later holding Mechthild's book and promising to preserve it. See II, pp. 26, 7-10; 68.

[7] Tobin, *Mechthild*, p. 91. "Der selber keinen vriden hat, der mag mir keinen vriden geben." II 24, pp. 51-2; 60.

[8] This is the second temptation in Luke and the third in Matthew.

These first two temptation scenes demonstrate well the interplay of tradition and creative drive in Mechthild. She borrows mainly from the gospels but adds touches from other sources. Through narratives relating the lives of the desert fathers, as these were used in sermons and in other forms of religious instruction, the common folk were exposed to many stories in which devils figure prominently. This material then merged with pagan ideas already present in the popular imagination. When Mechthild has the devil appear as an angel of light and disappear in a cloud of black smoke after offering a final obscene gesture, she is relying on popular tradition.[9]

The dialogue, however, I take to be largely her own creation. In both scenes the dialogue has been expanded beyond that in the gospels and, in the second scene, some of Mechthild's retorts have been fashioned in the assonance rhyme peculiar to her. In other words, we have here a literary artist at work who sees the dramatic possibilities in the material and cannot help but respond to them. Not without a twinge of conscience, however. In the second scene, to head off the oft-repeated spiritual admonition that one should not dispute with the devil but should simply flee him, she justifies her verbal jousting by interjecting the remark that "his idle talk annoyed her greatly; nevertheless, she listened to it freely so that she could become more shrewd."[10] Despite her assertion to the contrary, she obviously enjoys these verbal contests from which she comes away the winner. And it is the devil who must eat humble pie.

Three other personal encounters with the devil which Mechthild describes are not presented in the evangelical temptation format. Rather, they are based on more popular sources, such as holy legend, the lives of the saints, and folk literature. Her description of her encounter with a second devil, immediately following upon the second temptation scene just treated, is the most detailed of the three. All of them manifest didactic tendencies more directly than the temptation scenes.

This second devil assigned to her, Mechthild asserts, is a "trouble maker and master of concealed lewdness,"[11] whom God does not allow to attack her directly but rather through evil people who try to spoil good things for her and rob her of her honor, and even through good people whose idle unchaste talk distresses her. One night—the time when he is most likely to appear—he visits Mechthild still at her prayers. He is gigantic, with a short tail and crooked nose, his head large like a tub. Fiery sparks and black flames dart from his mouth as his raucous voice cunningly speaks and laughs. However, his cunning

---

[9] See Jeffrey Burton Russell, *Lucifer: The Devil in the Middle Ages* (Ithaca: Cornell University Press, 1984), p. 68.

[10] Tobin, *Mechthild*, p. 141. ". . .und si verdros vil sere siner unnützen merem, iedoch so horte si gerne, uf das si deste wiser were." IV 2, pp. 59-60; 111.

[11] Tobin, *Mechthild*, pp. 141-2. "ein fridenbrecher und ein meister der hellichen unkúscheit" IV 2, pp. 71-2; 112.

seems to desert him as he openly reveals what weaknesses he looks for in people in religious life and how he then proceeds. Mechthild then asks why, if he is evil, he is relating all this spiritually helpful information to her. He replies that he can only do what God commands, so firmly is he in God's hands (IV 2, 71-98).

Mechthild again does battle with a devil later in Book IV over the soul of a beguine. He is huge, fiery, bloody, and black; with claws, horns, and glassy eyes. He trundles over her like a sack of water. Mechthild blesses herself and falls asleep, but an angel from the fourth choir then explains what this visitation is all about.[12] It all has to do with the fact that Mechthild has been opposing him in the case of a lady torn between living her life at court or as a beguine. The devil—one of the worst, we are told—returns to shoot excruciating fiery rays at Mechthild.[13] Because, however, she submits to anything and everything God may allow the devil to do to her, he sees his power diminishing. With quasi-divine authority Mechthild commands him: "by the living God" and "by the last judgment" to identify himself and his business with the lady.[14] He finally capitulates. His name, he says, is Raging Anger, and he destroys spiritual hearts by fostering arrogance, cunning, and lust in his victims. Again, in this spiritual anecdote narrated by Mechthild in the first person, the devil provides the reader with spiritual insight.

In a third dialogue with another devil (VI 7, 1-33; 213-14), following much the same pattern as the one just mentioned, the object of contention is a stubborn, self-willed beguine under Mechthild's supervision. The lesson learned is that the devil can only assail those who freely allow him to do so. God, however, is not so gentle with this recalcitrant beguine and tells Mechthild he cannot help the person with kindness and will soon strike her lame, dumb, and blind. At the same time he warns that what one does to this woman one does to him. When these afflictions indeed befall the woman fourteen days later, Mechthild exclaims, "Alleluia," presumably at seeing God's power revealed and not just in relief at being free of the woman.

A third format or structure Mechthild uses in dealing with the diabolical —in addition to temptation scenes and encounters based on legend, folk tales, and the like—is one in which theatrical qualities are predominant. While all her encounters with the devil have inherent dramatic qualities in that dialogue, and particularly a drama-style dialogue, is an underlying feature, Mechthild's vision

---

[12] Mechthild often refers to the different choirs or ranks of angels, a doctrine stemming from the writings of Pseudo-Dionysius.

[13] The devil was popularly thought to be able to abuse good people physically, and he is pictured in medieval art shooting fiery arrows at the soul. See Russell, *Lucifer*, pp. 72 and 212.

[14] Tobin, *Mechthild*, p. 160. "Bi dem lebenden got mane ich dich . . . bi dem jungesten tage!" IV 17, pp. 25-8; 131.

described in V 23 (1-190; 174-81), which one could call her Annunciation and Christmas pageant, contains visual elements reminiscent of medieval stage productions.[15] In this long vision Mechthild witnesses—much like a member of the audience at a mystery play—gospel events from the angel Gabriel's visit to the Virgin to Jesus' retreating to the desert. In passing, we can note that this is an "interactive" vision or performance, since Mechthild is able to stop the action to ask questions and receive responses from Mary. Interestingly enough, it is the devil scenes in this portrayal of gospel events that have most in common with what we know about medieval drama. Could Mechthild have been influenced by stage productions that she herself witnessed? It is tempting to suppose that she did, but the evidence is less than conclusive, as a brief review of available material will show. First, however, we should look at the scenes themselves.

Satan first appears on the scene together with the star of Bethlehem and follows the three kings to the Christ child. Mustering the infant with an evil look, he delivers a sixteen-line monologue in assonance-rhyme verse in which he wonders whether this might be the child of whom the prophets spoke and who is destined to undo hell's domination on earth. Satan decides to discuss the matter with his master Lucifer, and the scene changes to hell, where Lucifer commands Satan to return to earth and teach the powerful and learned in the land how they might kill the child before he comes of school age. Satan then returns to earth and, in a few lines having no theatrical characteristics, enters into Herod's heart to move him to kill the innocents. Jesus, however, is hidden from Satan's gaze by an angelic light until he turns thirty.

Later in the same chapter the devil perceives Jesus in the desert and goes to the Jewish masters to instruct them on how to resist him with perverse words. He then returns to hell for a long dialogue with Lucifer in which he confesses his impotence to deal with his superior foe. The two of them puzzle over who Jesus is and what powers he has, and they discuss the best way of dealing with him.

In examining Mechthild's possible relationship to actual plays, we can begin by noting that the emergence of medieval drama occurred early enough for Mechthild to have felt its effects. At least this is true with respect to the earliest plays—those written and produced in Latin and flourishing from the thirteenth to the fifteenth century. This was a *European* drama, which spread

---

[15] In calling the dialogues with the devil just treated *dramatic*, I do not wish to imply that Mechthild in any way derived them from medieval drama. An examination of extant texts of dramas close to Mechthild in time reveals nothing remotely similar. The "pageant" in V 23, however, does show characteristics of the medieval Christmas cycle plays. Yet because of the presence of narrative sections, one cannot consider the chapter as something actually resembling a draft for a stage play.

easily across linguistic and ethnic boundaries.[16] Most surviving manuscripts of these plays are from German-speaking areas, which attests to their popularity there.[17] It is assumed, however, that very many manuscripts have been lost, especially in lands that became Protestant.[18] Despite the fact that these plays presenting or expanding on a biblical text were performed in Latin, they were performed for and enthusiastically received by the unlettered folk who were well able to understand and follow the action.[19] Though these plays arose chiefly as a pedagogical means of instructing the simple folk and were first performed in church as an extension of the liturgy with clerics as actors, even early on a spirit of playful frivolity and "liturgical buffoonery of the *clerici*" entered into such performances.[20] The introduction of the devil or devils was, of course, a natural occasion for introducing both silliness and horror. Such perceived abuses evoked the wrath of reformers and resulted in ecclesiastical prohibitions. Gerloh of Reichersberg (1093-1169) opposed all involvement of the church and clerics in plays. He mentions nativity plays in particular and finds it especially offensive that actors, presumably clerics, transform themselves into women, soldiers, and devils.[21] Harrad of Landsberg (1167-95), abbess of the monastery of Hohenburg, in her *Hortus deliciarum* also condemns the plays because of their excesses despite the pious intentions connected with their origins, and she approves of the actions of those among the higher clergy who forbade such plays.[22]

Indeed, such prohibitions were forthcoming. Pope Innocent III issued a decree to the whole church in 1210 ordering that bishops see to it that such theatrical excesses be rooted out of their churches.[23] Interestingly enough, the original decree in 1207 had been addressed to the Archbishop of Gnesen (Gneizno), whose jurisdiction included eastern sections of German-speaking territories.[24] Similar decrees were issued repeatedly by synods in German-

---

[16] See E. K. Chambers, *The Medieval Stage* (Oxford: Clarendon, 1903), II, p. 22; and Hansjürgen Linke, "Drama und Theater," in *Die deutsche Literatur im späten Mittelalter, 1250-1370*, zweiter Teil: *Reimpaargedichte, Drama, Prosa*, ed. Ingeborg Glier (Munich: Beck, 1987), p. 153.

[17] Linke, "Drama und Theater," p. 157.

[18] Chambers, *The Medieval Stage*, II, p. 64.

[19] Linke, "Drama und Theater," pp. 159-60; and Karl Young, *The Drama of the Medieval Church* (Oxford: Clarendon, 1933), II, p. 410.

[20] Young, *The Drama of the Medieval Church*, II, p. 410.

[21] ". . . se in daemonum larvas transfigurant." Gerloh of Reichersberg, *De Investigatione Antichristi*; quoted from Bernd Neumann, *Geistliches Schauspiel im Zeugnis der Zeit*, 2 vols. (Munich: Artemis, 1987), II, pp. 888-9. The mention of "masks of demons" should be particularly noted. It is easy to forget, when reading the texts of the plays, just how important the *spectacle* aspect was in evoking audience response.

[22] See Neumann, *Geistliches Schauspiel*, Neumann, II, pp. 984-95.

[23] See Neumann, *Geistliches Schauspiel*, II, pp. 869-70.

[24] Neumann, *Geistliches Schauspiel*, II, p. 869.

speaking areas during subsequent centuries, which confirms both the popularity of the plays and the abuses which often accompanied them.[25] One oft-repeated objection to the plays seems to have been how the demonic elements are portrayed (*monstra larvarum*, which no doubt included devils), or that a devil (*angelus satane*) was transformed into an angel of light.

The devil already makes an appearance in the earliest form of liturgical drama, the Easter plays, as part of the so-called harrowing of hell. After his crucifixion, Jesus descends to the gates of hell and issues his command: *Tollite portas*, to which the devil within replies (in the words of Psalm 24): *Quis est iste rex glorieae?*[26] Also, Lucifer's fall was a main subject of a play performed in Regensburg in 1194.[27]

In the plays of Christmas as well, we find the devil making an early appearance. In the Benediktbeuern play, which originated in the German-speaking South between 1200 and 1250, he appears to the shepherds three times, attempting to convince them that they are being duped by the angelic messenger and should not go to the manger. His efforts are, however, ultimately in vain. Later, in the part of the Benediktbeuern cycle entitled *Ludus de rege Aegypti*, Herod, after the slaughter of the innocent children of Bethlehem, sinks from his throne and, eaten by worms, is received into the arms of a host of rejoicing devils.[28]

From all this we can conclude that Mechthild probably had the opportunity to experience and borrow from the medieval theater. As in several of the plays, Mechthild casts Satan in the role of Lucifer's chief emissary. And, as the two deliberate about just who this Jesus might be, one is reminded of the devil's (Lucifer's) perplexity in the Easter plays when Jesus appears at the gates of hell. Yet Mechthild, despite the obvious dramatic possibilities of the material, never portrays a harrowing of hell and transfers Lucifer's baffled state

---

[25] Neumann, *Geistliches Schauspiel*, II, p. 870-72.

[26] See, for example, the Easter plays of Muri and Klosterneuburg, both originating in the first half of the thirteenth century.

[27] "Anno Domini MCXCIIII celebratus est in Ratispona ordo creacionis angelorum et ruina Luciferi et suorum et creacionis hominis et casus et prophetarum sub Celestino papa regnante Heinrico imperatore et semper augusto et Chuonrado regente inibi episcopatum VII. id[us] Februarii." Neumann, *Geistliches Schauspiel*, I, p. 610.

[28] Linke, "Benekiktbeurer Weihnachtsspiel," *Die deutsche Literatur des Mittelalters: Verfasserlexikon*, 2 ed. Kurt Ruh (Berlin: de Gruyter I, 1978), p. 697. Devils comport themselves wildly on the stage early on in other situations as well. In a Norman or Anglo-Norman play of the twelfth or thirteenth century referred to as the *Adam*, the devil plays a prominent role tempting our first parents. The stage directions call for devils to run about the stage (paradise) pointing at the forbidden fruit. After Eve and then Adam fall into sin, the tempter, accompanied by three or four other devils, chain the necks of them both, and push and pull them into hell, where they are greeted with a rowdy welcome by yet more devils. See Chambers, *The Medieval Stage*, II, pp. 80-82.

of mind to the Christmas story. There she has Satan move Herod to kill the innocents but does not have him approach the shepherds or have devils welcome Herod to hell.

There are elements linking medieval drama and Mechthild more directly, but they occur in texts from the later Middle Ages. For example, in the *Hessisches Weihnachtsspiel* (after 1450), the devils do deliberate on how to deal with the new-born Christ.[29] And in a French play of the fifteenth century, Satan redeems himself before Lucifer for having brought the bad news that the new-born Jesus might be the Messiah by proposing that he return to Herod and suggest to him that he kill the innocents.[30]

A final similarity Mechthild's devils share with stage devils is found in three passages where she has devils rage about wildly. In the first, Mechthild reports a vision she has of her own end. Virgins and angels proceed down toward her followed by our Lord and his mother: "On both sides of the procession was a throng of devils. There were so many of them that I was unable to encompass them all with my sight. Still, I was not afraid of a single one. They thrashed about with great ferocity and they clawed each other like madmen."[31] In the final pages of her book Mechthild again returns to the theme of her own death. As she lies terribly ill, she again sees celestial beings preparing to welcome her, while the evil ones come from the north to witness her judgment. They are "all tangled together and tied up like whipped dogs. Choking at the collar, they try to get at me."[32] But to no avail and, much to her chagrin, she recovers. Finally, in another chapter, Mechthild recreates the chagrin devils feel when a soul departs for heaven. They comport themselves wildly and blame each other in their bitterness and in fear of the punishment awaiting them for their failure. Upon their return to the court of hell, their master chides them in verse for their failure and condemns them to remain in hell. In their place he decides to send learned scholars to blind the understanding of good people and thus destroy their zeal for God (VII 39, 31-4; 288). Passing over Mechthild's dig at learned masters who might well succeed in perverting the hearts of the god where devils have failed, we note that here again Mechthild's efforts resemble a theatrical scene.

---

[29] Rolf Bergmann, *Katalog der deutschsprachigen geistlichen Spiele und Marienklagen des Mittelalters* (Munich: Beck, 1986), pp. 174-6.

[30] Russell, *Lucifer*, p. 265.

[31] Tobin, *Mechthild*, p. 214. "Beidenhalben der procession was ein schar tüfelen, der was also vil, das mir das nit mohte geschehen, das ich si moehte übersehen; iedoch so voerchte ich keinen. Si undersluogen sich mit grossem grimme und si undercratzten sich als die unsinnigen." V 32, pp. 19-22; 192.

[32] Tobin, *Mechthild*, pp. 334-5. "si hatten sich zesamen gewunden und waren getwungen als die besclagenen hunde; si wurgetent mit irme halse ze mir." VII 63, pp. 18-19; 309.

One cannot conclude one's remarks on the devil without mention of the strong visual images Mechthild is able to create in her visions of hell (III 21) and of purgatory (III 15 and V 14). Actually, these visions center on hell and purgatory as places.[33] We shall focus our attention on the devils within them. In the case of hell, however, it is impossible to separate Lucifer as a person from the place. Although Mechthild expends much effort describing hell as a place, Lucifer so dominates the landscape that he seems to fill it entirely. He resides in its "deepest abyss. There flows forth unceasingly out of his fiery heart and out of his mouth" all evil.[34] He greets the newcomers thrusting the proud under his tail, sucking the Sodomites down his throat into his belly and expelling them out again with a cough. Each kind of sinner receives Lucifer's personal attention in a manner appropriate to his sin. After the last day he shall don a new garment fashioned from the manure of all the filthy sins he suggested to men and angels.[35] Then "he will swell up enormously and his muzzle shall open very wide," as he devours evil Christians, Jews, and heathens.[36] Hell and Lucifer seem to melt into a single entity as Mechthild describes the top of hell as a head with many fiery eyes shooting flames into the lowest part of purgatory. Here the breath of Lucifer tortures those who have barely escaped hell. And, she reminds us, hell's mouth is always open.[37]

Purgatory, too, is under the charge of a devil,[38] and countless hosts of them are engaged in tormenting the souls there. In two separate visions Mechthild vividly describes their punishments. Like toads, they are boiled and roasted in the fiery pitch and muck and the accompanying smoke and stench. Devils rub them, wash them, eat them, and strike them with fiery scourges (III 15, 29-52; 95-6). In revealing what awaits bad priests in purgatory Mechthild's vision draws on the gospel image of priests as fishers of men (Mt 4:19). Here it is the erring priests who are the fish and the devils who are the fishers pursuing them in fiery boiling water with their fiery claws. After bringing these fish to shore, they throw them into a boiling pot and jab them with pitchforks to see if they are done. They gobble up the poor fish with their beaks and expel them out behind. Then the whole process begins again (V 14; 167).

---

[33] For an excellent analysis of Mechthild's hell and its meaning, see Tax, "Die große Himmelsschau," pp. 126-36.

[34] Tobin, *Mechthild*, p. 128. "... in dem nidersten abgrúnde ... und im flússet ane underlas von sinem fúrigen herzen us und usser sinem munde...." III 21, pp. 16-18; 100.

[35] This, no doubt, corresponds in Mechthild's thinking to the new crown Jesus is to receive after the last day. See VII 1, pp. 254-8.

[36] Tobin, *Mechthild*, p. 131. "So sol er sich ze stunden drinten also gros und sin grans wirt im vil wit, da versluket er mit eime zuge sines atemes inne die cristan, juden und heiden." III, pp. 21, 86-7; 102-3.

[37] Hell, as a gigantic maw, is already present in early medieval iconography. See, for example, Russell, *Lucifer*, 143.

[38] "der túfel, der des vegefúres pfliget...." V, pp. 33, 13-14; 193.

In summing up the functions of the devil or devils for Mechthild, one might emphasize two points. First, she does very little theologizing about them, preferring rather to portray them through images and dialogue. Second, devils have for her a certain ambivalence. Her devils are both serious and comic figures. Lucifer, the lord of hell, generally speaks with a sober dignity and is intellectually miles above his chief lieutenant Satan and his other minions. Aside from Lucifer, devils seem to be tragicomic figures. They are physically grotesque, when not in disguise, and are presented with the ambiguities that often accompany grotesqueness. They are powerful, yet ultimately powerless. They are intensely evil, and yet a bit ridiculous. Mechthild recounts the devil's assaults on her but assures us (at least three times! II 24, 62; 60; IV 17, 10; 131; and VII 63, 19; 309) with a bravado based perhaps in part on her feeling some trepidation, that she has no fear of him. Drawing on a variety of traditions and sources difficult to determine with any precision, she uses the devil to drive home to her audience moral lessons; but, being pedagogically savvy, she knows that often the best way to teach is to entertain.

Antichrist

Mechthild's treatment of the material surrounding Antichrist is characterized by the same interplay of tradition and creativity evident in her approach to the devil. She concentrates on three topics or themes in regard to the last days: the appearance of the holy brothers, the return of Enoch and Elijah, and the rise of Antichrist.[39] She twice deals with these themes in great detail (first in IV 27, and again in VI 15), and her elaborations show her to be well versed in medieval prophecies and ruminations about the last days and to be ready to exploit the visual images and dramatic possibilities inherent in the material.

We might begin by noting that in both these chapters Mechthild chooses a way of introducing them modeled on the well-known final chapter of Book II, where Mechthild, concerned about dire threats to her book, takes refuge in prayer and is rewarded by the Lord's appearing to her holding the book and telling her that one cannot burn the truth (II 26, 1-9; 68). In IV 27 Mechthild worries about the future of the Dominicans, who are being attacked by false teachers (*valsche meister*) and sinners. God answers her prayers by assuring her that they, too, have his protection and will continue to the end of the world.[40] In VI 15, occupied with thoughts of dying, Mechthild begs the Lord that her holy desire to praise him and to suffer for him continue on after her

---

[39] Mechthild's treatment of the holy brothers or "viri spirituales" is her closest point of contact with the writings of the Calabrian abbot Joachim of Fiore, but even here she obviously adds much that is her own.

[40] This gives God the opportunity to mention to Mechthild the coming of a new order of brothers.

death. As before, so here the Lord consoles her, telling her that her desire cannot die because it is eternal.

Both chapters contain elements of drama and stark visual images, but they are not the only features nor are they present throughout. Indeed, in IV 27, where Mechthild devotes eighty-two of the first ninety lines to a description of the life of the holy brothers, though she begins her elaborations with the standard *do sach ich* (then I saw) used to preface a vision, there is little that is visionary about her description of them. Knowingly or not, she is obviously drawing on the thought of Joachim of Fiore in her description of the brothers, but many of the details are certainly her own. We are told, for example, how they are to dress, how they should wash and care for their hair and beards, how they should undertake their journeys, and what food and other alms they may accept, when they are to hold chapter meetings, and what the administrative structure of the order shall be.

One can best explain this long descriptive digression, which has none of the immediacy of the reporting of a vision, by seeing it as an example of Mechthild's almost programmatic tendency to explore and enlist all genres of writing, both literary and those less literary for her book. The forms in evidence span almost all possibilities known at the time, from the courtly lyric (as manifested in such sub-genres as the exchange or *Wechsel*, the messenger's song or *Botenlied*, and the lover's complaint), through various kinds of folk literature (such as the fairy tale, nursery rhymes, and folk sayings), and general forms (such as the letter, the anecdote, autobiography, and epigram), to religious forms (such as the litany, spiritual instruction, and, of course, the vision). What Mechthild is most likely doing here is trying her hand at writing a rule for a religious order. This explains the number of specific regulations she includes, which she infuses with statements reflecting the spirit and idealism she expects from this new order.

After writing her "rule" in the first part of IV 27, Mechthild switches from a descriptive style to narrative in relating how, despite the efforts of the holy brothers, Antichrist seduces both secular and church rulers by exploiting their greed. The holy brothers, however, resist him and even convert some Jews and heathens (IV 27, 91-105; 146). Then Mechthild adopts a much more visual mode as she relates the tortures and deaths of many of the holy brothers and their followers. Though the portrayal of these events could well be the direct expression of a spiritual vision as defined by Augustine, they certainly are stageworthy as well. We see Antichrist's henchmen stab the holy preacher with an iron pole and carry him thus impaled and writhing before the eyes of the children of God to be displayed from the place where he had preached. Then his faithful followers have their heads lopped off and thrown into the water. Finally, after the appearance of Elijah and Enoch, Antichrist's henchmen hurl

Christian men onto sizzling griddles while their wives and children are thrown into a fiery pit and have wood and straw heaped upon them.

When Mechthild returns to the Antichrist story in VI 15, she continues to use strong visual and dramatic images. Christians are clubbed to death like mad dogs, and the faithful watch Elijah hang for three days nailed to a lofty cross before expiring. The chapter closes with a charged dramatic dialogue, as Enoch and Antichrist engage in a verbal duel before Enoch utters his final prayer. To this Mechthild appends God's reply to his servant Enoch which, she confides, she "saw and read in the Trinity."[41] Thus, though not entirely dramatic or theatrical, much of the last days material as presented by Mechthild could readily be turned into a stage production.

When we address the theatrical elements present in these chapters, it is helpful to compare Mechthild's treatment of the material to that given it in the *Ludus de Antichristo* which was probably written by a monk at the monastery at Tegernsee (Bavaria) between 1178 and 1186.[42] The play enjoyed some degree of popularity, as attested to by the fact that lines of the play turn up in the Benediktbeuern Christmas cycle play (*circa* 1200-1250) and in at least one other manuscript.[43] Because of differences in content and manner of treatment, however, a direct link between the Tegernsee play and Mechthild seems unlikely. Mechthild's version lacks the pro-imperial political dimension so obvious in the play. Also, though Mechthild gives attention to the fate of the Jews, there is no *Synagoga* figure in her account.

For artistry and stageworthiness, however, Mechthild's presentation strikes one as being the better version. Of course, staging Mechthild's account would be a difficult undertaking, but the Tegernsee play, with its eleven scene changes and sixty actors (not all of whom speak), has also left scholars with many unanswered questions about how text and action might have been presented on stage. Mechthild's treatment, if it were faithfully performed, allows for a richer variety of stage events than are present in the Tegernsee play. Also, the verbal battle between Antichrist and the last prophet (Elijah in the play and Enoch in Mechthild's version) is longer and literarily more ambitious as formulated by Mechthild than the more linear argumentation presented in the play. What links Mechthild to the author of the play especially is that they share a strikingly cosmic perspective in what they portray. It is the whole world which both attempt to embrace. Christians, Jews, and heathens are all drawn into the action on a vast world stage. The play adds the divine element to the scene by means of the thunderclap which destroys Antichrist.

---

[41] "das sah ich und las es in der heligen drivaltekeit." VI 15 pp. 83, 225.

[42] *Ludus de Antichristo*: Edition und Übersetzung, ed. Gisela Vollmann-Profe (Göppingen: Kümmerle, 1981). English version: *The Play of Antichrist*, translated with an introduction by John Wright (Toronto: Pontifical Institute, 1967).

[43] Linke, "Drama und Theater," p. 224.

Mechthild accomplishes something similar by *seeing* and *reading* God's response to Enoch's final prayer in the Trinity.

Finally, it should be noted that both chapters in which Mechthild deals with Antichrist come to an abrupt end. In the first, after coming to a definite closure by showing how the good men die roasting on the griddles and how their wives and children burn to death in the pit, Mechthild adds a final paragraph reintroducing Elijah and Enoch. She relates how an angel brings them from paradise, how they shudder at coming back to earth, how they receive earthly appearances, and how, besides receiving sustenance from God, they eat honey and figs and drink diluted wine (IV 27, 164-70; 148). This is hardly a moment at which a curtain should fall.

When she returns to this material in Book VI, a book thought by some to have been written perhaps as an afterthought some years later, she takes up the story again in a manner that allows one to consider this chapter more or less a continuation of the material presented in IV 27. The abruptness of the ending of this chapter, which concludes with Enoch's final prayer and God's response to it, leaves one again with a feeling of incompleteness. The reader instinctively asks why Mechthild stops here and refrains from describing the fall of Antichrist with all the theater and drama this would afford her. One response is that we should return to the beginning of the chapter and note that the vision granted Mechthild here was to focus on Enoch, "the last human being to cultivate the spiritual life."[44] The vision was not to be one that described the last days in their entirety.

And yet the question persists. Why, given her obvious interest in the material and her talent for visual description and dramatic dialogue, did Mechthild not return and finish her personalized account of the last days? To conjecture here is no more than to admit ignorance. Nonetheless, on the basis of what we do have, one would seem to be justified in assuming that her portrayal would have been vivid, mixing tradition with innovation, and that it would have taken its place among the most moving depicitons of the end which the Middle Ages produced.

---

[44] "Enoch sol der jungste mensche wesen, der geistliches lebennes sol pflegen." VI 15, pp. 20-21; 222.

2 The Spirituality of *Piers Plowman*

M. Clemente Davlin, O.P.

Piers Plowman has been called "the supreme English testament of Christian faith and practice."[1] Written in the fourteenth century by William Langland for an audience of laity (men and women) and clergy, it was very popular for several centuries. In the last fifty years, after a period when it had been almost inaccessible, it has become a focus for scholarly study with an annual of its own and dozens of books and articles analyzing it each year. A few summers ago, an NEH Summer Institute invited influential university teachers to study *Piers Plowman* together with Chaucer, and the most recent editions of college textbooks such as the *Norton Anthology of English Literature* have finally recognized it as a standard part of the canon; undergraduate students are finding it attractive. Currently, at least five paperback translations are in print.[2] One hopes that it is on the verge of becoming available and useful to readers even outside the universities, people like its first readers in the fourteenth and fifteenth centuries.

Written in a Middle English laced with hundreds of Latin quotations, mostly from the Bible and liturgy, *Piers Plowman* is a book-length narrative of a man called Will who, in his youth, goes out to see wonders and has a series of ten dreams about the world, himself, and God.[3] In the course of the poem, Will confers with many allegorical interlocutors, Holy Church, the powers of his own psyche (such as Knowledge, Conscience, the Soul, and Imagination), biblical figures like Abraham and the Good Samaritan, Nature, and the title-figure, Piers the Plowman. A symbolic figure, Piers is a farmer, perhaps a prophet; at one point, he is identified with Christ and at another point, with Peter. Following Piers, Will comes to experience Christ directly during Holy Week, when he dreams of his passion, death, harrowing of hell, and

---

[1] J. A. W. Bennett, *Poetry of Passion* (Oxford: Clarendon Press, 1982), p. 85.

[2] The translations currently in paperback are by Donaldson (1990), Schmidt (1992), Covella (1992), Goodridge (1959), and Economou (1996).

[3] There are three or four versions of *Piers Plowman*, called the Z, A, B, and C Texts. Z and A are short, B and C long (book-length). I shall be speaking principally of the B-Text and using Schmidt's 2nd edition; translations are my own. A few of the ideas in this essay had their beginning in a talk at a conference on spirituality at the Kentucky Metroversity, 1978.

resurrection. In the last two dreams, Will sees the corruption of the world of his time and wakes as Conscience goes to seek Piers the Plowman to reform it.

A generation ago, Hilary Pepler, O.P., wrote a series of essays on the spirituality of this poem, developed later in his book on *The English Religious Heritage*.[4] He saw *Piers Plowman* as "a mirror of the common spirituality" of medieval England, "a truly English and liturgical type of spirituality, that must have been characteristic of the devout members of the Church, both ecclesiastical and lay."[5] Since his work, many other studies of the religious aspects of the poem have appeared on such topics as action and contemplation,[6] the "three lives,"[7] the image of God,[8] spiritual growth,[9] sincerity,[10] the Trinity,[11] mysticism,[12] social justice),[13] patience,[14] Christology,[15] God's action,[16] liturgy,[17]

---

[4] Parts of Pepler's work also appeared in *Life of the Spirit* 1.

[5] Hilary Pepler, O.P., "The Spirituality of William Langland," *Blackfriars* 29 (1939): 846-54.

[6] T. P. Dunning, "Action and Contemplation in *Piers Plowman*, pp. 213-25 in S. S. Hussey, ed., *Piers Plowman* (London: Methuen, 1969).

[7] S. S. Hussey, "Langland, Hilton, and the Three Lives," *Review of English Studies* 7 (1956): 132-50.

[8] Daniel Murtaugh, *Piers Plowman and the Image of God* (Gainesville: University Presses of Florida, 1978); and Barbara Raw, "Piers and the Image of God in Man," pp. 143-79 in Hussey, *Piers*.

[9] Stephen Manning, "Langland and the Tradition of Spiritual Growth," *Yearbook of Langland Studies* 7 (1993): 77-95.

[10] Guy Bourquin, "*Piers Plowman* ou l'ascèse de la sincérité," *La Vie Spirituelle* 131 (1977): 686-714.

[11] Lawrence M. Clopper, "Langland's Trinitarian Analogies as Key to Meaning and Structure," *Medievalia et Humanistica* 9 (1979): 87-110.

[12] Edward Vasta, *The Spiritual Basis of Piers Plowman* (The Hague: Mouton, 1965); and A. V. C. Schmidt, "Langland and the Mystical Tradition," pp. 17-38 in Marion Glasscoe, ed., *The Medieval Mystical Tradition in England* (Exeter: University of Exeter Press, 1980).

[13] David Aers, *Community, Gender, and Individual Identity* (London: Routledge and Kegan Paul, 1988); David Aers, "Justice and Wage Labor after the Black Death," pp. 164-90 in Allen Frantzen and Douglas Moffat, eds, *The World of Work* (Glasgow: Cruithne, 1994); Geoffrey Shepherd, "Poverty in *Piers Plowman*," pp. 169-89 in T. H. Aston, et al., eds, *Social Relaitons and Ideas* (Cambridge: Cambridge University Press, 1983); Christopher Dyer, "Piers Plowman and Plowmen: A Historical Perspective," *Yearbook of Langland Studies* 8 (1994): 155-76; Derek Pearsall, "Poverty and Poor People in *Piers Plowman*," pp. 167-85 in E. D. Kennedy, R. Waldron, and J. S. Wittig, eds, *Medieval Studies Presented to George Kane* (Cambridge: D. S. Brewer, 1988).

[14] Anna Baldwin, "The Triumph of Patience in Julian of Norwich and Langland," pp. 71-83 in Helen Phillips, ed., *Langland, the Mystics, and the Medieval English Religioius Tradition* (Cambridge: D. S. Brewer, 1990).

[15] Elizabeth Kirk, "Langland's Narrative Christology," pp. 17-35 in Robert R. Edwards, ed., *Art and Context in Late Medieval English Narrative* (Cambridge: D. S. Brewer, 1994).

marriage,[18] and knowledge and love.[19] However, the poem has not yet become a standard part of courses in the history of spirituality, nor of popular reading, even by people already acquainted with Julian, Hildegard, Eckhardt and other medieval religious writers. Thus, it is not recognized as the rich resource it could be for self-understanding by the Christian community. In tribute to Mary Giles, whose life has blended scholarship with spirituality, I should like here to sketch some of the characteristics of the spirituality of this great religious poem.

By spirituality, I mean, in Carolyn Bynum's definition, "the attitudes and assumptions that underlie the ways in which people believe in, approach and worship God,"[20] or, in Simon Tugwell's words, "people's ways of viewing things, the ways in which they try to make sense of the practicalities of christian [sic] living and to illuminate christian hopes and christian muddle."[21] One might argue, with Jean Leclercq, that there is only one Christian spirituality since there is only "one Gospel."[22] But as he himself points out, "many factors— . . . surroundings . . . historical circumstances . . . vocations . . . cause variations in the concrete application of the Gospel to a human life,"[23] and thus, Christian spirituality has many modes of religious sensibility and style, even though it is one in faith. *Piers Plowman* is a Christian poem with a sensibility and style, attitudes and assumptions, and ways of viewing things which are unique and particularly attractive to readers of the late twentieth century who come to know it. The best way of enjoying these is through a thorough study of the poem, which, like the *Divine Comedy* and Julian's *Shewings*, is so rich that it will yield insights on many aspects of spirituality. In an attempt to summarize

---

[16] John Lawlor, "Imaginative Unity of *Piers Plowman*," *Review of English Studies* 8 (1957): 113-26.

[17] Raymond St. Jacques, "Conscience's Final Pilgrimage in *Piers Plowman* and the Cyclical Structure of the Liturgy," *Revue de l'Université d'Ottowa* 40 (1970): 210-23; Raymond St. Jacques, "Langland's Bells of the Resurrection and the Easter Liturgy," *English Studies in Canada* 3 (1977): 129-35; Raymond St. Jacques, "Langland's Christ-Knight and the Liturgy," *Revue de l'Université d'Ottowa* 37 (1967): 144-58; Raymond St. Jacques, "The Liturgical Associations of Langland's Samaritan," *Traditio* 25 (1969): 217-30; and M. Teresa Tavormina, "*Piers Plowman* and the Liturgy of St. Lawrence: Composition and Revision in Langland's Poetry," *Studies in Philology* 84 (1987): 245-71.

[18] M. Teresa Tavormina, *Kindly Similitude: Marriage and Family in Piers Plowman* (Cambridge: D. S. Brewer, 1995).

[19] James Simpson, "From Reason to Affective Knowledge: Modes of Thought and Poetic Form in *Piers Plowman*," *Medium Aevum* 55 (1986): 1-23.

[20] Carolyn Walker Bynum, "Franciscal Spirituality: Two Approaches," *Medievalia et Humanistica* 7 (1976): 195.

[21] Simon Tugwell, O.P., *Ways of Imperfection* (Springfield: Templegate, 1985), p. viii.

[22] Jean Leclercq, "Preface," *Spirituality of Western Christendom*, E. Rozanne Elder, ed. (Kalamazoo, Michigan: Cistercian Publications, 1976), p. xi.

[23] Leclerq, "Preface," pp. x-xi.

this richness, I will discuss four characteristics of this spirituality: it is biblical and liturgical, social and personal, God-centered, and intended not just for clergy, but also for a lay audience of women and men.

Perhaps the most obvious characteristic of this spirituality is its deeply Biblical and liturgical character. Kuczynski calls the poem "psalmic,"[24] and Morton Bloomfield goes so far as to say that the author "speaks Bible,"[25] not only because so many Biblical quotations are woven into the fabric of the text,[26] but also because the Biblical books, especially the psalms and Wisdom literature, including John, form the thought and style of the poem.[27] The chief "original" name for God in *Piers Plowman*, for example, (i.e., in addition to "God," "Lord," and "Jesus Christ") is "Truth," a name Biblical in origin.[28] Biblical stories of Adam and Eve, Abraham, Moses, David, and the life of Christ are retold. Moreover, the ethics the poem teaches are, as Pepler says, "thoroughly evangelical," since "Love is the heart of Langland's message.[29]

The spirituality is biblical also in its affirmation of material creation. In its first description of creation, the poem specifies the creation of the body as well as the soul and describes Truth's concern that human physical needs be met with such specifics as wool and linen, to "make you comfortable":

> For he is fader of feith, formed yow alle
> Bothe with fel and with face and yaf yow fyve wittes
> For to worshipe hym therwith the while that ye ben here.
> And therfore he highte the erthe to helpe yow echone
> Of wollene, of lynnen, of liflode at nede
> In mesurable manere to make yow at ese. (1.14-9)

[For he is father of faith, formed you all

---

[24] See Michael P. Kuczynski, *Prophetic Song* (Philadelphia: University of Pennsylvania Press, 1995), pp. 189-90: "the Psalms command a special, even preeminent place in Langland's literary and moral imagination . . . extending rather than interrupting his discourse. . . . When Langland thought and wrote, he did so (much of the time) in psalmic ways."

[25] Morton Bloomfield, *Piers Plowman as a Fourteenth-Century Apocalypse* (New Brunswick, New Jersey: Rutgers University Press, 1961), p. 37.

[26] John Alford, *Piers Plowman: A Guide to the Quotations* (Binghamton, New York: Medieval and Renaissance Texts and Studies, 1992), has collected and identified these. In the B-Text, he finds just over 200 citations of the Hebrew Scriptures, and 200 of the New Testament.

[27] For uses of the psalms, see Kuczynski, *Prophetic Song*; for uses of Wisdom literature and John, see Mary Clemente Davlin, O.P., "*Piers Plowman* and the Books of Wisdom," *Yearbook of Langland Studies* 2 (1988): 23-33; and Mary Clemente Davilin, O.P., "*Piers Plowman* and the Gospel and First Epistle of John," *Yearbook of Langland Studies* 10 (1996): 89-127.

[28] Used about 50 times, by my count.

[29] Pepler, "Spirituality, " p. 852.

> Both with skin and with face, and gave you five wits
> To worship him with while you are here.
> And therefore he ordered the earth to help each of you
> With wool, with linen, with what you need to live
> In a temperate way, to make you comfortable]

The phrase "formed you all" suggests the innumerable medieval manuscript illuminations and stained glass and mosaic representations of God bending to form Adam and Eve with his hands. "Father of faith" can mean both "origin of what we believe" and "faithful father," the latter exemplified by God's concern for the well-being of his creatures, ordering the earth to help them.

Later in the poem, God's creative work is seen as the model and source of human labor, sexual love, and artistry.[30] This affirmation is characteristic of the spirituality of the entire poem, to the point that in Passus 9, God is identified with Nature (Kynde):

> "Kynde," quod Wit, "is creatour of alle kynnes thynges,
> Fader and formour of al that evere was maked—
> And that it the grete God that gynnyng hadde nevere,
> Lord of lif and of light, of lisse and of peyne." (9.26-9).

> "Nature," said Wit, "is creator of all kinds of things,
> Father and former of all that ever was made—
> And that is the great God that never had beginning,
> Lord of life and of light, of bliss and of pain."

In Passus 11, Will is called by Kynde to see "the wonders of this world . . . and to learn/ Through each creature to love Kynde, my creator" in a passage which affirms the natural world, the body, and human and animal sexuality, and accepts the whole creation as a lesson in divine love. This affirmation, developed in contrast to a powerful sense of the horror and pain of evil, gives the poem a sense of hope and joy in God who is

> The light of al that lif hath a londe and a watre,
> Confortour of creatures—of hym cometh alle blisse. (16.189-90)

> The light of all who have life on land or water,
> Comforter of creatures; of him comes all bliss.

These biblical insights are made accessible, celebrated, and understood in the poem largely through the liturgy. That is, biblical quotations are often those already familiar through the liturgy, the official communal Christian worship;

---

[30] On marriage and sexuality in the poem, see Tavormina, *Kindly*, esp. 78-82, 99-102, 107-9, 135, 176-90.

within the narrative, too, common prayer, celebrations of sacraments, and participation in feasts of the church are occasions for recalling Bible stories and language. For example, the climax of the poem comes during Holy Week. Will goes to sleep during Palm Sunday Mass and sees in his dream the meaning of the Holy Week services, watching a mental dramatization of the gospel story from the crucifixion to the resurrection of Christ. On Pentecost, again he goes to Church, and in a dream he sees the Holy Spirit descend upon the apostles. Another dream represents a communal celebration of the sacrament of penance or reconciliation (Passus 5).[31]

Pepler notes that "Langland's attitude toward the Person of Christ seems to reflect the restrained, austere and majestic treatment of the liturgy."[32] Because the liturgy is common worship, its prayers rarely use highly subjective or emotional expressions of devotion; they tend to be restrained, dignified, and tranquil, regulated by rubric. There is no place in liturgy for violence, surprise or singularity, though at the same time the nature of the sacraments and the aims of worship make the liturgy intensely realistic and deeply personal. In these ways, too, Langland's religious sensibility and spirituality are distinctively liturgical.

Because it is liturgical, the spirituality of *Piers Plowman* is social. In fact, in describing the poem's spirituality as "fundamentally liturgical" Pepler means that within it, "prayer is communal; . . . [the] approach to God is not isolated or solitary."[33] Religious experience in *Piers* is public, much of it taking place in the Field of Folk. There, Holy Church comes to teach Will, sinners confess, Piers tells of his intimate life with Truth (God), Truth sends his pardon, Unity Holy Church is built, and the "fools" resist Antichrist—all exteriorly, in full light, in the midst of large groups of people. The genres used in the poem to explore religious questions, such as debate, dialogue, sermon, and allegorical instruction[34] are public forms. Even in the most deeply interior scenes, dreams within dreams, experience is always perceived as communicable. As Bloomfield says,

> *Piers* is first of all socially oriented . . . in its view of perfection. . . .
> The journey of the individual soul to God is perhaps also implied, but
> it is not central . . . Conscience, Kind Wit, and Reason in the poem are

---

[31] See, for example, Greta Hort, *Piers Plowman and Contemporary Religious Thought* (New York: Macmillan, 1936); Dom D. Rutledge, "Langland and the Liturgy," *The Dublin Review* 228 (1954): 405-16; P. Di Pasquale, "The Form of *Piers Plowman* and the Liturgy," diss. University of Pittsburgh, 1965; the works of St. Jacques, cited above, note 17; and Tavormina, "*Piers*."

[32] Pepler, "Spirituality" p. 853.

[33] Hilary Pepler, O.P., *English Religious Heritage* (London: Blackfriars, 1958), pp. 52-3.

[34] On the genres in the poem, see especially Bloomfield, *Piers*, 8-34.

not personal or subjective, as in the modern psychological approach to the self, but objective though inward. They reflect an older type of psychological interest, antedating the intensity of men like Bernard of Clairvaux and Richard of St. Victor, as well as later mystics.[35]

At a time when many religious writers, under the influence first of Bernard and later of the Franciscans, were emphasizing "devotion to the humanity of Jesus, particularly to those moments in his life that aroused sentiments of love and compassion: his infancy and his passion,"[36] *Piers Plowman* exemplifies what both Bloomfield and Pepler call "objective" rather than "subjective" spirituality.[37] God is seen as father, brother and companion, judge and lord, teacher and physician, creator, redeemer and comforter, champion and mother, names which suggest open, shared, universal relationships. There are over eighty names for God in the poem, but these do not include "spouse" or "lover," and this absence of erotic imagery is surprising in an age when the *Song of Songs* pattern of allegory was so influential in England.[38] Richard Rolle, for example, an earlier contemporary of Langland, describes union with God as reaching one's beloved spouse: "dilecte cum dilecto coniunccio consequatur"; Langland describes it as the deeply personal but universally shared relationship of child to father with a hushed sense of interior attention, loving obedience and adoration:

> Thow shalt see in thiselve Truthe sitte in thyn herte
> In a cheyne of charite, as thow a child were,
> To suffren hym and segge noght ayein thi sires wille. (5.606-8)

> Thou shalt see in thyself Truth sit in thine heart
> In a chain of charity, as if thou wert a child,
> To let him be, and say nothing against thy sire's will.

For Rolle, characteristics of love are mostly erotic or private: love is "burning, violent, inflamed, impetuous, invincible, inseparable, unique. . . ."[39] Precious as it is to Langland ("the dearest thing . . . most precious") love is figured in exterior, objective, public, even political images, rather than in subjective or romantic ones:

---

[35] Bloomfield, *Piers*, pp. 105, 116.
[36] Richard Kieckhefer, *Unquiet Souls* (Chicago: University of Chicago Press, 1984), p. 90.
[37] Pepler, *Religious*, p. 59.
[38] Tavormina points out one exception, i.e., that the Church is said to be the spouse of Christ and mother of his children (*Kindly*, p. 146).
[39] "flag rans, vehemens, estuans, impetuosus, invincibilis, inseparabilis, singularis . . ." (*Melos* xlvii, xlvi (II:13, p. 5, and L:39, p. 159).

> ... love is triacle of hevene:
>
> ... the levest thyng and moost lik to hevene,
> And also the plante of pees, moost precious of vertues:
>
> ... ledere of the Lordes folk of hevene,
> And a meene, as the mair is [inmiddes] the kyng and the commune;
>
> Love is leche of lif ...
> And also the graithe gate that goth into hevene.
>
> (1.148, 151-2, 159-60, 204-5)
>
> ... love is the sweet nourishment of heaven
>
> ... the dearest thing and most like to heaven,
> And also the plant of peace, most precious of virtues.
>
> ... leader of the lord's folk of heaven,
> And a mediator, as the mayor is, between the commons and the king.
>
> Love is physician of life ...
> And also the straight road that goes into heaven.

Even in its figuration of Christ's passion as a knightly tournament, a figure used earlier in the "Ancrene Riwle" and religious lyrics within a courtly love convention, *Piers Plowman* "leaves out entirely the espousal motif, ... [producing] a change in tone from the romantic to the heroic," as Wilbur Gaffney pointed out (166).[40]

This social, objective quality of the spirituality of *Piers Plowman* is related to a profound sense of the obligations of social justice. A plowman is the exemplar and symbol of holiness in the poem; he is perhaps the source for Chaucer's good plowman in the Prologue to the *Canterbury Tales*.[41] By using this idealized image of the good peasant, both poets go counter to the attitudes of their own society which had a "work ethos" despising the poor as lacking "aggressive individualism."[42] Langland writes with "unsentimental loving compassion and ... raw truth" about the poor,[43] so that, as Christopher Dawson declared many years ago, *Piers Plowman* "is the first and almost the

---

[40] Wilbur Gaffney, "Allegory of the Christ-Knight," *PMLA* 46 (1931): 166.

[41] See Jill Mann, *Chaucer and Medieval Estates Satire* (Cambridge: Cambridge University Press, 1973), pp. 67-74. See also Aers, "Justice," pp. 177-181; Shepherd, "Poverty"; Dyer, "Historical Perspective"; and Elizabeth Kirk, "Langland's Plowman and the Recreation of Fourteenth-Century Religious Metaphor," *Yearbook of Langland Studies* 2 (1988): 17-35.

[42] Aers, *Community* pp. 55, 59.

[43] Pearsall, "Poverty," p. 180.

only utterance in literature of the cry of the poor."[44] For example, in Passus 9, the poem says,

> Sholde no Cristene creature cryen at the yate
> Ne faille payn ne potage, and prelates dide as thei sholden.
> A Jew wolde noght se a Jew go janglyng for defaute
> For alle the mebles on this moolde, and he amende it myghte.
> Allas that a Cristene creature shal be unkynde til another!
> Syn Jewes, that we jugge Judas felawes,
> Eyther helpeth oother of hem of that that hym nedeth.
> Whi nel we Cristene [be of Cristes good as kynde]
> As Jewes, that ben oure loresmen? Shame to us alle!
> The commune for hir unkyndenesse, I drede me, shul abye.
> Bisshopes shul be blamed for beggeres sake;
> [Than Judas he is wors] that yyveth a japer silver
> And biddeth the beggere go, for his broke clothes. (80-92)

> No Christian creature should cry at the gate
> Nor lack bread nor soup, if prelates did as they should.
> A Jew would not see a Jew go whistling for his supper
> For all the goods in the world, if he could help it.
> Alas that a Christian creature should be unkind to another!
> Since Jews, that we judge the companions of Judas
> Help one another with what they need.
> Why will we Christians not be as kind with the goods of Christ
> As Jews, our teachers? Shame to us all!
> The community, for their unkindness, I fear, shall suffer.
> Bishops shall be blamed for the beggars;
> He is judged as worse than Judas who gives an entertainer silver
> And tells the beggar to go, for his torn clothes.

Such passages, "without any sentimentalization . . . force readers to shift outside the ethos in which able-bodied vagrants are swiftly classified as drunken scroungers, drones, wasters."[45] The "beggars" with "torn clothes" who "lack bread" and "soup" are yet "Christian creature[s]," persons with dignity, part of the community, to whom the rest of "us all" owe "kindness." In this spirituality, care for the poor is not a matter of unusual charity, but of justice. The poor have a right to "bread" and "soup" and "silver," a right as "Christian creature[s]" not to be excluded, not to be left to "cry at the gate." Thus, against the worldly mores of his time and ours, Langland gets to the heart of Christian teaching, implicating the whole community: "Shame to us all." This attitude is subversive, not of the church, but of oppressive wealth.

---

[44] Christopher Dawson, *Medieval Essays* (London: Sheed and Ward, 1953), p. 250.
[45] Aers, *Community*, p. 61.

Another subversive perception in this passage from the B-Text[46] is the example of kindness Langland gives: the care of the Jewish community for one another. Langland is as aware as Chaucer of antisemitic feeling. The adjectival clause, "that we judge companions of Judas" sounds as if the speaker identifies with such feeling. But this judgment itself is judged a few lines later: Christians who are spendthrifts, bishops contemptuous of the poor, are worse than what they falsely judge Jews to be—"worse than Judas." And the use of the example at all suggests that the Jews who enact love and kindness are not only not "companions of Judas," but are kin to the One whose names are "Kynde" and "*caritas,*" God, for whom kindness, the virtue of these Jews, is named. Clearly, then, the spirituality of this poem is not easy or fashionable. It is based on a deeply prophetic and very unusual understanding of Christ's message of love.

In addition to being social and rooted in social justice, the spirituality of the poem is deeply personal, without being subjective or romantic. Its narrative is the story of a lay Christian struggling to come to know God and himself. Holy Church, at the beginning, teaches him that "When all treasures are tried, truth is the best" (1.207) (When alle tresors ben tried, Treuthe is the beste.). Truth is the moral virtue of honesty, sincerity, and faithfulness. As Guy Bourquin has shown, the asceticism of truth is the movement from duplicity to sincerity,[47] but if it is to be true and meritorious, it must be loving as well. Holy Church emphasizes this point with a joke:

> For though ye be trewe of youre tonge and treweliche wynne,
> And as chaste as a child that in chirche wepeth,
> But if ye loven leelly and lene the povere,
> Of swich good as God yow sent goodliche parteth,
> Ye ne have na moore merite in masse ne in houres
> Than Malkyn of hire maydenhede, that no man desireth.
> (1.179-84).

> For even if you are true of your tongue, and earn your living honestly,
> And are as chaste as a child who weeps in church,
> Unless you love faithfully and give to the poor,
> Share freely such goods as God gives you,
> You have no more merit in Mass nor in prayers

---

[46] This passage is absent from the C-Text. See Elisa Narin van Court, "The Hermeneutics of Supersession: the Revision of the Jews from the B to the C Text of *Piers Plowman,*" *Yearbook of Langland Studies* 10 (1996): 43-87 on the change in attitude toward the Jews in the C-Text.

[47] Bourquin, "*Piers,*" p. 593.

Than Malkyn has for her maidenhood that no one wants.

Will learns to repent of sin and tries to learn to "Do-well, Do-better, and Do-best," making mistakes that are comic and humbling. Finally, after years of trying to know what "Do-well" really is, he comes face to face with his own soul who tells him, "You are imperfect and one of Pride's knights" (15.50) ("Thanne artow inparfit," quod he, "and oon of Prides knyghtes!"). The shock of this reprimand frightens and shakes him. In his desperation, he comes to see and love Christ as the Good Samaritan and as a young knight who will fight against the fiend, falseness, and death in a tournament. In this vision of Christ, many of the problems of Will's personal search are resolved, and both he and the reader begin to realize that the search for God and holiness is only one side of the spiritual life, for all the time that Will has been searching for God, God has been searching for him.[48]

Thus, while *Piers Plowman* can be called the story of a person's search for God, on another level it is a poem about the nature of God, and its spirituality is God-centered. God is a mystery, never simplified by the poet, a mystery which the poem invites the reader to enter and probe by faith and love. The Trinity, the incarnation, the indwelling of God in human hearts, and the nature of the Church and her sacraments are presented to Will and the reader for contemplation, and each of these great mysteries is shown to have implications for the spiritual life of the individual and the group.

In presenting the mystery of the Trinity, for example, the Samaritan compares it to a torch, "As wax and wick twisted together and then a fire flaming forth out of both" (17.205-6) (As wex and a weke were twyned togideres,/ And thanne a fir flawmynge forth out of bothe). What seems a simple simile becomes a source of insight as he continues, first with a theology of the Trinity: "So grace of the Holy Spirit melts the great might of the Trinity to mercy" (230-31) (So grace of the Holy Goost the greet myght of the Trinite / Melteth to mercy), and then with a moral lesson:

> Thus is unkyndenesse the contrarie that quencheth, as it were,
> The grace of the Holy Goost, Goddes owene kynde.
> For that kynde dooth, unkynde fordooth. (271-3)

> Thus is unkindness the contrary that quenches, as it were,
> The grace of the Holy Spirit, God's own nature.
> For what Kynde[49] makes, unkindness destroys.

---

[48] See Lawlor, "Imaginative."
[49] "Kynde" is a pun meaning Nature/the kind one/God. See Tavormina, *Kindly*, pp. 49-50, 59.

The fire of the Holy Spirit, strong enough to "melt the great might of the Trinity to mercy," can be quenched by human unkindness which thus destroys the possibility of mercy. The nature of God as Trinity, inconceivable in its mystery, is the reason humans are to live in loving community, and thus the sin of unkindness against another human is a sin against the nature of God who, in three Persons, is a communion of love.

As this example shows, the poem is intellectually challenging because instead of settling for attractive emotional images of Jesus, it insists upon exploring the great mysteries of Jesus' teaching. Jesus himself is always "God-man," never simply divine or simply human. In him, "God is born," and "God dies," the noun denoting divinity, the verb humanity. In a crucifixion scene in Passus 5, the poet writes,

> "*Consummatum est*," quod Crist, and comsede for to swoune,
> Pitousliche and pale as a prison that deieth;
> The lord of lif and of light tho leide hise eighen togideres.
> The day for drede withdrough and derk bicam the sonne.
> The wal waggede and cleef, and al the world quaved. (18.57-61)

> "*Consummatum est*," said Christ, and began to swoon.
> Piteous and pale as a prisoner dying,
> The Lord of life and of light then closed his eyes.
> The day for dread withdrew and dark became the sun.
> The wall waved and broke, and all the world quaked.

Here, typically, the poet expresses "the most elevated of religious feelings in the simplest terms,"[50] showing "the ambiguity of the Christian experience as lived in the person of the crucified/resurrected Christ."[51] Langland weaves the Bible narrative into the English line and adds very little to the Biblical account except details from human experience, like the swoon and the closing of the eyes.[52] The scene includes elements of pathos, the swoon, the piteous paleness of the young man closing his eyes in death, the gentle alliterating sounds of *s*, *p*, and *l*. Yet the poet complements these pathetic elements with something which causes us to see the crucifixion not simply as a moment of pathos, but also as the revelation of a great mystery. The young man, "Christ" (the name which

---

[50] Charles Muscatine, *Poetry and Crisis in the Age of Chaucer* (Notre Dame: University of Notre Dame Press, 1972).

[51] Mary E. Giles, *The Book of Prayer of Sor Maria of Santo Domingo* (Albany: State University of New York Press, 1990), p. 116.

[52] As Bennett, *Poetry*, points out, Langland "reduces rather than inflates the gospel narrative" (p. 106); but Kirk also points out ("Langland's Narrative") that this passage presents the "events as *witnessed*" and surrounds the crucifixion with "a kaleidoscope of superimposed images ... and contexts" (pp. 23, 30). See also Simpson, *Piers*, p. 211.

implies his divinity),[53] is "the Lord of life and of light." The paradox of the Lord of life dying, the Lord of light closing his eyes, the pun in the next line ("and dark became the sun"), familiar from liturgical hymns associating the Son of God with the glorious sun of light, and the terrifying reactions of nature to the crucifixion, retold from the gospel account with onomatopoetic power—all these emphasize the divinity of Christ and the paradox of the death of God. One side of the paradox is never allowed to swallow up the other: human and divine, tenderness and awe, grief and wonder together are part of the intellectual toughness of the lines which require the reader to look squarely at mystery, at what cannot be fully understood.[54]

As must be obvious to readers of Julian, *Piers Plowman* has much in common with the teaching of some of the mystics,[55] especially Julian of Norwich, who was a later contemporary of Langland. A. V. C. Schmidt asserts "the fundamental oneness of Langland's teaching with Julian" because of "parallels of thought and phrase,"[56] suggesting that Julian had read *Piers Plowman.* For example, both writers transgress the ordinary borders of gender by considering Jesus as Mother. To Julian, "our saviour is our true Mother, in whom we are endlessly born and out of whom we shall never come. . . . We are all enclosed in him and he is enclosed in us."[57] He is "our true Mother in nature by our first creation, and . . . our true Mother in grace by his taking our created nature."[58] Julian's text repeats this affirmation of the motherhood of Jesus and of God more frequently than the poem does, but both Julian and Langland write of the birth of the church from Jesus' body and the invitation to suck at Jesus' motherly breasts. Julian writes, "The mother can give her child to suck of her milk, but our precious Mother Jesus can feed us with himself, and does, most courteously and most tenderly, with the blessed sacrament, which is the precious food of true life . . . ."[59] In *Piers Plowman*, Will is told,

> For Crist cleped us alle, come if we wolde—
> Sarsens and scismatikes, and so he dide the Jewes:
> *O vos omnes sicientes, venite . . .*

---

[53] Bennett, *Poetry*, p. 101.

[54] Some of the preceding section is taken from my "Chaucer and Langland as Religious Writers," forthcoming in Kathleen Hewett-Smith, ed., *William Langland's Piers Plowman: a Book of Essays*, with permission.

[55] See Mary E. Giles, *The Poetics of Love* (New York: Peter Lang, 1986), p. 1: "Mysticism is union with God, and a mystic is one who falls in love with God and seeks to live in conformity with the divine will. Complexity enters, as does difficulty, with the mystic's efforts to describe the experience and the scholar's to explain it."

[56] Schmidt, "Langland" p. 20.

[57] Edmund Colledge and James Walsh, trans., *Julian of Norwich: Showings* (New York: Paulist Press, 1978), p. 292.

[58] Colledge and Walsh, *Julian*, p. 296.

[59] Colledge and Walsh, *Julian*, p. 298.

> And bad hem souke for synne save at his breste
> And drynke boote for bale. (11.119-22)
>
> For Christ called us all, to come if we would—
> Saracens and schismatics, and the Jews:
> O all you who thirst, come—
> And bade them suck a cure for sin at his breast
> And drink good for evil . . . .

Calling on the reader's preconscious experience of intimate dependence upon a mother as powerful source of satisfaction for all one's needs, the image destabilizes gender-boundaries and daringly evokes absolute divine power and immediacy. Here, as in Julian's book, Christ's milk is likely a figure for the eucharist. As Carolyn Bynum points out, "To medieval natural philosophers, milk was transmuted blood[,] and a human mother—like the pelican that also symbolized Christ, fed her children from the fluid of life that coursed through her veins."[60] To "suck . . . at his breast" is to take within one's own body, as in the eucharist, the healing, saving substance of Christ's body.

Another passage also destabilizes gender-boundaries, this time in a context of birth:

> For alle are we Cristes creatures, and of his cofres riche,
> And bretheren as of oo blood, as wel beggeres as erles.
> For at Calvarie, of Cristes blood Cristendom gan sprynge,
> And blody bretheren we bicome there, of o body ywonne. (11.198-201)
>
> For we are all Christ's creatures, and rich from his coffers,
> And siblings of one blood, beggars as well as earls.
> For at Calvary, Christendom began to spring from Christ's blood
> And blood brothers we became there, won by/out of one body.

Bynum gives a number of examples of the commonplace that the church was born from the body of Christ on the cross,[61] and we seem to have another example here. Delivered in birth from the body of Christ the Mother, all people are siblings. The openings, the fissures in Christ's body made by nails and spear, the passages made by violation, are birth-passages, channels of life. Again a profound mystery has powerful moral implications: here, beggars must be accepted even by earls as "blood brothers."

As these last passages suggest, the spirituality of *Piers Plowman* is for lay people, women and men, as much as for clergy. In it, as Anne Middleton

---

[60] Carolyn Walker Bynum, *Jesus our Mother* (Berkeley: University of California Press, 1982), p. 270.

[61] Bynum, *Jesus*, pp. 110-69; and Carolyn Walker Bynum, *Fragmentation and Redemption* (New York: Zone, 1991), p. 97.

shows, a commoner addresses himself to the commonweal, to the spiritual and material welfare of his whole society.[62] Christopher Dawson called the poem "a voice from another world—the submerged world of the common Englishman . . . the authentic voice of the English people."[63] Although the protagonist and the poet admire Benedictine monks and value the work of virtuous religious, priests, and bishops, both protagonist and poet are themselves lay.[64] Marriage and family life are the context of the narrative and the spirituality it embodies; as M. T. Tavormina has shown, the poet presents "the economy of salvation in language drawn from the familial."[65] Dozens of kinship terms occur in the poem, for example, used both literally and figuratively. There are brethren, sisters, and siblings, godfathers, fathers, forefathers, lineage and heirs, children and godchildren, bastards, babies and youngsters; there are women, lovers, mothers, dames, and widows, cousins and metaphorical aunts, kith and kin of all kinds, as well as fellows and peers, mates, and mediators. The number and variety of such terms show how highly developed the poet's awareness of kinship was. His whole society, of course, was profoundly aware of kinship and must have valued it greatly; medieval law books abound in "trees of consanguinity" and "trees of affinity," and Bibles and stained glass windows illustrate the genealogy of Christ in the tree of Jesse, as history books graph the genealogy of rulers. Boccaccio even traced the family trees of the ancient gods.[66] It is not surprising, therefore, that especially to a poet probing the mystery of the relationship of people to the Triune God, and the mystery of church as the people of God, kinship is an important image.[67] "From the very fact of the Incarnation all [hu]mankind has become related to God . . . even those outside the Church."[68]

It is not too much to say that in *Piers Plowman*, salvation is attained only through kinship. "Words, works and will" are of course important in "the scheme of salvation,"[69] but virtue itself is a form or proof of kinship with God,

---

[62] Anne Middleton, "The Idea of Public Poetry in the Reign of Richard II," *Speculum* 53 (1978): 100-101.

[63] Dawson, *Medieval Essays*, p. 242.

[64] Or they were "minor" clerics, married and singing psalms for a living.

[65] Tavormina, *Kindly*, p. 225.

[66] A few manuscripts with such trees are Vat. Pal. lat 441, f. 19 verso, Vat. Pal. lat. 629, f. 260 verso, and Vat. lat. 1383, f. 3 verso; I am grateful to the Vatican Film Library, St. Louis University, for the opportunity to see these in microfilm. For Boccaccio, see Wilkins; one manuscript of his *genealogia deorum* is at the Regenstein Library, University of Chicago.

[67] Pepler connects Langland's emphasis on blood relationships to his conception of the church ("Spirituality," p. 850). On kinship, see Tavormina, *Kindly*, ch. 4, esp. pp. 191-202, and Lawlor, *Piers*, pp. 170-73.

[68] Pepler, *English*, p. 56.

[69] The first term is Burrow's; the second of Robert Worth Frank, Jr., *Piers Plowman and the Scheme of Salvation* (New Haven: Yale University Press, 1957).

as it is the bond of kinship which makes both virtue and salvation possible. Passages from two major turning points in the poem illustrate the centrality of kinship in the spirituality of *Piers Plowman*.

The first comes at the end of the confession scene. Piers offers to lead the repentant to Truth, but the road he prescribes for their pilgrimage is a hard one. He concludes:

> Ac ther are seven sustren that serven Truthe evere
> And arn porters over the posternes that to the place longeth. . . .
>
> And but if ye be sibbe to some of thise sevene,
> It is ful hard, by myn heed, any of yow alle
> To geten ingong at any gate but grace be the moore!   (5.618-19, 627-8)

> But there are seven sisters that always serve Truth
> And are porters of the postern that belong to that place.
>
> Unless you are sibling to some of these seven,
> It will be very hard, by my head, for any of you
> To get entrance at any door, unless grace be very great.

The seven sisters prove to be abstinence, humility, charity, chastity, patience, peace, and liberality, hard-won virtues with which some of the pilgrims feel no kinship. Even Piers' sentence structure is discouraging. He begins with "But" as if to place an obstacle, and concludes in a sentence with two "unless" clauses, the first almost a threat, the second tentative about grace. Understandably enough, the less savory types lose hope:

> "Now, by Crist!" quod a kuttepurs, "I have no kyn there."
> "Ne I," quod an apeward, "by aught that I knowe."
> "Wite God," quod a wafrestere, "wiste I this for sothe,
> Sholde I never ferther a foot for no freres prechyng."   (5.630-33)

> "By Christ!" said a cut-purse, "I have no kin there."
> "Nor I," said an ape-keeper, "by aught I know."
> "God knows," said a wafer-maker, "if I knew this were the truth,
> I'd never go a foot further for any friar's preaching."

And after all, what hope is there? Having read the journey which precedes this passage, one perhaps expects Piers to try to reconcile these ignorant sinners to a less perfect goal than the vision of God in their hearts, or at best to recommend a long, severe alternate route of penance so that they may become kin to the virtues. Instead, one of the most poignant and beautiful moments of the poem occurs as the soul of Piers is suddenly flooded with a new insight:

> "Yis," quod Piers the Plowman, and poked hem alle to goode,

> "Mercy is a maiden there, hath myght over hem alle;
> And she is sib to alle synfulle, and hire sone also,
> And thorugh the help of hem two—hope thow noon oother—
> Thow myght gete grace there—so thow go bityme." (5.634-8)

> "Yes!" said Piers the Plowman, and urged them to good,
> "Mercy is a maiden there with might over them all,
> And she is sister to all the sinful, and her son is their brother,
> And through the help of those two, (hope in no other),
> You might get grace there, if you go quickly."

The utter simplicity of the lines and of the solution bears conviction, and the shift in the basis of kinship is itself an image of grace. Whereas kinship to abstinence is only for the abstinent, kinship to chastity for the chaste, kinship to "Christ and . . . his clean mother" (5.511)[70] is for all sinners. Allegorical kinship to virtues has a kind of mechanical justice about it; but kinship with the sinless Christ and his mother, a kinship which "has might over" kinship with virtue, enacts mercy; it is available only to the "sinful," and it is the hope of salvation.

Later, at the climax of the poem, this passage is echoed and fulfilled in the great reconciling speech of Christ. Christ defends his right to be merciful to all humans at the last judgement, "at such a need where help is needed" (18. 400) (at swich a nede ther nedes help bihoveth.). His argument is based upon his nature, his *kynde*, and upon his natural relationship, his kinship, with all humans: "But to be merciful to man, my nature demands it" (18.376) (Ac to be merciable to man thanne, my kynde it asketh.). He concludes,

> For blood may suffre blood bothe hungry and acale,
> Ac blood may noght se blood blede, but hym rewe. . . .
>
> Ac my rightwisnesse and right shal rulen al helle,
> And mercy al mankynde bifore me in hevene.
> For I were an unkynde kyng but I my kyn holpe. (18.395-6, 397-9)

> For blood may bear blood being hungry and cold
> But blood may not see blood bleed without pity.
>
> But my righteousness and justice shall rule all hell,
> And mercy all humankind before me in heaven.
> For I would be an unnatural, unkind king, unless I helped my kin

This is an astounding passage, guaranteeing the salvation of all human beings. Christ as God is "*deus caritas*"; his nature is love. As a man, he shares blood

---

[70] Skeat, the first great modern editor of the poem, says, "*Mercy* here is the Virgin Mary." See W. W. Skeat, *The Vision Concerning Piers the Plowman*, vol. 2 (Oxford: Oxford University Press, rpt. 1978), p. 105, n. 288.

with all humans, and so both his natures demand (he says) that he help his kin. If he did not, he would be acting against his divine and human natures, and thus, in being unkind, he would be unnatural. Salvation thus depends upon the natures of Christ and his kinship with all people.

One of the implications of the spirituality of kinship demonstrated in these two passages is that goodness and holiness lie not in single actions or habits alone, nor in intentions alone, but in the relationships which persons make or allow. Relationships with God and with other humans are crucial; kinship guarantees certain rights and privileges, chief among which is love. Thus, another implication of a spirituality of kinship is the intended permanence and security, perhaps the irrevocability, of good relationships, and the right all people have to be able to count on others, including God, the trustworthy Truth.

In this broad spirituality of kinship, both genders are essential and valuable. Although the protagonist, like the poet, is masculine, his stories (like the parables of Jesus) tend to have as many women characters as men, good and bad. Names for God are what a twentieth-century person would call "inclusive," not only in the expected medieval sense that God is mother as well as father, but also in another sense. Many of the poet's favorite names for God, such as Truth, Love, Kind Nature, Grace, are neither masculine nor feminine, and thus they create inclusive images of God, attractive to both women and men.[71]

Like the work of the mystics whom Mary Giles has made so well known, *Piers Plowman* teaches a spirituality attractive to people of the late twentieth century not only because of the beauty of the poem itself, but also because of its Biblical and liturgical character, its emphasis both upon the need for the individual to "do well" and upon the bonds of kinship and love in society; its tender sense of God as neither feminine nor masculine but the source of both, infinitely good, mysterious, but permanently bonded to human beings; its affirmation of marriage and lay life; and its hope for universal salvation.

---

[71] It seems that the qualities by which Mary Giles, ed., *The Feminist Mystic* (New York: Crossroad, 1982) defines "the feminist mystic": "unique, solitary, contemplative, social, sexual" ("Introduction," p. 5) are exhibited by Langland and his protagonist, except that they do not seem to be "solitary."

3 Doubled Truth: Skeptical Fideism, Pseudo-Dionysius, and the *Second Shepherds' Play*

Robert Boenig

In her analysis of Chaucer's underlying skepticism, *Chaucer's House of Fame: The Poetics of Skeptical Fideism*,[1] Sheila Delany draws connections between the English poet's juxtaposing contradictory truths and/or traditions and certain developments in late medieval philosophy which admitted the existence of contradictory truths, particularly between observed nature and God's revelation. The so-called skeptical fideists—specifically the thirteenth-century philosophers Boethius of Dacia[2] and Siger of Brabant[3] but also to a certain extent their predecessors like Abelard and successors like William of Ockham—held that what we would now term mutually exclusive beliefs could each be true,[4] with the Church's officially recognized dogma taking precedence through a motion of faith. Thus Boethius and Siger could assert the ultimately Aristotelian "truth" of the eternal nature of the world[5] while accepting concurrently and

---

[1] Sheila Delany, *Chaucer's House of Fame: The Poetics of Skeptical Fideism* (Chicago: University of Chicago Press, 1972).

[2] See John F. Wippel, trans., *Boethius of Dacia: On the Supreme Good, On the Eternity of the World, On Dreams* (Toronto: Pontifical Institute of Mediaeval Studies, 1987).

[3] See. B. Bazan, ed., *Siger of Brabant: Questiones in Tertium de Anima, De Anima Intellectiva, De Aeternitate Mundi* (Louvain: Paris, 1972).

[4] Wippel, in his introduction to his *Boethius of Dacia*, argues that the thirteenth-century philosopher did not strictly hold to the doctrine of doubled truth, since he asserts the priority of Christian revelation. The difference is semantic. Boethius writes: "Thus the Christian speaks the truth when he says that the world and the first motion began to be. . . . The natural philosopher also speaks the truth when he says that such things are not possible from natural causes and principles. . . ." (pp. 52-3). Later Boethius asserts the priority of Christian truth: "We maintain, therefore, that the world is not eternal but was created *de novo*. . . ." (p 56). In other words, using the tools of each discipline (natural science or theology), one comes to contradictory positions, and in the terms of each discipline, each is true. But, through a motion of faith (hence the term "fideism"), the truth of religion takes priority.

[5] The debate over reconciling Aristotle's doctrine of the eternal, uncreated nature of the world with the biblical claim of creation was at the heart of the debate over skeptical fideism. Other medieval philosophers besides the skeptical fideists also looked with sympathy

privileging the Church's insistence on God's initiatory act of creation. Delany sees in Chaucer's juxtaposing contradictory beliefs in *The House of Fame* sympathy with this philosophical stance. Thus Aeneas can be seen in Chaucer's poem simultaneously through the lenses of Virgil's praise of him and Ovid's condemnation of his desertion of Dido,[6] and both Orpheus and Homer can be seen in a positive and a negative light. Delany cites Chaucer's "God turne us every drem to goode"[7] (line 1, compare lines 57-8, ". . . the holy roode / Turne us every drem to goode!") as the fideistic solution to the co-existence of mutually contradictory truths.

The purpose of my article is to extend this idea in two directions. First, I maintain that a skeptical fideistic approach is equally applicable to the Wakefield Master's *Second Shepherds' Play*.[8] Second, I point out a corollary double-truth hypothesis in a body of work much closer to fourteenth- and fifteenth-century English thought than the speculations of two rather obscure thirteenth-century philosophers—the writings of the Middle English mystics most heavily influenced by the doubled-language theories of Pseudo-Dionysius.

Near the beginning of *The Second Shepherds' Play*, after Coll the *primus pastor* has complained about the weather and the oppressive gentry who lord it over peasants like him and after the *secundus pastor* has complained about the weather and his masterful wife, Daw, the *tertius pastor*, shows up, complaining about the weather:

> Was neuer syn noe floode / sich floodys seyn;
> Wyndys and ranys so rude / and stormes so keyn;
> Som stamerd, som stod / in dowte, as I weyn;
> Now god turne all to good / I say as I mene,
>   ffor ponder. (127-31)

The accumulated woes of all three sheperds—the foul weather, the ills of an oppressive social order, domestic infelicity—amount to an implied philosophical conundrum, the existence of evil in a world created by a good God, the so-called problem of pain. Daw's solution is skeptically fideistic—may God turn all to good, doubtless a proverb but seemingly a quotation of Chaucer, the very phrase Delany highlights. There is no solution to the problem posed by the woes the shepherds endure, only an assertion that God will turn things to good.

---

to Aristotle's eternal world, notably Averroes. See Marcia L. Colish, *Medieval Foundations of the Western Intellectual Tradition, 400-1400* (New Haven: Yale University Press, 1997), pp. 147, 151, 299.

 [6] Delany, *Skeptical Fideism*, pp. 48-57.

 [7] Quotations from Chaucer's works are taken from Larry D. Benson, ed., *The Riverside Chaucer* (Boston: Houghton, Mifflin, 1987).

 [8] The edition of *The Second Shepherds' Play* I use is George England and Alfred W. Pollard, eds, *The Towneley Plays* EETS, E.S. 71 (London: Oxford University Press, 1897, 1966).

Thus we have a juxtaposition of contradictory truths: the world is full of evil / the world is controlled by a good God. We are close, of course, to the solutions of Boethius of Dacia and Siger of Brabant to the problem of reconciling Aristotle's eternal universe with Genesis 1; we are in some ways even closer to Julian of Norwich's assertion at the heart of her account of her near-death visions: All will be well and all manner of things will be well.[9]

Let us, though, stay at the juncture between *The Second Shepherds' Play* and Chaucer before turning to the Middle English mystics. Coll echoes the words of both Chaucer and Daw about half way through the play in an exchange that in another way is both Chaucerian and fideistic. After the three shepherds awake from the sleep that enables Mak to filch one of their sheep and before he returns to feign sleep, they debate the nature of the dreams they have had:

> *primus pastor.* Resurrex a mortuis! / haue hald my hand.
> Iduas carnas dominus! / I may not well stand:
> My foytt slepys, by ihesus / and I water fastand.
> I thoght that we layd vs / full nere yngland.
>   *Secundus pastor.* A ye!
> lord! what I haue slept weyll;
> As fresh as an eyll,
> As lyght I me feyll
>   As leyfe on tre.
>
> *Tercius pastor.* Benste be here in! / so my [hart] qwakys,
> My hart is outt of skyn / what so it makys.
> Who makys all this dyn? / so my browes blakys,
> To the dowore wyll I wyn / harke felows, wakys!
>   We were fowre:
> se ye awre of mak now?
> *primus pastor.* we were vp or thou.
> *iius pastor.* Man, I gyf god a vowe,
>   yit yede he nawre.
>
> *iiius pastor.* Me thoght he was lapt / in a wolfe skyn.
> *primus pastor.* So are many hapt / now namely within.
> *iius pastor.* When we had long napt / me thoght with a gyn
> A fatt shepe he trapt / bot he mayde no dyn.
>   *Tercius pastor.* Be styll:
> Thi dreme makys the woode:
> It is bot fantom, by the roode.

---

[9] In Julian's Middle English, this is "alle shalle be wele"; see Edmund Colledge, O.S.A. and James Walsh, S.J., eds, *A Book of Showings to the Anchoress Julian of Norwich* (Toronto: Pontifical Institute of Mediaeval Studies, 1978), p. 405.

> *primus pastor.* Now god turne all to good,
>   If it be his wyll.
>
> *iius pastor.* Ryse, mak, for shame! / thou lygys right lang.
> *Mak.* Now crystys holy name / be vs emang!
> what is this? for sant Iame / I may not well gang!
> I trow I be the same / A! my nek has lygen wrang
>   Enoghe;
> Mekill thank, syn yister euen,
> Now, by sant stevyn,
> I was flayd with a swevyn,
>   My hart out of sloghe. (350-85)

Two-thirds of the way through this exchange Coll despairs of finding a solution to the problem of what kind of dream they have had, remarking, "Now god turne all to good, / If it be his wyll." The coincidence, of course, is here striking, for in Chaucer's poem the two references to the fideistic solution of God turning all to good frame his long dissertation on the nature of dreams, one in which he develops terminology about dreams taken from Macrobius's *Commentary on the Dream of Scipio*:[10]

> God turne us every drem to goode!
> For hyt is wonder, be the roode,
> To my wyt, what causeth swevenes
> Eyther on morwes or on evenes,
> And why th'effect folweth of somme,
> And of somme hit shal never come;
> Why that is an avision
> And why this a revelacion,
> Why this a drem, why that a sweven,
> And noght to every man lyche even;
> Why this a fantome, why these oracles,
> I not. . . .
> For I of noon opinion
> Nyl as now make mensyon,
> But oonly that the holy roode
> Turne us every drem to goode!
>   (*HF*, 1-12, 55-8)

"Dreme," "fantom," and "swevyn" are the words the two passages share in addition to the fideistic line already considered. More important is the similarity in content: Chaucer wonders about the truth and significance of the dream he is

---

[10] See William Harris Stahl, trans., *Macrobius: Commentary on the Dream of Scipio* (New York: Columbia University Press, 1952). Macrobius's treatment of dreams is found on pp. 87-92.

about to recount; the shepherds wonder if the dream of Mak making away with a sheep is a reliable guide to their real, waking world. It is tempting in the extreme to suggest that the Wakefield Master has read Chaucer's *House of Fame*.[11] Chaucer's persona's swearing "By seynt Thomas of Kent!" (*HF*, 1131) and Daw's anachronistic assertion that the dream was true and either Mak or his wife Gyll are guilty, "Now trow me, if ye will / by sant thomas of kent, / Ayther mak or gyll / was at that assent" (ll. 458-9) do little to make one resist that temptation.

But more important for us is the use Coll makes of the Chaucerian word "fantom." According to Delany, who devotes an entire chapter to the concept,[12] "phantom" refers to a dream that occurs *between* waking and sleeping (Macrobius), and "image which serves as intermediary between perception and understanding" (Aristotle), and a synonym for fraud (as in Old French literature), and as such it helps establish Chaucer's "absence from [*The House of Fame*] of a fixed narrative point of view."[13] Boethius of Dacia himself wrote a treatise entitled *On Dreams*,[14] whose subject is the extent to which dreams can represent reality. In *The Second Shepherds' Play* these meanings give the narrative an ironic twist: Daw calls his dream of Mak stealing the sheep a "fantom, by the roode" (374)—a deceptive, disorienting type of dream that cannot be relied upon as conveying truth. Yet Mak has indeed stolen the sheep. The result is a certain doubling of language: do we deny it as only a "dreme" (373) or affirm it as reality? Is it true or is it not? Has the theft occurred or is the dream a prophesy of a future theft? The use of the word "fantom" causes us to distrust the dream, yet as omniscient viewers of the pervious action, we know that Mak has already made off with the sheep. The passage might, in other words, strike us as Chaucerian, but it belongs to the conceptual world of Boethius of Dacia, Siger of Brabant, and, as I will show later, Pseudo-Dionysius and the mystics.

The play's larger structures bespeak this same doubled truth even more than the level of individual words.[15] There are of course two mutually contradictory manger scenes, the first in which a sheep supplants the place of a baby so that Mak and Gyll might hide their crime from the shepherds. Daw

---

[11] For fifteenth-century English authors, Chaucer was of unparalleled authority, the one author from the past that most seemed to have read. For his influence on the fifteenth century, see D. S. Brewer, ed., *Chaucer and Chaucerians: Critical Studies in Middle English Literature* (University, Alabama: University of Alabama Press, 1967).

[12] Delany, *Skeptical Fideism*, pp. 58-68.

[13] Delany, *Skeptical Fideism*, p. 67.

[14] See Wippel, *Boethius of Dacia*, pp. 68-78.

[15] For the parodic nature of the play, see Lois Roney, "The Wakefield *First* and *Second Shepherds' Plays* as Complements in Psychology and Parody," *Speculum* 58 (1983): 696-723.

calls him/it "that lytyll day starne"[16] (577) when he goes to offer his sixpence gift to the child, immediately before its ovine face shatters his affective response to the child in the manger: "what the dewill is this? / hi has a long snowte" (585). Is it a baby or is it a sheep? The two, of course, are mutually exclusive, but it is empirical evidence, not a fideistic leap, that solves this problem.

But the other manger scene, juxtaposed immediately with the first, counters this assertion. Offering their gifts, the shepherds, in *secundus pastor*'s words, find a "Lytyll day starne" (727) who does not metamorphose into a sheep. The baby in the manger is Mary's—a true baby, one who in the ensuing months and years doubtless finds more use for the bob of cherries, bird, and tennis ball[17] the three offer him than the sheep finds in Daw's sixpence.

But this baby, of course, is just as problematic as the first. He is the Lamb of God. Is it a baby or God in this manger? These are two mutually contradictory constructs juxtaposed—a conundrum that had a long history of fideistic solutions before Boethius of Dacia and Siger of Brabant posited their solution to the problem of the world's eternal and created natures.

Beyond the judgment of the nature of each cradle's occupant is the larger juxtaposition of them against each other. The Wakefield Master seems at pains to draw out their similarities. But he makes little effort to establish the religious manger-scene over the secular cradle-scene. If the manger gets priority because it concludes the play, because the singing angels punctuate the preceding action with a full stop and redirect it towards Bethlehem, and because the play's whole *raison d'être* is the Christmas story, the cradle scene gets priority because its narrative sequence is much the longer of the two (637 lines versus 117) and because its comic energy overwhelms the conventional if touching manger scene. Which should we choose as the interpretive center of the play? The reader/viewer is in a skeptically fideistic dilemma.

The play's theological language, of course, contributes to its fideistic nature. Once the three shepherds have entered her house, for instance, Gyll[18] resorts to hyperbole to disprove the obvious, that the child in the cradle is really the lost sheep:

> I pray to god so mylde,
> If euer I you begyld,
> that I ete this chylde

---

[16] For this allusion, see Martin Stevens, *Four Middle English Mystery Cycles: Textual, Contextual, and Critical Interpretations* (Princeton: Princeton University Press, 1987), p. 175; and Thomas J. Jambeck, "The 'Day Star' Allusion in the *Secunda Pastorum*," *Modern Language Quarterly* 50 (1989): 297-308.

[17] See Lauren Lepow, "Daw's Tennis Ball: A Topical Allusion in the *Secunda Pastorum*," *English Language Notes* 22 (1984): 5-8.

[18] For an interesting treatment of Gyll, see Mary Stearns, "Gyll as Mary and as Eve: Order and Disorder in *Secunda Pastorum*," *Fifteenth-Century Studies* 11 (1989): 295-304.

that lygys in this credyll. . . (535-8)

"Mild" is an adjective usually reserved for God *as* the child in the manger. Eating the child in the manger amounts, of course, to a reference to the Eucharist, and many Eucharistic visions include a child seemingly sacrificed at the altar by a priest celebrating Mass.[19] Thus in a comically ironic moment in the play tending even towards blasphemy we here have doubled theological vision: is the child in the cradle a eucharistic Christ child or the stolen sheep, a candidate for literal rather than sacramental consumption?

The doubled nature of "vyrgyn" (676) as applied to Mary, who has just given birth, is so well documented that it needs little further explication here, except perhaps to mention Chaucer's line from the Prioress's Prologue, "O mooder Mayde, O mayde Mooder free!" (*CT*, VII, 467). But one other use of theological language in *The Second Shepherds' Play* deserves some attention. Daw greets the baby Jesus with these words:

> hayll, derlyng dere / full of godhede!
> I pray the be nere / when that I haue nede.
> hayll! swete is thy chere! / my hart wold blede
> To se the sytt here / in so poore wede. . . . (728-31)

The great Godhead clothed in poverty is a doubled perspective at the heart of Incarnational theology, with roots in the earliest Christian writings, most specifically in St. Paul's Epistle to the Philipians:

> Let the same mind be in you that was in Christ Jesus, who, though he was in the form of God, did not regard equality with God as something to be exploited, but emptied himself, taking the form of a slave, being born in human likeness. And being found in human form, he humbled himself and became obedient to the point of death—even death on a cross. Therefore God also highly exalted him and gave him the name that is above every name, so that at the name of Jesus every knee should bend, in heaven and on earth and under the earth, and every tongue should confess that Jesus Christ is Lord, to the glory of God the Father.[20] (Phil 2:5-11)

The effect of Daw's words is to juxtapose seemingly irreconcilable truths: is Christ powerful or weak, God or man, rich or poor, eternal or just born?

---

[19] For this eucharistic vision, see Robert Boenig, *Saint and Hero: Andreas and Medieval Doctrine* (Lewisburg: Bucknell University Press, 1991), pp. 61-3; and Miri Rubin, *Corpus Christi: The Eucharist in Late Medieval Culture* (Cambridge: Cambridge University Press, 1991), pp. 135-9. For the topic of eucharistic theology in general, see Gary Macy, *The Theologies of the Eucharist in the Early Scholastic Period* (Oxford: Clarendon Press, 1984).

[20] Wayne A. Meeks, ed., *The Harper Collins Study Bible: New Revised Standard Version* (New York: Harper Collins, 1993).

Similar in effect to the doubled theological language is the play's anachronism. The characters swear by St. Thomas of Kent (458), Mary and John (443), and our Lady (553), refer to the pater noster (104) and resurrection (350), and for all intents and purposes seem like ordinary fifteenth-century English peasants. Yet to his horror Coll has dreamt that he was *near* England, reminding us that contrary to all appearances the shepherds are resident in the far-off Holy Land almost 1500 years earlier. The doubled perspective caused by the anachronism, of course, is quite effective art, drawing in the original spectators in fifteenth-century Wakefield almost as participants in the holy story, thus contemporizing that story.[21] Far from being the naiveté that some have imagined it, the anachronism is a sophisticated gesture in the direction of skeptical fideism and pseudo-Dionysian mysticism. It is to the pseudo-Dionysian nature of *The Second Shepherds' Play* that we now must turn.

Pseudo-Dionysius was an anonymous late fifth-century Syrian[22] who appropriated the persona of Dionysius the Areopagite, the Athenian philosopher converted by St. Paul in Acts, chapter 17. Among his treatises are two which posit the juxtaposition of affirmation and denial as a means of access to mystical knowledge of God. For Pseudo-Dionysius, even more than for the skeptical fideists, language was by its nature doubled.

The Divine Names discusses the words and concepts, drawn from the Bible, that we associate with God. Its aim is to define how we might know about God rather than to describe the structure of reality, so its interests are more properly epistemological than metaphysical. Briefly put, in *The Divine Names* Pseudo-Dionysius defines affirmative theology versus negative theology (what will be transformed into the later *via positiva* and *via negativa*), claiming affirmative theology as the main subject of the present treatise. Affirmative theology accepts the concepts related to God in the Bible as true insofar as they proceed from revelation. There is a hierarchy of these terms and

---

[21] The effort to draw the reader into the sacred events of the Bible is a venerable one, arguably begun by the Cistercian Abbot Aelred, from the Abbey of Rievaulx, just to the north of Wakefield. In his *De Institutione Inclusarum*, he advises his sister to use her senses to imagine herself literally present in her readings of the gospels (see John Ayto and Alexandra Barratt, eds, *Aelred of Rievaulx's De Institutione Inclusarum* EETS 287 [London: Oxford University Press, 1984]). A widespread topos of late medieval England, this meditative technique was promulgated by the Franciscans and left its mark in the lyrics and drama of the age. See David L. Jeffrey, *The Early English Lyric and Franciscan Spirituality* (Lincoln, Nebraska: University of Nebraska Press, 1975). Later, the technique was taken up by the Jesuits, being incorporated into his *Spiritual Exercises* by Ignatius of Loyola, whence it had a strong influence on seventeenth-century English poetry (see Louis Martz, *The Poetry of Meditation* 2nd ed. (New Haven: Yale University Press, 1962).

[22] For Pseudo-Dionysius, see Paul Rorem, *Pseudo-Dionysius: A Commentary on the Texts and an Introduction to their Influence* (New York: Oxford University Press, 1993); for the standard English translation, see Colm Luibheid, trans., *Pseudo-Dionysius: The Complete Works* (New York: Paulist Press, 1987).

concepts—from highest to lowest: Good, Being, Life, Wisdom, Power, and the other abstractions down to the more anthropomorphical representations of God—i.e., God's strong arm and God's beard. The bulk of *The Divine Names* is devoted to discussing the abstractions. He lays primary emphasis on the concept of the Good—recognizable, of course, in its Platonic and Neoplatonic[23] aspects as well as its Christian. These words or "names" proceed from God, and we accept them in turn in their emanation outwards from the God who is unity towards the multiplicity and plurality of the revealed concepts about God.

But these names must be denied in the return from plurality towards unity. Pseudo-Dionysius briefly discusses this return in *The Divine Names*, but it is given fullest—and most influential—treatment in *The Mystical Theology*. In the christianized Neoplatonic return, we reject each name, starting from the lowest, most anthropomorphic and ending with the abstractions so close to our accepted notion of God's nature: No, God has no beard, no strong arm; no, God is not power, wisdom, life, being, the Good. The denial of being to God, of course, has nothing to do with the God-is-dead theology of the American 1960s, for Pseudo-Dionysius posits simply that these terms are too narrow to define God. He presents a bevy of terms, using the prefix *super-* (in Greek *hyper-*): God is not Being, he is Super-being (i.e., above being); God is not Good, he is above goodness, etc. Such theology might strike one as dangerous, and indeed in the 1320s Meister Eckhart died while under investigation by the Inquisition for, among other things, promulgating these ideas too enthusiastically.[24] The last Pseudo-Dionysian denial in the *via negativa* is the paradoxical denial of denial itself. It is worth quoting his concluding words of *The Mystical Theology* as indication both of this concept and of the dense and difficult style he employed in all his treatises:

> There is no speaking of it [i.e., the Godhead], nor name nor knowledge of it. Darkness and light, error and truth—it is none of these. It is beyond assertion and denial. We make assertions and denials of what is next to it, but never of it, for it is both beyond every assertion, being the perfect and unique cause of all things, and, by virtue of its preeminently simple and absolute nature, free of every limitation, beyond every limitation; it is also beyond every denial.[25]

---

[23] For the Neoplatonic elements of Pseudo-Dionysius, see Stephen Gersh, *From Iamblichus to Eriugena: An Investigation of the Prehistory and Evolution of the Pseudo-Dionysian Tradition* (Leiden: E. J. Brill, 1978).

[24] See Edmund Colledge, O.S.A. and Bernard McGinn, trans., *Meister Eckhart: The Essential Sermons, Commentaries, Treatises, and Defense* (New York: Paulist Press, 1981), pp. 12-15.

[25] Luibheid, *Works*, p. 141.

The theories of Pseudo-Dionysius thus imply a gap between signifier and signified[26] and a fideistic solution to the epistemological problems this gap implies.

The ideas of Pseudo-Dionysius reached England through several channels.[27] There was some knowledge of him among the Anglo-Saxons, for Bede mentions him, Ælfric wrote a homily on his (legendary) life, and several of his works were known to be in Anglo-Saxon libraries.[28] More importantly, Pseudo-Dionysian ideas entered England in the late twelfth century through the associates of that same Thomas Becket of Kent both Chaucer and the Wakefield Master invoke: Becket's friend John of Salisbury commissioned John Sarracenus to produce a fresh translation of Dionysius's treatises. The legend has it that Becket's last words were an invocation to St. Denis. In the thirteenth century the Friars, particularly the Dominicans, promulgated Dionysian ideas in England. In the fourteenth century the writings of the great mystics Walter Hilton and the author of *The Cloud of Unknowing* were permeated with Dionysian ideas. The *Cloud*-author translated *The Mystical Theology* (under the title of *Deonise Hid Diunite*[29]) and claimed in *The Cloud of Unknowing*:

> þe moste goodly knowyng of God is þat, þe which is knowyn bi vnknowyng. & treuly, who-so wil loke Denis bookes, he schal fynde þat his wordes wilen cleerly aferme al þat I haue seyde or schal sey, for þe biginnyng of þis tretis to þe ende.[30]

By the fifteenth century, Pseudo-Dionysian ideas were endemic to English mystical and devotional texts; the scriptoria of the Brigettine house of Syon and the Carthusian house at Mount Grace just north of Wakefield were particularly active in copying texts that were at heart Dionysian. Julian of Norwich, writing in the early fifteenth century, mentions St. Denis and, in her major theological pronouncements, can juxtapose God-as-Father with God-as-Mother.

The juxtaposition of mutually exclusive terms, doubled language where words signify and simultaneously fail to signify, and a final fideistic privileging

---

[26] It is interesting that well into his career Jacques Derrida discovered the affinity of his language theories with those of Pseudo-Dionysius and Meister Eckhart. See Jacques Derrida, *Psyché: Inventions de l'autre* (Paris: Galilée, 1987), pp. 535-96.

[27] See David Luscombe, "The Reception of the Writings of Denis the Pseudo-Areopagite into England," pp. 115-43 in Diana Greenway, Christopher Holdsworth, and Jane Sayers, eds, *Tradition and Change: Essays in Honour of Marjorie Chibnall* (Cambridge: Cambridge University Press, 1985); and Robert Boenig, "Pseudo-Dionysius and the *Via* towards England," pp. 21-38 in William F. Pollard and Robert Boenig, eds, *Mysticism and Spirituality in Medieval England* (Woodbridge: D. S. Brewer, 1997).

[28] See J. D. A. Ogilvy, *Books Known to the English, 597-1066* (Cambridge, Massachusetts: Mediaeval Academy of America, 1967), pp. 155-8.

[29] See Phyllis Hodgson, *Deonise Hid Diuinite and Other Treatises on Contemplative Prayer* EETS 231 (London: Oxford University Press, 1955).

[30] Phyllis Hodgson, ed., *The Cloud of Unknowing* EETS 210 (London: Oxford University Press, 1944). pp. 125.

of one truth over another are all characteristics of the Dionysian mystics as well as the skeptical fideists like Boethius of Dacia and Siger of Brabant. Two passages will serve as examples.

In *The Cloud of Unknowing* the author directly addresses the problem of how spiritual language simultaneously signifies and fails to signify. In defining the "cloud" of his title, he explains:

> & wene not, for I clepe it a derknes or a cloude, þat it be any congelid of þe hummurs þat fleen in þe ayre, ne ȝit any derknes soche as is in þin house on niȝtes, when þi candel is oute. For soche a derknes & soche a cloude maist þou ymagin wiþ corioste of witte, for to bere before þin iȝen in þe liȝtest day of somer; & also aȝenswarde in þe derkist niȝt of wynter þou mayst ymagin a clere schinyng liȝt. Lat be soche falsheed; I mene not þus. For when I sey derknes, I mene a lackyng of knowyng; as alle þat þing þat þou knowest not, or elles þat þou hast forȝetyn, it is derk to þee, for þou seest it not wiþ þi goostly iȝe.[31]

The cloud is a metaphor, an allegory even, of a truth that belies the literal truth that masks it. The one truth must be denied (spiritual unknowing is not a "real" cloud) but only after it is affirmed (we cannot arrive at the spiritual meaning without first imagining the literal). We are not too far away here from the Wakefield Master's lamb/Lamb in the cradle: he first affirms a literal poor family with an exceptional baby admired by shepherds before denying it by providing its spiritual equivalent in the Holy Family.

The second example is taken from Julian of Norwich. Her visions of Christ on the cross occurred during the crisis of a near-fatal disease. In the midst of her own sufferings, she meditates on the problem of pain: why did a perfect God allow sin into the world? She writes:

> . . . and me thought yf synne had nott be, we shulde alle haue be clene and lyke to oure lorde as he made vs. And thus in my foly before thys tyme often I wondryd why, by the grete forseyng wysdom of god, the begynnyng of synne was nott lettyd. For then thoucht me that alle shulde haue be wele. Thys steryng was moch to be forsaken; and nevyrthe lesse mornyng and sorow I made therfore withouȝte reson and dyscrecion. But Jhesu that in this vysyon enformyd me of alle that me nedyd answeryd by thys worde and seyde: Synne is behouely, but alle shalle be wele, and alle shalle be wele, and alle maner of thynge shalle be wele.[32]

---

[31] Hodgson, *Cloud*, p. 23.
[32] College and Walsh, *Showings*, pp. 404-5.

Note how skeptically fideistic this, arguably the most famous[33] passage in Julian's book, is. She posits one truth—that sin has marred the world—then another—that sin is "behouely," i.e., necessarily in God's will. She concludes with a fideistic solution not far from Chaucer's and the Wakefield Master's "God turn everything to good"—"All will be well," emphatically repeated twice. What is operative in this passage is the Pseudo-Dionysian idea that God's goodness is beyond human comprehension: we affirm that God's creation is good, deny it in the face of a sinful world, and affirm that God's concept of the Good somehow supersedes our own. When all will be well, it will be so with Dionysian hyper-goodness.

The whole fabric of *The Second Shepherds' Play* replicates this very idea. All the discontented language from the three shepherds about the bad weather, bad lords, and bad domestic strife belies the goodness of the creation. So does Mak's theft of the sheep. The shepherds' actions reaffirm goodness, for they choose to toss Mak in a blanket[34] rather than prosecute him for theft, a crime in fifteenth-century England punishable by death. Their goodness is immediately answered by the angels' summons to visit the child in the manger, a vision, as it were, of Dionysian hyper-goodness.

---

[33] It is, of course the passage T. S. Eliot alludes to in "Little Gidding": Sin is Behovely, but / All shall be well, and / All manner of thing shall be well" (T. S. Eliot, *The Complete Poems and Plays, 1909-1950* [New York: Harcourt, Brace, and World, 1971], pp. 142-3).

[34] For this action, see Thomas J. Jambeck, "The Canvas-Tossing Allusion in the *Secunda Pastorum*," *Modern Philology* 76 (1978): 49-54; John C. Hirsh, "Mak Tossed in a Blanket," *Notes and Queries* 226 (1981): 117-8; and Míceál Vaughan, "Tossing Mak Around," pp. 146-50 in Richard K. Emmerson, ed., *Approaches to Teaching Medieval Drama* (New York: Modern Language Association, 1990).

4 Ecstasy, Prophecy, and Reform: Catherine of Siena as a Model for Holy Women of Sixteenth-Century Spain

Gillian T. W. Ahlgren

Scholars have made much of the contributions of Cardinal Francisco Jimenez de Cisneros to fostering a reform-oriented climate of spiritual renewal in early sixteenth-century Spain. But we have been slower to appreciate the content of the texts Cisneros commissioned, and we are only beginning to address the extent to which such texts produced gendered models of spirituality. This is an urgent task for several reasons. First, we know that the translation of medieval mystical texts constituted a central part of the reforming interests of Cisneros and the humanist university of Alcalá. A revival of spirituality and mystical experience was consistent with the notion of reform in the early sixteenth century: change the inner person and gradually Christendom would be renewed and revitalized. Second, several of these texts address areas of religious experience of primary importance to spiritual women of the sixteenth century. Catherine of Siena in particular was a medieval mystic who had extensive visionary experiences, produced texts, and engaged in church reform, overcoming scrutiny, resistance, and even opposition to her role as a reformer. Most female reformers in sixteenth-century Spain had similar experiences and could look to the model of Catherine's life for support and even in self-defense. In replicating Catherine's prayer experiences later women found continued justification for their public reforming roles.

In this paper I would like to begin to explore how a medieval model of female holiness which integrated intercessory prayer, visions, ecstasy, and humility was translated into the milieu of sixteenth-century Spain by considering the influence of the Castilian translation of Raymond of Capua's *Life of Catherine of Siena* on three Spanish women and their defenders: María de Santo Domingo, Teresa of Ávila, and Francisca de los Apóstoles. Capua's *Life of Catherine* was translated into Castilian by Antonio de la Peña and published at Alcalá in 1511 as part of Cisneros's program of religious reform. A second edition of the same translation was published in Medina del Campo in 1569.

While Catherine's own works were also influential in Spain,[1] Raymond's *Life* established a hagiographical model which women in sixteenth-century Spain could assimilate. Canonized in 1461, Catherine was a public, prophetic church reformer, and her *Life* contained a blueprint for later women to continue her tradition of visionary and intercessory prayer leading to ecclesiastical reform. Or so it seemed.

Catherine of Siena was born in 1347,[2] the 24th of 25 children. Her father was a wool dyer. At the age of fifteen, in defiance of her parents' desire for her to marry, she joined the sisters of penance, a group of laywomen associated with the Dominican order. She led a severe ascetical life and experienced mystical phenomena, including spiritual marriage and the stigmata. By 1374, at age 27, Catherine became involved in mediating conflict between political factions in Siena and Florence. In that same year she gained a new spiritual director, Raymond of Capua. In 1376 she moved to Rome, where she lived with a community of followers and had several meetings with Pope Gregory XI. Although Catherine was unsuccessful in resolving political disputes, she exerted a certain influence on the Pope in matters of church reform and in the question of returning his residence to Rome. Gregory made a solemn entry into Rome in January 1377 (from Avignon) and remained there until he died in March 1378. Controversy erupted over his successor. The election of the Archbishop of Bari, Bartolomeo Prignano, as Urban VI was roundly rejected in many quarters and spawned the election of another pope, Clement VII, in September of 1378. Probably in a move to gain increased credibility, Urban VI invited Catherine and Raymond to return to Rome, where he enjoyed their support until Catherine's death in 1380.

Raymond of Capua began his biography of Catherine in 1385. He spent ten years compiling stories about her and constructing a hagiographical portrait. In the prologue Raymond sets out his purpose in recording the *Life*: to demonstrate how Catherine was sent to the world by God to accomplish the

---

[1] The translation of Catherine's letters and prayers was also ordered by Cisneros and it, too, is said to be the work of Antonio de la Peña; it was also published by Brocar in Alcalá on November 22, 1512. See *The Book of Prayer of Sor María of Santo Domingo: A Study and Translation*, ed. Mary E. Giles (Albany: State University of New York Press, 1990), p. 55: "The first edition was printed by Brocar on March 27, 1511 and the second appeared on June 26, 1511." But see Pre-NUC listing. A Catalan edition of the *Life* was published in Valencia on September 17 1511, but this could be by Tomas de Vesach; see Alvaro Huerga, "Santa Catalina, Precursora de Santa Teresa" in *Cuadernos de investigación histórica*, 10 (1986): 197-214 at 213, n. 12.

[2] There is some controversy over this date, as Raymond of Capua makes much of Catherine being 33 at the time of her death, the age tradition ascribes to Christ. Robert Fawtier claims that it is more likely that Catherine was 43 at the time of her death. See Robert Fawtier, *Sainte Catherine de Sienne, essai de critique des sources*. Vol. 1: Sources hagiographiques. (Paris: Editions de Boccard, 1921).

healing and sanctifying mission of its conversion and reform. Acknowledging that she experienced spiritual marriage with Christ, Raymond suggests that she was specifically instructed, encouraged, and enabled by Christ as her spouse to act in the ways she did. As current scholarship on late medieval female saints has shown, Raymond of Capua's *Legenda maior* was extremely influential in both the actual practices and the textual construction of later saints. Indeed, John Coakley suggests that in Raymond of Capua's life of Catherine a hagiographical model very fruitful for the church is established. He writes: ". . .[H]ere we have the most harmonious and ambitious male vision of the female saint, in the sense that her powers complement those of the church, and she and Raymond form together a sort of androgynous unit for the salvation of Christendom."[3] The *Legenda* did much to influence the canonization process of Catherine which was initiated in 1411 and concluded with her canonization in 1461.

Raymond of Capua's case for Catherine's holiness is an interesting blend of two philosophical currents. First, consistent with the thought of Thomas Aquinas, Capua sought to show how Catherine was an extraordinary example of how grace works with human nature to enable individuals to advance in the life of holiness. Second, consistent with another strand of Aquinas's thought, that the nature of womanhood is a deficient form of human nature, Capua showed how in Catherine of Siena grace had actually overcome all that was deficient in human nature and produced an extraordinary occurrence: "an angelic maiden," who "in a way surpassing all human reckoning, penetrated into the abyss of divine wisdom as deeply as any soul who is still a pilgrim here below may do, and opened up and unfolded its mysteries to the rest of us."[4] Thus his argument consists of demonstrating the combination of Catherine's humility and her spiritual powers; the perfect balance of these two qualities insured each other.

To reinforce the reader's estimation of Catherine's holiness, Capua sets up in the Prologue evidence that she embodied "the foundation and support of all the other virtues, humility." A good indicator that Catherine "possessed humility perfectly," Capua notes, is "that not only did she invariably choose to be made lower than the lowest of all, man or woman, and to be regarded as beneath everyone else, but she was also unshakably convinced that she herself

---

[3] Coakley, "Friars as Confidants of Holy Women," p. 246.
[4] Raymond of Capua, *The Life of Catherine of Siena*, trans. Conleth Kearns (Wilmington, Delaware: Michael Glazier, 1980), p. 6. Compare p. 8: "You would have seen some, wise in their own eyes and learned in human knowledge, put their finger on their lips in amazement on hearing what she had to say. 'How does she know letters,' they muttered to each other, 'when she never learned? Where did this weak woman get this deep wisdom? Who taught her so perfectly? Who instructed her so profoundly?' Such facts, surely, are proof sufficient that she did indeed possess the key of the abyss; the key, namely, of the deep things of the wisdom of God."

was the cause of all the evils which others suffered."[5] Accordingly, Catherine's life was characterized by deliberate self-subjection, an attitude and practice inspired, as Capua explains, by "a genuine inner conviction that she was in fact beneath all others."[6] Indeed, the very effect of Catherine on others was to produce humility in them. Capua describes how those who came to her "to deride and belittle her, left her presence in tears. Stiff-necked, their hearts puffed up with pride, they came to her; in tears, and with heads bowed down, they left her."[7]

Self-subjection, however, did not always lead Catherine to be out of control of the circumstances of her own life and without a reforming vision to which she committed herself. But, as Capua constructs the narrative, God intervened frequently, enabling Catherine to overcome opposition and social prejudice. When it looked as if her family would not allow her to join the Sisters of Penance, for example, God gave her a life-threatening illness which convinced them to acquiesce to her desires. When Catherine took on a more public reforming role she complained to God of the enormity of her task. "How can anyone like me, feeble and no account, do any good for souls? My very sex, as I need not tell you, puts many obstacles in the way. The world has no use for women in such work as that. . . ." God responded to Catherine by explaining that "wise and learned men" needed to be "put back in their place by a just judgment." God would accomplish this by "sending to them, to humble their pride, mere women—women who of themselves will be ignorant and frail, but whom I will fill with the power of God and the wisdom of God."[8]

The structure of Capua's biography has God consistently rewarding Catherine for expressions of self-abnegation. As only one incident of this phenomenon I cite the disturbing example of when Catherine tended the wound of a woman with the cancer of the breast—of whom we will say more shortly—and, to overcome her nausea at the infection, drank the water with which she had just washed the woman's wound. In direct response to this action, Catherine received a vision of Christ's body in which she was invited to drink from Christ's wounded side. As Christ leads her to his side, he tells her why she has been allowed this extraordinary privilege: "Yesterday the intensity

---

[5] Capua, *Life of Catherine*, trans. Kearns, p. 10.
[6] Capua, *Life of Catherine*, trans. Kearns, p. 12.
[7] Capua, *Life of Catherine*, trans. Kearns, p. 8.
[8] Capua, *Life of Catherine*, trans. Kearns, pp. 116-7. Compare excised passage on women in Teresa of Ávila, *Camino de perfección* (El Escorial text) 4:1 in which Teresa says: "Isn't it enough, Lord, that the world keeps us silenced and incapable of doing anything of value for You in public and we don't dare speak of truths we bewail in secret, but you won't hear our rightful petition? I don't believe it of such a good and just lord; you are a just judge, not like the world's judges, who, since they are sons of Adam, and are, in short, all men, there is no female virtue they don't view as suspect." See Gillian T. W. Ahlgren, *Teresa of Ávila and the Politics of Sanctity* (Ithaca, New York: Cornell University Press, 1996), p. 88.

of your ardent love for me overcame even the instinctive reflexes of your body itself: you forced yourself to swallow without a qualm a drink from which nature recoiled in disgust. In response to this I now say, that as you then went far beyond what mere human nature could ever have achieved, so I today shall give you a drink that transcends in perfection any that human nature can provide or has ever heard of."[9]

By responding with humility to extraordinary spiritual gifts, women both opened themselves up to continued graces and made a strong case for their authenticity. Capua describes Catherine's struggle in this regard, that when she first received revelations she was "very nervous, afraid that it might be an illusion of that Enemy who often transforms himself into an angel of light." Indeed, as Capua represents it, Catherine's attitude of suspicion about her revelations was highly appropriate: "Nor was our Lord at all displeased at her misgivings. On the contrary, he commended her timorousness." In response to Catherine's humble confusion, God explains to her the principles of discerning spirits. "This is a basic principle: I am the Truth. From this it follows that a vision which comes from me gives the soul a better grasp of the truth. Now the truth that matters most to the soul is the truth about me and about itself; and when it truly knows me and knows itself, it will hold itself in slight regard and me in highest honour. To bring this about is the proper function of humility. From all this it follows that by visions which come from me the soul grows more and more in humility, learns more and more to acknowledge its own nothingness, and holds its own worth ever more and more in low esteem."[10]

As Catherine experienced more supernatural gifts she took on a more public prophetic and reforming role and, in turn, attracted criticism and suspicion from some of her contemporaries. In the second part of the *Life* Raymond describes four basic kinds of opposition Catherine faced. Some criticized the extremities of her fasting; others criticized her for singularity, which they claimed was a manifestation of spiritual pride; others accused her of having been deceived by the devil; and still others accused her of intentionally deceiving her contemporaries as a fraudulent mystic.[11] Capua defends Catherine against the first two groups, who complained about extremity and singularity, by appealing to her extraordinary humility. "Admittedly," he writes, "a person should not spontaneously go in for singularities; but when God imposes singularities upon certain people they have no choice but to bow to his will and be thankful."[12] Against accusations of deception by the devil Capua argues that the combination of Catherine's continued dedication to fasting and penance and the spiritual joy and peace she experienced was outside the power

---

[9] Ahlgren, *Teresa*, p. 156.
[10] Ahlgren, *Teresa*, pp. 77-8.
[11] See Ahlgren, *Teresa*, p. 166.
[12] Ahlgren, *Teresa*, p. 168.

of the devil to provoke. Finally, Capua dismisses accusations that Catherine deliberately misled people saying, "These are better answered by silence than by words. . . . Only by silently ignoring them will they be reduced to silence themselves."[13]

To summarize, then, the spiritual model of Catherine as Raymond has constructed it, is one in which spiritual progress is measured in terms of the soul's growth in humility and the corresponding supernatural rewards the soul receives. This spiritual preparation bears fruit in the public realm as well since the person becomes God's instrument for reform in the world. Indeed, as Raymond portrays her, Catherine's penances and petitions to God to end the papal schism were the cause of her death; thus, she was in fact a martyr for the church.[14]

Antonio de la Peña, the Castilian translator of the *Life of Catherine of Siena*, was in a unique position to appreciate both the theological message of Capua's text and the rhetorical strategies of his portrait. Antonio de la Peña was a spiritual director of the beata María de Santo Domingo (d. 1524), a charismatic woman whose raptures and spiritual power were controversial in her day. Along with María's other confessor Diego de Vitoria, Antonio became María's public defender in an investigation into her orthodoxy in 1509-10. His defense was successful, as Maria was exonerated by Cisneros and the Consejo of the Inquisition in March of 1510. In 1518 María went on to dictate a book of prayer; reportedly while in a state of rapture, as Catherine of Siena had experienced. Mary Giles has reviewed some of the similarities between María's

---

[13] Ahlgren, *Teresa*, pp. 169-70.

[14] See Ahlgren, *Teresa*, pp. 321-2: "For when our Lord once more, as before, urged the claims of his justice, she replied: 'My Lord, since it is impossible that your justice should be set aside, listen, I beg, to this request of your handmaid: Whatever punishment is due to this people, let it be worked out upon this body of mine. I am more than ready, for the honour of your name and for your holy Church, to drink this chalice of suffering and death. You can bear me witness yourself, that this has all along been truly my desire, ever since I first began, by your grace, to love you with my whole heart and my whole mind.' To these words, which she uttered with her soul rather than with her body, the voice of God which had been speaking within her made no rejoinder. This meant that her request was to be granted. In fact from that moment the mutterings of the people began little by little to grow less, and finally died away. But on Catherine herself, for all her virtue, fell the full weight of the suffering she had asked for. For now, by God's permission, those infernal serpents were allowed to treat as they would the wasted body of this virgin, and wreaked their fury on it with such savagery that no one who had not seen it could believe what she had to undergo . . . . From now on, that frame of hers began to undergo a daily agony of suffering beyond even what it had hitherto been accustomed to. It appeared as if reduced to skin and bone, not the body of a living person but of someone who had already faded away from the earth. Yet all this time she kept on her feet, and continued her labours and her prayers without intermission, looking to the eyes of those who saw her, more like a spectre than a creature of flesh and blood. Her torments grew more agonising from day to day. It was plain to every eye that they were devouring her bit by bit."

book of prayer and the writings of Catherine of Siena, and Jodi Bilinkoff, after studying María's case, suggests that María de Santo Domingo and her supporters represented a "Catherinist" movement with a charismatic orientation to prayer and penance which challenged contemporary Thomistic revival in the universities.[15]

Clearly Antonio de la Peña was part of this agenda as an interpreter and propegator of the living and textual models of María and Catherine, perhaps responding to what Rudolph Bell has called "the general, marked increase of male suspicion of extraordinary behavior among pious women about 1500."[16] Antonio's contribution to Capua's *Life of Catherine of Siena* was to reinforce in his introduction the strategy of paradoxical representation Capua had employed. Thus de la Peña added a brief introduction to the reader in which he stressed that in Catherine the weakness of natural womanhood was overcome by divine grace, and the result was an astonishing expression of prophetic power. In presenting Catherine to the reader, Antonio writes:

> The eternal God gave to many illustrious women the prophetic spirit as a sign that he did not want them to be kept from his divine secrets. . . . Thus it is not for nothing that the church teaches about God that among the things which most demonstrate his omnipotence is in exhibiting the victory of martyrdom in something so weak as a woman.[17]

The Life of Catherine of Siena clearly influenced the Carmelite reformer and mystic Teresa of Ávila (1515-82). What evidence is there that Teresa knew Raymond of Capua's text? Teresa could have known of Catherine only through

---

[15] See Giles, *The Book of Prayer*, p. 88 and Jodi Bilinkoff, "Charisma and Controversy: The Case of María de Santo Domingo" in Magdalena S. Sánchez and Alain Saint-Saens, eds, *Spanish Women in the Golden Age: Images and Realities* (Westport, CT: Greenwood Press, 1996), pp. 23-35 at pp. 30-31.

[16] Johb Coakley, "Friars as Confidants of Holy Women in Medieval Dominican Hagiography" in Renate Blumenfeld-Kosinski and Timea Szell, eds *Images of Sainthood in Medieval Europe*. (Ithaca, New York: Cornell University Press, 1991), pp. 222-46 at 245. Compare Rudolph Bell, *Holy Anorexia* (Chicago: University of Chicago Press, 1985), pp. 150-51.

[17] Raimundo de Capua, *Vida de la bienaventurada sancta Catharina de Sena*, trans. and prólogo Antonio de la Peña. Alcalá 1512. Reed. Medina del Campo: Francisco de Canto, 1569 (BN: R/562): "[iii] A muchas mugeres ilustres dios eterno de spiritu prophetico en señal q[ue] no las queria estrañar de sus divinales secretos, porque no tuviera ocasion de desesperar su flaqueza, una biuda propheta . . . nos es puesta por exemplo en el santo evangelio. . . . Y tambien nos lo muestra lactantio firmiano en el libro primero de las divinas instituciones en las sibillas, de las quales haze mencion el Aurelio doctor Sant Augustin en el xviii libro de la cibdad de Dios." [iiii] Por tanto no en vano la yglesia dize a Dios que entre las cosas en que el mas muestra su omnipotencia es en dar la victoria del martyrio en cosa tan flaca como son las mugeres.

Catherine's own texts or she could have known about Catherine through other, more generic collections of saints' lives—books which she herself confesses she loved to read.[18] However, I believe that a reference Teresa made to Catherine in a letter to Isabel de San Geronimo and María de San José dated May 5, 1579 is enough to demonstrate that she was well aware of this text. The specificity of the event, detailed only in Raymond's biography, leads me to this conclusion. In this letter Teresa writes cryptically about troubles with the Inquisition the Discalced Carmelites were experiencing in Seville, reminding the women of the example of Catherine of Siena. She writes: "Remember what saint Catherine of Siena did to the woman who accused her of being a bad woman, and let us consider with fear what evil we would do if God took his favor from us."[19] This is an apparent reference to a section in Capua's *Life* in which Catherine faced accusations of lack of chastity from a cancer-stricken member of Catherine's own group of sisters of penance in Siena. According to Raymond's account, as Teresa incorporates it into her own context, Catherine used the incident to demonstrate further her charity toward the woman, and through her charity her holiness increased.[20] The parallel in Teresa's own experience is that

---

[18] See *Vida*.

[19] Carta 284:10: " . . .[A]cuérdense de santa Catalina de Sena lo que hizo con la que le había levantado que era mala mujer, y temamos, temamos, hermanas mías, que si Dios aparta su mano de nosotras, qué males habrá que no hagamos?"

[20] See Capua, *Life of Catherine of Siena*, trans. Kearns, pp. 374-6: "There was in the city of Siena, (as recorded already in the last part of that same fourth chapter of Part Two), an old woman belonging to the same religious group as Catherine herself. In a way they have in that region, this woman had a man's name adapted to a feminine form, and was called Andrea. She was suffering from a cancer of the breast which had so eaten into her flesh and had become so corrupt, that no one could go near her without holding their nostrils, so foul was the odour it gave off. For this reason she found it practically impossible to get anyone to attend on her or do any service for her. When Catherine heard this, without an instant's hesitation she dedicated herself to the service of Andrea. Undeterred by the odour or the corruption, not holding her nostrils, but with joy in her heart and in her countenance, she attached herself to that cancer-ridden patient, attended on her with the most diligent care, uncovered the sore, swabbed it, and washed it clean of pus, bandaged it without the slightest haste or disgust; and when nature itself was nauseated by all this, by a supreme act of mortification of her own flesh, pressed her face upon the mass of corruption and forced herself to bear that foul odour until she was on the point of fainting. "But Satan entered into Andrea, as he had formerly entered into Palmerina. Little by little she went on from suspicions against the one who had made herself her servant to whispering against her. In the end her folly reached the pitch of making false and shameful charges against Catherine's good name, even before the Sisters of Penance, alleging that this pure maiden had lost her virginity by a sin against chastity. On hearing this report Catherine was cut to the heart with an anguish beyond all power to describe. Nevertheless, once she had rebutted the charge by truthfully asserting her innocence, and had called on the help of her Bridegroom by tears and prayers, she showed no falling off in her devotion to the invalid. On the contrary, she now showed her even greater attention and attachment than before. And by her unshakable patience she overcame the other's malice. In reward for her patience and in witness of her

Teresa and the discalced Carmelites in Seville had been accused by members of their own Carmelite order of unchaste conduct; Teresa herself had been accused of soliciting the young women of Seville, under the pretext of becoming nuns, into prostitution.[21] In this case, Teresa used a hagiographical text with remarkable parallels to Teresa's own situation to advocate patience, charity and confidence that God would vindicate her cause.

The above passage is the most telling direct reference to Catherine in all of Teresa's writings; indeed, outside of her letters Teresa makes only one passing reference to Catherine in her formal mystical texts.[22] However, a comparison of Raymond's *Life* and Teresa's *Vida* reveal significant parallels, including the stunningly similar descriptions of conversions facilitated by Mary Magdalene. In both texts these conversions signal the beginning of a deeper spiritual experience as well as commitment to a zealous reform of monastic life. Capua describes Catherine's experience in this way:

> Now, after the death of her sister, she discerned with clearer eye than ever the emptiness of the world, and began to seek again the endearments of her eternal Spouse with warmer affection and keener eagerness than before. Crying aloud her own guilt, she abased herself with Mary Magdalene, coming behind at the feet of our Lord, and shedding floods of tears. She begged him for mercy, nor would she leave off praying and grieving for her sin until, with Mary Magdalene, she would have won from him the words: "Your sins are forgiven you." From that time she began to have a special devotion to the Magdalene, for it was then that she began, from her inmost heart, to imitate her in seeking forgiveness for her sins. This devotion grew apace, so that in the end the Spouse of holy souls and his glorious Mother gave the

---

sanctity, she was displayed transfigured before the eyes of her traducer, who plainly saw her surrounded by rays of brilliant light, and with her face shining like an angel's.... With tears she begged Catherine's pardon, and sending for all those to whom she had defamed her, loudly proclaimed herself a guilty wretch, and described with tears and cries the sight that she had seen. Recanting all the false charges she had made, she proclaimed that Catherine was not only a pure virgin but was a choice flower of sanctity in the eyes of God. This, she said, she was now convinced of beyond all shadow of doubt. And so it came about that Satan, in trying to blacken the good name of Catherine, succeeded, in his own despite, only in adding lustre to it. It was the Lord who brought this about, using Catherine's patience as his instrument."

[21] For more information on this incident see Ahlgren, *Teresa*.

[22] See *Vida* 22:7: "Yo he mirado con cuidado, después que esto he entendido, de algunos santos, grandes contemplativos, y no iban por otro camino. San Francisco da muestra de ello en las llagas; San Antonio de Padua en el Niño; San Bernardo se deleitaba en la Humanidad; Santa Catalina de Sena, otros muchos que vuestra merced sabrá mejor que yo."

Magdalene herself to Catherine as her teacher and her mother. . . .[23]

Within the framework of Catherine's life, Teresa's description of her own conversion in chapter 9 of *The Book of Her Life* gains coherence. Teresa relates how she was moved by a statue of Christ's passion:

> . . . I felt as if my heart were breaking, and I threw myself down beside Him, shedding floods of tears and begging Him to give me strength once for all so that I might not offend Him. I had a great devotion to the glorious Magdalen and often thought of her conversion, especially when I received communion, for, knowing that the Lord was certainly within me then, I would place myself at His feet, thinking that my tears would not be rejected. I did not know what I was saying; but in allowing me to shed those tears He was very gracious to me, since I so soon forgot my grief; and I used to commend myself to that glorious Saint so that she might obtain pardon for me.[24]

Another important point of comparison is in Teresa's conceptualization both of the role of humility in the mystical journey and her very definition of humility. Teresa identifies humility as the most important aid to spiritual growth—the cement of the soul's interior castle; throughout the journey toward intimacy with God humility indicates the soul's spiritual progress; deeper experiences of God propel the soul toward growth in self-knowledge and therefore with increasing clarity it sees that, in itself, it is nothing.[25] And in her *Life* Teresa chronicles her continued suspicion of her mystical experiences and her fear of being deceived by the devil. Like Raymond, who approved of such behavior in Catherine, Teresa's early confessors advocated this kind of response to visionary and mystical phenomena. Reflecting more generally on the problem of being deluded by the devil, Teresa argues that humility can be an important guarantor of authenticity, writing in the *Life*: "Especially for women is this worse: the devil may provoke some kind of illusion, although I know for certain that the Lord does not consent him to do harm to anyone who seeks him with humility."[26] Reflecting on the importance of humility toward the end of her

---

[23] Capua, *The Life of Catherine of Siena*, trans. Kearns, p. 44.

[24] Teresa of Ávila, *Life*, 9:1-2.

[25] See for example, *Vida* 12:4, 19:2, 20:7, 29:2; *Camino de perfección* (Valladolid text) 17:3; *Moradas* I:2:9; I:2:13; IV:2:9; VI:5:10. See also *Moradas* VII:4:8: ". . .[T]odo este edificio, como he dicho, es su cimiento humildad."

[26] Teresa of Ávila, *Vida* 12:7: "Torno otra vez a avisar que va mucho en no subir el espíritu si el Señor no le subiere; qué cosa es, se entiende luego. En especial para mujeres es más malo; que podrá el demonio causar alguna ilusión, aunque tengo por cierto no consiente el Señor dañe a quien con humildad se procura llegar a El; antes sacará más provecho y ganancia por donde el demonio le pensare hacer perder." Compare *Moradas* VI:9:12: "Aunque las visiones no fuesen de Dios, si tenéis humildad y buena conciencia, no os dañará

Interior Castle Teresa relates:

> Once I was considering why Our Lord was so fond of this virtue of humility and it came to me—it seemed to me without [being part of my] reflection but rather suddenly [as if from inspiration] this: that it is because God is supreme Truth and to be humble is to walk in the truth .... [27]

Finally, Teresa skillfully adopted Capua's rhetorical strategy of paradoxical representation with which he argues for the legitimacy of Catherine's mystical experiences as well as her adoption of a public reforming role. In *Teresa of Ávila and the Politics of Sanctity* I have observed and characterized this self-portrayal in Teresa's works as the combination of the strategy of subordination and the strategy of instrumental authority, effective because it appealed to the central paradox of Christianity: God upholds the lowly.[28] Perhaps more daring because Teresa employed the strategy herself in a sort of auto-hagiography, this strategy is easily explicable given the climate of opposition to visionary and ecstatic experiences, particularly those of women.

The domestication of the visionary/reforming model through such heavy emphasis on humility explains its success in the case of Teresa as well as its failure in cases where women were judged to be insufficiently humble in their expressions of their mystical experiences. The case of Francisca de los Apóstoles, a contemporary of Teresa tried by the Inquisitional Tribunal of Toledo between 1574 and 1578, demonstrates that Catherine's model of prophetic church reform was not universally accepted. During her trial Francisca described her own experiences of ecstatic visions in which God asked her to offer herself up to expiate the sin of others and referred explicitly to sections of *The Life of Catherine of Siena*, where Catherine was asked to do the same. For Francisca reading *The Life of Catherine of Siena* helped give meaning to her own religious experience and helped her to see herself as part of a larger Christian tradition of intercessory prayer. The inquisitor, however, found that Francisca was not sufficiently humble in her attitude toward her religious experiences: that she appeared unwilling to doubt and test her experiences for his was evidence that they were inauthentic.[29]

---

el demonio."

[27] Teresa, *Moradas* VI:10:7: "Una vez estaba yo considerando por qué razón era nuestro Señor tan amigo de esta virtud de la humildad y púsoseme delante, a mi parecer, sin considerarlo sino de presto, esto: que es porque Dios es suma Verdad y la humildad es andar en verdad." Compare *Vida* 40:1-4. For context on the phrase "a mi parecer" see Ahlgren, *Teresa of Ávila and the Politics of Sanctity*, pp. 70-71.

[28] See Ahlgren, *Teresa*, pp. 83-4.

[29] See Ahlgren, "Francisca de los Apostoles: A Visionary Voice for Reform in Sixteenth-Century Toledo" in Mary E. Giles, ed., *Women in the Inquisition: Spain and the*

The Life of Catherine of Siena took on significance in women's own self-construction, but it was also a model for those—men and women—who wished to recognize other women's holiness. There are many interesting points of comparison here between Capua's *Life* and the testimonials and biographies of Teresa; however, I want to highlight textual strategies of instrumental authority (where the woman is seen as a vehicle for divine activity in the world) and paradoxical representation. Teresian scholars will have no difficulty recognizing the parallels between Raymond's description of Catherine the writer and the many testimonials about Teresa when she wrote. Of Catherine Raymond writes:

> She used to dictate those letters of hers with such rapidity, without the slightest pause to take thought, that one would have fancied she was reading out her words from a book lying open before her. I myself often saw her dictating at the same time to two different secretaries, two different letters, addressed to two different persons, and dealing with two different subject-matters; and in the process neither secretary ever had to wait the fraction of a second for the dictation he was taking, nor did either of them ever hear from her anything but what belonged to his own subject-matter at the moment. When I expressed my astonishment at this I was told by several who had known her before I did, and who had very frequently watched while she dictated, that she would sometimes dictate in this way to three secretaries, and sometimes even to four, with equal rapidity and sureness of concentration. To me the existence of such a capacity in that weak woman's body of hers, worn out as it was by vigils and fasting, was a sign that it was miraculous and supernaturally infused, and no mere natural talent.[30]

Compare that description to the one given by María del Nacimiento during the collection of testimonies for Teresa's canonization:

> When she wrote it was with great speed and with such great beauty in her face that it caused this witness to admire her, and she was so absorbed in what she was writing that if there were any noise it never disturbed her; so this witness understood that everything she wrote was written while she was in [a state of] prayer.[31]

For Raymond of Capua, the greatness of Catherine's accomplishments is

---

New World (Baltimore, MD: Johns Hopkins University Press, 1998), pp. 119-33

[30] Capua, *Life*, trans. Kearns, pp. 6-7.

[31] Testimony of María del Nacimiento in Silverio de Santa Teresa, ed., *Biblioteca mística carmlitana* (Burgos: El Monte Carmelo, 1934-49), p. 18:315. For commentary, see Ahlgren, *Teresa*, pp. 78-9.

enough to convince Raymond that "this woman of whom we speak was not [actually] a woman, but rather an angel on earth, or if you like, more a celestial man than a woman."[32] Many of Teresa's male biographers concurred; for them the theory of divine inspiration was the only way to account for the fact that a woman could explain such exalted doctrine.[33] Given the challenges to their religious authority both women faced, it is no wonder that Teresa's last words were said to have been, "At last I die, a daughter of your church," a situation which recalls Capua's description of Catherine as a martyr for the church.

Some Conclusions

Raymond of Capua's *Life of Catherine of Siena* offered a compelling model for female holiness which on the one hand argued that women could serve prophetic and intercessory functions in the church but on the other hand established norms for conduct and self-representation to control access to those public roles. Both the *Life of Catherine of Siena* and the sixteenth-century texts it influenced develop an understanding of female virtue that incorporated heroic expressions of physical penance, patient forebearance of opposition, and humility meant to authenticate embodied religious experiences and their prophetic content. Understanding this dynamic can help us achieve a balanced interpretation of the function of humility in women's mystical texts.

Further, the blending of the two techniques of subordination and instrumental authority, while not unique to *The Life of Catherine of Siena*, forms a substantial part of the text and provides a rhetorical form for the expression of women's holiness within a climate of opposition to women's theological and ecclesiastical authority. Thus *The Life of Catherine of Siena* should be viewed as influential for its hermeneutical and rhetorical contributions to sixteenth-century texts written by women religious and their defenders. We have seen how this strategy was employed in Raymond of Capua's *Life of Catherine* and then ably studied and imitated by Teresa as she worked out the defense of her life. What remains is to observe this pattern in other spiritual texts and to reflect on the relationship between rhetorical strategy and mystical doctrine.

---

[32] Raymond of Capua, *Vida*, fol. 10[r]: "Porque esta virgen, de quien aqui dezimos, no era muger, mas angel en la tierra, o si mas quisieres, mas era hombre celestial que muger."
[33] See Ahlgren, *Teresa*, pp. 156-9, 164-5.

5 Bernardino de Laredo's *Treatise on the Mysteries of St. Joseph* and the Evangelization of Mexico

Joseph F. Chorpenning

The Observant Franciscan friar Bernardino de Laredo (1492-*circa.* 1540) is best known, in the history of Christian spirituality, for his book *Ascent of Mt. Sion* (first edition, 1535; second edition, 1538, subsequent editions: 1540, 1542, 1590, 1617). This renown is owed to the *Ascent* being part of St. Teresa of Ávila's spiritual reading, as the saint herself testifies in her autobiography (ch. 23). What is less known about Laredo and his *Ascent* is that appended to the latter is a short treatise on St. Joseph—the first written in the Spanish language at a moment when devotion to this saint was on the verge of burgeoning. Laredo titles his brief treatise *Josephina*, and it treats "the mysteries of the glorious St. Joseph,"[1] the word "mysteries" meaning, as it does in St. Ignatius Loyola's contemporary *Spiritual Exercises*, events or episodes in the life of the saint.[2]

An equally significant point about Laredo's *Josephina* is that it offers one of the earliest testimonies about the devotion to St. Joseph which flourished in Mexico from the dawn of the Colonial period. Laredo records that, in the region of Yucatán, a papal bull had been promulgated granting an indulgence of five hundred days for praying an *Ave* (Hail Mary) and a *Pater* (Our Father) in honor of the saint (72). He further reveals that the first bishop of Mexico, the Franciscan friar Juan de Zumárraga (*circa.* 1468-1548), requested that the author send a hundred or more copies of his *Josephina* for distribution in his

---

[1] All references are given parenthetically in the text and are to Bernardino de Laredo, *Tratado de San José*, facsimile of the 1538 edition with transcription in modern Spanish (Madrid: Rialp, 1977); English translations are my own. The fundamental work on Laredo is Fidèle de Ros, *Un inspirateur de sainte Thérèse: le frère Bernardin de Laredo* (Paris: J. Vrin, 1948). Also see E. Allison Peers, *Studies of the Spanish Mystics*, 3 vols. (London: Sheldon Press, 1927-60), 2:41-76, and Robert Ricard's article, with bibliography, on Laredo in the *Dictionnaire de spiritualité*, vol. 9 (Paris: Beauchesne, 1975), pp. 277-81.

[2] See Ignatius of Loyola, *The Spiritual Exercises and Selected Works*, edited by George E. Ganss, with the collaboration of Parmananda R. Divarkar, Edward J. Malatesta, and Martin E. Palmer, The Classics of Western Spirituality (New York: Paulist Press, 1991), p. 421.

diocese (72). In fact, Laredo's *Ascent* was commonly found in Franciscan libraries in sixteenth-century Mexico, as well as included on manifests of cargo ships destined for Mexico during the same period.[3]

The purpose of this essay is to indicate that the Franciscan friars charged with the evangelization of Mexico would have found in Laredo's *Josephina* a valuable resource for their efforts to effect this spiritual conquest, specifically by promoting veneration of the guardian and protector of Jesus and Mary. Before turning to Laredo's treatise, however, the constitutive elements of the veneration of St. Joseph which flourished in Mexico will be examined, in order to understand better the context in which the *Josephina* was received and its possible role in helping to define and support the contours of the saint's cult there.

Veneration of St. Joseph in New Spain

It might be expected that veneration of St. Joseph in the New World lagged behind initiatives promoting this devotion in Europe. On the contrary, the saint's cult took canonical and liturgical forms in New Spain (present-day Mexico, Central America, and the Philippines) that anticipated by several decades its evolution in the Old World. Not only a strong, positive image of St. Joseph, but also popular devotion to him, was well established and widespread in New Spain years before Teresa of Ávila began to popularize his veneration in Spain.[4] The ubiquitousness of the figure of St. Joseph—universally depicted as the youthful, vigorous, and handsome husband of Mary, earthly father of Jesus, and divinely appointed head and protector of the Holy Family—in the devotional art of New Spain bears eloquent testimony to the popularity of his cult there. Reflection on, or images of, Joseph in New Spain always relate the saint to Jesus and Mary. Thus, the cult of St. Joseph blends imperceptibly into that of the Holy Family.

---

[3] Fidèle de Ros, *Un inspirateur*, p. 181.

[4] John McAndrew, *The Open-Air Churches of Sixteenth-Century Mexico: Atrios, Posas, Open Chapels, and Other Studies* (Cambridge: Harvard University Press, 1965), p. 396. For a review of scholarship on the question of Laredo's influence on St. Teresa's devotion to St. Joseph, see Simeón Tomás Fernández, "Las *Josefinas* de Bernardino de Laredo (1535) y de Andrés de Soto (1593), franciscanos," *Cahiers de Joséphologie* 25 (1977): 223-54, especially pp. 242-8. On the basis of close comparison of twelve texts from Laredo and from Teresa, Fernández concludes: "We do not claim to affirm that Teresa's devotion to, and 'knowledge' of, St. Joseph depends solely on Laredo, nor are we able to establish the exact moment when the saint came into contact with the *Josephina*. But . . . we are convinced that we have discovered and can affirm a very profound, very marked, and very ample influence of Laredo's *Josephina* on St. Teresa's devotion to, doctrine on, and enthusiasm for St. Joseph, as presented in chapter six of her autobiography" (248).

Official ecclesiastical approbation of the great devotion and veneration accorded St. Joseph by all the faithful, Amerindians and Spaniards alike, occurred very early in the history of New Spain. On June 29, 1555, at the First Provincial Council of Mexico, St. Joseph was declared patron of the ecclesiastical Province of Mexico, which included the archdiocese of Mexico City (established as a diocese in 1530, it was raised to an archdiocese in 1546) and its nine suffragan dioceses (all those in Mexico, plus several others, most notably Guatemala and Nicaragua).[5] Henceforth, St. Joseph's feast day was a holy day of obligation—sixty-six years before Pope Gregory XV (reigned 1621-23) so designated it for the Universal Church in 1621. In 1585, the Third Provincial Council of Mexico renewed the Province's dedication to St. Joseph, noting, in its conciliar decrees, "the extraordinary devotion with which the most chaste Patriarch and lord St. Joseph, husband of the most holy Virgin Mary, is honored, courted, and revered in this ecclesiastical Province."[6] By this date, Mexico City had twelve suffragan dioceses, the most recent addition being Manila in the Philippines.[7] As sermons and devotional art of the Colonial period proclaim, St. Joseph ruled over New Spain, just as his Old Testament type, the Patriarch Joseph, ruled over the land of Egypt.[8]

Origins of St. Joseph's Cult in the New World

Within the first decade of the conquest of Mexico (begun in 1518 and completed in 1521), the Viceroyalty of New Spain had become, to use Émile Mâle's phrase, "the chosen land of St. Joseph."[9] The saint's cult was introduced by the first Observant Franciscan friars who came to evangelize the Americas. The name that dominates this story is that of the extraordinary Flemish lay brother Fray Pedro de Gante (1486-1572). An uncle or great-uncle of Charles V (1500-58), Pedro was educated by the Brothers of the Common Life, who highly esteemed the writings of Jean Gerson (1363-1429), the eloquent and prolific chancellor of the University of Paris, who was one of the earliest advocates of the cult of St. Joseph and the concomittant devotion to the Holy

---

[5] Juan Antonio Morán, "La devoción a San José en México en el siglo XVII," *Cahiers de Joséphologie* 29 (1981): 953-99, especially p. 959.

[6] Quoted in José Rubén Sanabría, "La devoción a San José en México en el siglo XVI," *Cahiers de Joséphologie* 25 (1977): 663-76, at p. 673.

[7] On the history of the archdiocese of Mexico, see Daniel T. Olmedo, "Mexico, Archdiocese of (Mexicanus)," *New Catholic Encyclopedia*, 1967.

[8] Jaime Cuadriello, "José de Alzíbar (activo 1751-1804), *El ministerio de San José*, ca. 1771," in *Juegos de ingenio y agudeza: La pintura emblemática de la Nueva España*, exh. cat. (Mexico City: Museo Nacional de Arte, 1994), p. 382.

[9] *L'art religieux de la fin du XVIe siècle, du XVIIe siècle et du XVIIIe siècle: Étude sur l'iconographie après le Concile de Trente*, 2nd ed. (Paris: Librairie Armand Colin, 1951), p. 315.

Family.[10] Whatever devotion to St. Joseph to which Pedro may have been exposed, or even cultivated himself, during his student days would have been reinforced and strengthened when he entered the Franciscans.

One of the great masterpieces of early Franciscan devotional literature, the *Meditations on the Life of Christ*, authored by an anonymous Italian Franciscan friar *circa* 1300, reveals that the first generations of friars regarded St. Joseph and the Holy Family as models of mendicant poverty.[11] Veneration of St. Joseph acquired official status in the Franciscan Order in 1399, when, at a general chapter held at Assisi, a feast in the saint's honor, with a Mass and nine-lesson office, was adopted. Moreover, the Franciscans also actively promoted St. Joseph's cult in the late medieval Church at large. For example, the great Franciscan preacher and Doctor of the Church St. Bernardine of Siena (1380-1444) composed the most famous sermon on St. Joseph ever written, and the Franciscan Pope Sixtus IV (reigned 1471-84) introduced the saint's feast (March 19) at Rome in 1479.[12] In 1523, the year Pedro departed from Seville for the New World, the Observant Franciscans of the Flemish Province chose St. Joseph as their patron.[13]

The example and travails of St. Joseph and the Holy Family must have been a constant reference point for the Franciscans in general and for Pedro and his companions in particular. In addition to his primary role as a model of Franciscan poverty, St. Joseph took on other roles for Pedro and his fellow friars who traveled to the New World. The gospels testify that, under Joseph's protection, the Holy Family often traveled. The Holy Family's journey to and residence in Egypt, a pagan land hostile to Israelites, surely resonated in the experience of Pedro and his companions, as they embarked for an unknown, distant, pagan land. Like Jesus and Mary, they too must have journeyed under St. Joseph's protection. The flight into Egypt was also paradigmatic in another respect. In taking Mary and Jesus to Egypt, St. Joseph was credited with introducing Christianity to that pagan land.[14] The friars set out on a similar

---

[10] McAndrew, *Open-Air Churches*, pp. 369-70, 394.

[11] See *Meditations on the Life of Christ: An Illustrated Manuscript of the Fourteenth Century, Paris, Bibliothèque Nationale, Ms. Ital. 115*, translated and edited by Isa Ragusa and Rosalie B. Green (Princeton: Princeton University Press, 1961), pp. 36-7, 43, 51-2, 56-7, 72, 80, 100-101.

[12] Blaine Burkey, "The Feast of St. Joseph: A Franciscan Bequest," *Cahiers de Joséphologie* 19 (1971): 647-80, especially pp. 650-51, 655.

[13] McAndrew, *Open-Air Churches*, p. 394. For an overview of the history of the Franciscans and of constituent groups of the Order, such as the Observants, who, in opposition to the Conventuals, sought to observe the rule in its primitive severity, see Cyprian J. Lynch, "Franciscans," *New Catholic Encyclopedia*, 1967.

[14] Román Llamas, "San José evangelizador de América: Tema de un sermón barroco del siglo XVII," *Estudios Josefinos* 46 (1992): 27-52, especially 41. Compare Laredo, p. 46.

mission of evangelization, and historians of the Colonial period maintain that they entrusted this project to the patronage of St. Joseph.[15]

Once in Mexico, Pedro constantly proffered St. Joseph the craftsman and the head of the Holy Family to the Amerindians as a role model. To underscore this, in the late 1520s, Pedro placed the first school founded to instruct the Amerindians, not only in Christian doctrine, but also in fine arts and crafts, under the saint's protection. By the end of the same decade, the first place of worship named for St. Joseph in the Americas, the chapel of "San José de Belén de los Naturales" (St. Joseph of Bethlehem of the Natives) in Mexico City, was built. It was probably only the second or third church in the world ever dedicated to Joseph.[16] As the first parish established for Native Americans, "San José de Belén de los Naturales" has been aptly described as "the cradle of Christianity in the Americas."[17]

Bethlehem means "house of bread," and the name "San José de Belén de los Naturales" indicates that Pedro thought of this modest thatched chapel as a new Bethlehem, where Christ would again come into the world, under St. Joseph's watchful protection, under the form of the bread of the Eucharist. Just as St. Francis of Assisi (*circa* 1181-1226), had done three centuries earlier by presenting in tableau a living crèche, "San José de Belén de los Naturales" relived "the radiant poverty of the Nativity," thus recreating St. Joseph's world, in which the "poor like [Francis] are at home."[18] "San José de Belén de los Naturales" was the prototype for the many open chapels subsequently built for the Amerindians. These chapels were so frequently dedicated to the saint that "San José" became their familiar name.[19]

A Benevolent, Powerful, and Protective Father for an Oppressed People

In New Spain, the parents of Jesus also became the parents of the Amerindians. For example, St. Joseph was not only a role model for the Amerindians, he also became *their* father. The Conquest had a devastating impact on Native Americans. The worse effects were long-term. Most destructive were the ravages of the contagious diseases introduced by Europeans to the New World: smallpox, typhus, measles, and other as yet unidentified diseases. These

---

[15] Hermenegildo Ramírez Sánchez, "San José en la evangelización de América Latina," *Cahiers de Joséphologie* 39 (1991): 611-35, especially 613-14, and José Carlos Carrillo Ojeda, "San José en la Nueva España del siglo XVII," *Cahiers de Joséphologie* 35 (1987): 627-53, especially p. 632.

[16] McAndrew, *Open-Air Churches*, p. 397, and Rubén Sanabría, "La devoción," p. 667.

[17] Ramírez Sánchez, "San José," p. 614.

[18] Andrew Doze, *St. Joseph: Shadow of the Father*, translated by Florestine Audett (New York: Alba House, 1992), pp. 11-12.

[19] McAndrew, *Open-Air Churches*, p. 393.

diseases reached epidemic proportions, reducing the Indian population in central Mexico by about 90 per cent over the course of the first century after the Conquest. Other long-term effects of the Conquest included escalating demands for tribute on a shrinking indigenous population by a growing Spanish population, extensive social demoralization, and dislocation of many Indians from their own villages to Hispanic towns and cities. These pressures on Indian communities bred resentment and violence against the Spaniards, from whom Native Americans also sought protection.

A further social problem was that a sizable segment of the population of the New World did not know what it meant to have a father: most *mestizos* knew only their Indian mothers, but not their Spanish fathers. It has been estimated that the rate of illegitimacy in Colonial Spanish America was very high, ranging from 30 per cent to 60 per cent, depending on the region. One important way whereby the Church sought to offer the Amerindians protection and a sense of parenthood was by proffering Mary and Joseph not only as models of Christian faith, but also as *their* parents, thus extending to native peoples their heavenly patronage.[20] The Virgin Mary became their loving and compassionate mother, while Joseph became the father of this conquered and oppressed people who would protect and shelter them.[21]

While the idea of Mary's universal maternity was well established in the Christian tradition, the image of St. Joseph as a magnanimous, protective father, whose patronage was extended to all Christians, was just beginning to emerge as Spain's Colonial enterprise unfolded. The first person in Christian history to adopt St. Joseph as her father was St. Teresa of Ávila (1515-1582). In the *Book of Her Life* (begun in 1562 and completed in 1565), Teresa explains, in chapter 6, that she turned to this "doctor of heaven" to heal her from a crippling illness that afflicted her shortly after she entered the Carmelite monastery of the Incarnation in Ávila, since the "doctors of earth" were powerless to help her.[22] From the moment Teresa was healed through Joseph's intercession, he had a

---

[20] Edwin Williamson, *The Penguin History of Latin America* (New York: Penguin Books, 1992), pp. 35-6, 84-91; Thomas Calvo, "Calor de hogar: las familias del siglo XVII en Guadalajara," in *Sexualidad y matrimonio en la América hispánica*, edited by Asunción Lavrin (Mexico City: Grijalbo, 1991), pp. 309-38; Carlos Fuentes, *The Buried Mirror: Reflections on Spain and the New World* (Boston: Houghton Mifflin Company, 1992), 144-7; Maria Emma Mannarelli, *Pecados públicos: La ilegitimidad en Lima. Siglo XVII* (Lima: Flora Tristán, 1993); Clara López Beltrán, "La buena vecindad: Las mujeres de élite de la sociedad colonial del siglo XVII," forthcoming in *Colonial Latin American Review*. I am grateful to Professor Georgina Sabat-Rivers for sharing with me several references cited in this note.

[21] Compare Fuentes, *Buried Mirror*, pp. 145-6.

[22] *The Collected Works of St. Teresa of Ávila*, translated by Kieran Kavanaugh and Otilio Rodríguez, 3 vols. (Washington, D.C.: Institute of Carmelite Studies, 1976-85), vol. 1, p. 53.

preeminent place in her life, and henceforth she referred to him as "this father and lord of mine."[23] Teresa's speaking of St. Joseph as her father was unprecedented.[24]

Teresa's experience of St. Joseph's extension of his protection of Jesus and Mary to souls invoking his assistance must have had powerful reverberations in the Viceregal Americas, especially as her spirituality and Carmelite reform were exported there. In Mexico, her advocacy of devotion to St. Joseph would have supported and strengethened the vigorous cult of the saint which had already flourished there, undoubtedly due to the efforts of the Franciscans. With so many epidemics, Native Americans must have been instructed about St. Joseph's curative powers, which had delivered Teresa from a crippling paralysis. In the midst of oppression and of a fatherless society, St. Joseph was a benevolent, protective father who would defend and nurture those who recommended themselves to him, just as he saved the Christ Child from the murderous Herod and sustained the Son of God and His mother by the sweat of his brow.[25]

The most celebrated New World testimony to St. Joseph's role as an exemplary father figure in a fatherless society is that of the Mexican Hieronymite nun Sor Juana Inés de la Cruz (1648-1695). The premier female author of Mexican letters, Sor Juana, like so many of her contemporaries in Spanish America, was born out of wedlock. She deeply resented her father, regarding him as dishonorable, not only for his adamant refusal to marry her mother, but also for his promiscuity. For Sor Juana, St. Joseph stood in sharp contrast to her own father, as well as to the oppressive machismo of her day. Sor Juana was deeply attached to St. Joseph, a model husband and father who voluntarily renounced biological fatherhood, which in Jewish and Hispanic

---

[23] Kavanaugh and Rodríguez, *Collected Works*, 1:53.

[24] Doze, *St. Joseph*, pp. 15-17. In the next century, another great post-Tridentine saint and Doctor of the Church, St. Francis de Sales (1567-1622), professes, in a letter to St. Jane Frances de Chantal, that he is a son of St. Joseph as St. Teresa had been his daughter. The bishop of Geneva calls St. Joseph "the glorious father of our life and our love," as well as alludes to Mary and Joseph as the first Christians by speaking of the saint as Jesus' "first worshipper next to his divine spouse" (quoted in Doze, *St. Joseph*, pp. 41-2; Compare p. 32).

[25] Christopher C. Wilson, "Beyond Strong Men and Frontiers: Conquests of the Spanish Mystics," in *Temples of Gold, Crowns of Silver: Reflections of Majesty in the Viceregal Americas*, edited by Barbara von Barghahn (Washington, DC: George Washington University, 1991), pp. 116-27, especially pp. 122, 124, and "St. Teresa of Ávila's Holy Patron: Teresian Sources for the Image of St. Joseph in Spanish American Colonial Art," in *Patron Saint of the New World: Spanish American Colonial Images of St. Joseph*, exh. cat. (Philadelphia: Saint Joseph's University Press, 1992), pp. 5-17, especially pp. 7, 12.

society defined a man's identity, to raise another's child, the Son of the eternal Father.[26]

The Testimony of Images

Europeans were well aware that the invention of writing was one of the key cultural differentiations between themselves and the Amerindians, whereas pictorial images were something both groups had in common. The language of symbols enjoyed a privileged status, antedating the Conquest, among native peoples of the New World. Consequently, the friars who came to evangelize the Americas discovered that the Indians were deeply impressed by religious images. Thus, sight was given priority over sound as a means of catechization, and, consequently, religious images served not merely a decorative purpose in the many monasteries and churches constructed in the Americas, but as an essential medium of evangelization. Importing and producing devotional art became not only a priority, but also an industry.[27]

Numerous Mexican Colonial paintings seem designed to communicate that St. Joseph is a loving and benevolent father who, just as he defended the Christ Child from danger, will protect whomever invokes his intercession. Artists rely on gesture, another "language" shared by Europeans and Amerindians,[28] to convey this message. For example, St. Joseph may not only tenderly hold Jesus, but also protectively enfold Him within his cloak. Or the saint steadies the standing Christ Child with one hand, lest He fall, while he extends toward the viewer his other hand open, signifying protection, authority,

---

[26] Georgina Sabat-Rivers, *Sor Juana Inés de la Cruz and Sor Marcela de San Félix: Their Devotion to St. Joseph as the Antithesis of Patriarchal Authoritarianism* (Philadelphia: Saint Joseph's University Press, 1997).

[27] Peter F. Klaren, "Spain in America: The Viceroyalties of New Spain & Peru, 1521-1825," in *Temples of Gold, Crowns of Silver*, 1-15, especially 11; Luis Weckmann, *The Medieval Heritage of Mexico*, translated by Frances M. López-Morillas (New York: Fordham University Press, 1992), p. 180; Thomas Cummins, "From Lies to Truth: Colonial Ekphrasis and the Act of Crosscultural Translation," in *Reframing the Renaissance: Visual Culture in Europe and Latin America 1450-1650*, edited with an introduction by Claire Farago (New Haven: Yale University Press, 1995), 152-74, especially 153; Fernando R. de la Flor, "Jeroglíficos indígenas," in his *Emblemas: Lecturas de la imagen simbólica* (Madrid: Alianza, 1995), pp. 313-23.

[28] See Pauline Moffitt Watts, "Languages of Gesture in Sixteenth-Century Mexico: Some Antecedents and Transmutations," in *Reframing the Renaissance*, pp, 140-51.

power, and strength.[29] Or St. Joseph walks with the Christ Child leading Him by the hand, acting as His Guardian Angel.[30]

Laredo's Josephina: *a Resource for Evangelization*

There is a clear resonance between the theology of St. Joseph promoted by Laredo's *Josephina* and the shape which the saint's cult eventually took in New Spain. Bishop Zumárraga and his brother friars must have recognized in the *Josephina* their Order's strong traditional devotion to St. Joseph, as well as a potentially valuable resource in their efforts to introduce this veneration to the New World as part of their program of evangelization. In this connection, it is noteworthy that Laredo himself envisions his book being used principally for meditation and for preaching (12). Given the popularity of St. Joseph as a subject in Mexican Colonial painting, it is also significant that Laredo gives appreciable attention to the manner in which the saint is to be depicted in art. What are some of the important ideas which Laredo's confrères would have found in his *Josephina* and presumably disseminated in their ministry of evangelization?

For Laredo, St. Joseph is the greatest saint after the Virgin Mary because, after her, "there was no one who was more active, ardent, and perfect in charity. . . . [or] who served [Our Lord] for so many years" (10). St. Joseph was "chosen by . . . God from all eternity . . . from all the men on the face of the earth" for his sublime vocation as "the protector, companion, and helper" of the Virgin Mary and as father "of Him who on earth has no father" (10). St. Joseph's unique relationship with Jesus and Mary makes him the most powerful

---

[29] See J. E. Cirlot, *A Dictionary of Symbols*, 2nd ed., translated by Jack Sage (New York: Dorset Press, 1971), 137, and J. C. J. Metford, *Dictionary of Christian Lore and Legend* (London: Thames and Hudson, 1983), p. 116.

[30] Devotional writers, such as the Discalced Carmelite friar Jerónimo Gracián de la Madre de Dios (1545-1614), who was St. Teresa's religious superior, spiritual director, and closest friend and collaborator, argued that St. Joseph was entrusted with the office of serving as Jesus' Guardian Angel: see *Just Man, Husband of Mary, Guardian of Christ: An Anthology of Readings from Jerónimo Gracián's "Summary of the Excellencies of St. Joseph" (1597)*, translated and edited with an introductory essay and commentary by Joseph F. Chorpenning (Philadelphia: Saint Joseph's University Press, 1993), pp. 190-92. The image of St. Joseph leading the Christ Child by the hand iconographically parallels that of the Guardian Angel: see Mâle, 305-6; John B. Knipping, *Iconography of the Counter Reformation in the Netherlands: Heaven on Earth*, 2 vols. (Nieuwkoop: B. de Graaf/Leiden: A. W. Sijthoff, 1974) 1:126-7; Louis Réau, *Iconographie de l'art chrétien*, 3 vols. (Paris: Presses Universitaires de France, 1955-59), vol. 2, part 2, p. 757. For further discussion, with illustrations, of the portrayal of St. Joseph in Mexican art, see Joseph F. Chorpenning, "The Iconography of St. Joseph in Mexican Devotional *Retablos*," in *Mexican Devotional Retablos from The Peters Collection*, exh. cat. (Philadelphia: Saint Joseph's University Press, 1994), pp. 39-92.

of heavenly intercessors. In heaven, as on earth, Jesus obeys St. Joseph's paternal authority, and whoever takes St. Joseph as an intercessor also obtains Mary's intercession (72). Hence, St. Joseph's intercession could be invoked with the greatest confidence.

Another role which Mary and Joseph fulfill is that they were the first Christians. As the author of another, later, *Josephina* explains, "the Christian is one who knows, believes in, serves, and glorifies Christ after His coming into the world. . . . St. Joseph was the first who, after the Virgin Mary, knew and adored Christ incarnate."[31] For his part, Laredo puts it this way: "After the ever-virgin Mother, St. Joseph was the first to witness Christ's birth and benefited the most from it. And no one felt more keenly the dolorous pain of the circumcision of this King eight days after His birth. More than anyone, after the Virgin Mary, he suffered the travails of exile in Egypt. . . . And, during the three days when the Child was lost in Jerusalem, accompanying the Virgin, he suffered greater affliction than can be imagined. For almost thirty years he served the Virgin and Christ with such faithfulness that he merited . . . to be the person on earth, after the Virgin Mary, with whom Our Lord most often and most closely conversed" (18). This emphasis on Mary and Joseph as the first Christians who knew, believed in, served, and glorified the Word made flesh would have had a special value and poignancy as the Church worked to convert an entire indigenous population to the Catholic faith.[32]

According to Laredo, St. Joseph is inseparable from Mary and Jesus. The Church's liturgical calendar and sacred art attest to this truth. The events of Jesus' infancy and childhood, celebrated by the Church in liturgical feasts, such as the Lord's Nativity, Circumcision, and Presentation in the Temple, are "the door" whereby one enters into contemplation of Jesus, Mary, and Joseph (12). Likewise, in art "St. Joseph is almost always portrayed with the most holy Virgin . . . and with her Child, since [He] is not depicted during His childhood without the Virgin and St. Joseph. Neither is the Virgin painted giving birth nor in many other mysteries without St. Joseph and Her Son" (42). In accord with this principle, paintings of familiar events recorded in the gospels and of intimate scenes of the Holy Family's domestic life would abound in Colonial Mexico, while at the same time offering—for Native Americans' admiration, reflection, and imitation—the example of Mary and Joseph, who came into the closest contact possible with the Son of God, accepted Him in faith, and protected, sustained, and educated Him.

Laredo expresses special concern about how artists choose to depict St. Joseph, particularly his age at the time of his espousal to the Virgin. Following Gerson, Laredo argues that St. Joseph was "forty years of age, more or less, at the time when the eternal God ordained that he be married . . . to the ever-

---

[31] Chorpenning, *Just Man*, pp. 254-5.
[32] Compare Wilson, "St. Teresa of Ávila's Holy Patron," p. 13.

virgin Mary" (18).³³ This opinion is based on Scripture, specifically commentaries interpreting Isaiah 62:5, "a young man marries a young woman . . . the bridegroom rejoices over the bride," as referring to St. Joseph and the Virgin Mary (18). Moreover, Laredo argues, reason dictates that St. Joseph could not have been aged because Mary would have appeared as an adulteress and Jesus would have been suspected of being illegitimate (18). Laredo then invokes the authority of Gerson, who held that St. Joseph was most handsome, to criticize artistic representations which show the saint as otherwise (18).³⁴ Like a modern student of iconography, Laredo attempts to account for the practice of representing St. Joseph as elderly: "in the early Church there were heretics who held that St. Joseph was the biological father of Christ, and to refute this error the practice began of showing St. Joseph to be an old man" (20). But what was done in the past for good reason is now foolishness, and the saint should be depicted as "young, radiant, and most handsome, as the great Gerson avers, because it is to the great glory of God" (20). In the New World, these arguments must have been very persuasive for "Artists in Spanish America consistently portrayed [St. Joseph] as young and vigorous. It seems that people in this new and utopian world could not conceive of the man who protected from danger the Virgin and the young Son of God as being old and weak."³⁵

Conclusion

This brief sampling of some of the principal themes of Laredo's *Josephina* highlights several important ways in which this devotional treatise would have supported the evangelization of Mexico and also helped to shape the contours of the cult of St. Joseph as it would evolve in the Viceroyalty of New Spain. The doctrine which Laredo proffers is not new. He takes pains to note that it is in accord with the teaching of the Fathers of the Church, the saints, and the most orthodox theologians, such as Gerson (12).³⁶ In the Hispanic world, the theology of St. Joseph which Laredo propounds would become normative, first in the New World and then in the Old.

---

   ³³ Gerson held that St. Joseph was about thirty-six because this is the age which Aristotle identifies as the prime of life. See David Herlihy, *Medieval Households* (Cambridge, Massachusetts: Harvard University Press, 1985), p. 128.
   ³⁴ For an interesting discussion of Gerson's treatment of artistic representations of St. Joseph, see Meyer Shapiro, "*Muscipula Diaboli*: The Symbolism of The Mérode Altarpiece," in his *Late Antique, Early Christian, and Mediaeval Art: Selected Papers* (New York: George Braziller, 1979), pp. 1-11, especially pp. 6-7.
   ³⁵ Sabat-Rivers, *Sor Juana*, p. 5.
   ³⁶ For fuller treatment of the *Josephina*'s sources, see Fidèle de Ros, *Un inspirateur*, p. 168-73.

6 What's in a Name: On Teresa of Ávila's *Book*

Elizabeth Rhodes

In a renowned scene from *Romeo and Juliet*, the young protagonist asks the evening sky what difference a name makes, innocently reasoning, "That which we call a rose / By any other word would smell as sweet."[1] Although Juliet's idealism has become a cliché, the less overt, ironic function of her words remains potent, for her naive essentialism proves fatal. There is, indeed, much in a name, and the radiance cast by words around that which they denominate can be extremely influential.

Literary historians name texts according to genus, from whence the familiar *genre*, via a process which corresponds to a similar procedure in the natural sciences. Educators regale students with these categories from elementary school on, categories presented as the keys to understanding literature. Often binary opposites, such as fiction and non-fiction, these *genera* deeply condition the texts in them by creating predetermined expectations, for the most part of an oppugnant nature. Thus, a work is "true" or "not true," through the privileging of rationalism over other mimetic strategies. Neither transparent nor universal, this process of classification is bound to collide on occasion with samples the categories cannot accommodate. Such misfits, which also plague physical scientists, are often produced by places and (in the case of literature) authors whose existence was not factored into the classifications as they were designed, but whose products are urged into a place within the denominating grid regardless. This is the case with the oxymoron "magic realism," the name bestowed upon a specific type of twentieth-century Latin American fiction that stretches past the limits of both the "magic" and the "real" as defined by the European tradition. Women's writings often pose such challenges to canonical distinctions, as does religious literature.[2]

---

[1] William Shakespeare, *Romeo and Juliet. The Riverside Shakespeare* (Boston: Houghton Mifflin, 1974), ed. G. Blackmore Evans, 2.2.43-4.

[2] For discussion of how women's experience with the categorizing processes of the natural sciences is equally vexed, see Paula Findeln, "Essay Review: Danger and the Scientific 'Civilizing Process.'" *Journal of the History of Biology* 24 (1991): 331-8; David F.

THE MYSTICAL GESTURE

Teresa of Ávila composed such a misfit text when she wrote, originally under orders of her religious superiors, an account of her relationship with God. In the very first words of that text's prologue Teresa explains exactly what she was doing: "Quisiera yo que, como me han mandado y dado larga licencia para *que escriba el modo de oracinón y las mercedes que el Señor me ha hecho*, me la dieran para que muy por menudo y con claridad dijera mis grandes pecados y ruin vida" ["Since my confessors commanded me and gave me plenty of leeway *to write about the favors and the kind of prayer the Lord has granted me*, I wish they would also have allowed me to tell very clearly and minutely about my great sins and wretched life."][3] She repeats later, addressing her confessor: "pues tanto me ha importunado escriba *alguna declaración de las mercedes que me hace Dios en la oración*" ["since you have so importuned that I write *some statement about the favors granted me by God in prayer*"] (10.8; emphases mine).

The manuscript resulting from this religious exercise, itself the culmination of a long series of probes into Teresa's spiritual experiences, is now universally referred to as her *Vida* or *Life*. This nomenclature, which dates from the 1588 edition of her works, inscribes an isomorphic relationship between Teresa's historical person and the text's narrative persona and thereby invites positivist readings, among which those treating the text as an autobiography are by far the majority. Readers of all professions have taken Teresa's warm and compelling invitation to see the text through her "I," and accept it as a re-telling of her individual life. Biographies of the saint rely heavily on information contained in the same book. The supposed relationship between history and "non-fiction" is intimate, and it is no surprise that a piece of writing composed largely in first person be taken as such by readers at large. It is surprising, however, that cautionary flags warning against this procedure continue to be glossed over. Among these are Kavanaugh's exact declaration that "Teresa's book is not an autobiography. . . . What she deals with mainly are the supernatural (infused or mystical) realities of the interior life" and Weber's

---

Noble, *A World without Women: The Christian Clerical Culture of Western Science* (New York: Alfred A. Knopf, 1992); and L. J. Jordanova, "Gender, Science and Creativity," in Maureen McNeil, ed., *Gender and Expertise* (London: Free Association Books, 1987), pp. 152-7.

[3] *Vida*, Prólogo 1.1. Quotations from Teresa's Spanish texts are from the *Obras completas* (OC; eds Enrique Llamas et al., 3rd ed., Madrid: Editorial Católica, 1984) and cite chapter then paragraph number. Translations are by Kieran Kavanaugh and Otilio Rodríguez, "The Book of Her Life," in *Saint Teresa of Ávila: Collected Works*, 2nd ed. (Washington, DC: Institute of Carmelite Studies, 1987), vol 1, pp. 53-365. I have modernized the Spanish of other early modern sources, and translations of all other sources are mine.

discreet reminder of the "ambiguous appropriateness of this [autobiographic] generic attribution."[4]

The practice of reading not only Teresa's text, but women's religious testimonies in general, in terms of autobiographical standards is widespread and can be observed in studies of medieval holy women, early modern Hispanic nuns, and nineteenth-century black Methodists.[5] Following the titular lead that suggests Teresa's spiritual life story is indeed her *Life*, the vast majority of readers today either consider it an autobiography or describe it as "autobiographic."[6] This nomenclature conditions readers' approach to the narrative, creating expectations it cannot meet by means of a false pre-textual premise about its nature. As Lanser observes, "Textual expectations —including expectations about point of view—are first set up by the extrafictional voice, especially through the texts' title."[7]

Teresa's first long prose work is double-crossed by the name imposed upon it and the autobiographical ramifications that name has generated. It is compromised once by the autobiographical postulate of a subject whose

---

[4] Kieren Kavanaugh, "*The Book of Her Life*. Introduction," in Kavanaugh and Rodríguez, *Book*; Alison Weber, *Teresa of Ávila and the Rhetoric of Feminity* (Princeton: Princeton University Press, 1990), p. 42.

[5] Respectively, Jo Ann K. McNamara, *Sisters in Arms: Catholic Nuns Through Two Millennia* (Cambridge, Massachusetts: Harvard University Press, 1996); Electa Arenal and Stacey Schlau, *Untold Sisters. Hispanic Nuns in their Own Works*, trans. Amanda Powell (Albuquerque: University of New Mexico Press, 1989); Rodrigo Cánovas, "Ursula Suárez (monja chilena 1666-1749): La autobiografía como penitencia," *Revista chilena de literatura* 35 (1990): 97-115; Kathleen Myers, ed., *Word from New Spain: The Spiritual Autobiography of Madre María de San José (1656-1719)* (Liverpool: University of Liverpool Press, 1993); Sherry Marie Velasco, *Demons, Nausea, and Resistance in the Autobiography of Isabel de Jesús* (Albuquerque: University of New Mexico Press, 1996); Jean M. Humez, "'My Spirit Eye': Some Functions of Spiritual and Visionary Experience in the Lives of Five Black Women Preachers, 1810-1880," in Jo Ann K. McNamara and Barbara J. Harris, eds, *Women and the Structure of Society: Selected Research from the Fifth Berkshire Conference on the History of Women* (Durham, North Carolina: Duke University Press, 1984), pp. 129-43.

[6] To cite but a few: Ruth A. El Saffar, *Rapture Encaged: The Suppression of the Feminine in Western Culture*, London: Routledge, 1994); James D. Fernández, "La *Vida* de Teresa de Jesús y la salvación del discurso," *MLN* 105 (1990): 283-3020; Sonja Herpoel, "Bajo la amenaza de la Inquisición: Escritoras españolas en el Siglo de Oro," in Martin Gosman and Hub Hermans, eds, *España, teatro y mujeres: Estudios dedicados a Henk Oostendorp* (Amsterdam: Rodopi, 1989), pp. 123-31; Isabel Poutrin, *La voile et la plume: Autobiographie et sainteté féminine dans l'Espagne moderne* (Madrid: Casa de Velázquez, 1995); and Paul Julian Smith, "Writing Women in Golden Age Spain: Saint Teresa and María de Zayas," *MLN* 102 (1987): 220-40).

[7] Cited in Amy R. Williamsen, "Question of Entitlement: Imposed Titles and Intrepretation in Sor Juana and María de Zayas," *Revista de Estudios Hispánicos* 31 (1997): 106.

individuated identity is at odds with women's social experience, which has long been historically conditioned by relational identity. Autobiographical readings, in turn, disable it as a religious text, since religious writings necessarily invoke at least two subjects, the human being and the divine, contrary to the single-lensed "I" of autobiography."[8] As Teresa herself points out, her text recounts not the story of her life, but rather the most extraordinary moments in her relationship with God. Thus Kavanaugh insists, "the real object of her testimony is the supernatural."[9] Religious literature in first person, then, is inherently distinct from autobiography, for its subject shares the textual stage with a divinity.

Difficulties in categorizing Tersa's first long prose work are evident: it has been named a treatise on humility, a manual of spirituality, a self-defense, an apology, a chronicle of grace and sin, a text with links to the picaresque tradition, self-portraiture, the Augustinian confession, and the personal letter, for example. In the face of such florid variety, Carol Slade calls it a "dialogized heteroglossia," and suggests that it displays "the accents of several other genres."[10] This classificational wrestling, which presses Teresa's text into niches from which it inevitably and nimbly escapes, suggests that extant literary categories can not only fail to accommodate but can actually compromise women's writing, on the one hand, and religious texts, on the other.[11] Teresa's *Book*, perched astride the domains of both, doubly challenges literary history.

---

[8] Religious literature by women constitutes most of the textual evidence used by Mary Mason, "The Other Voice: Autobiographies of Women Writers," in Bella and Celeste Schenck Brodzki, eds, *Life/Lines: Theorizing Women's Autobiography* (Ithaca, New York: Cornell University Press, 1988), p. 180, to suport her contention that in women's autobiography: "the 'I' is mediated by the agency of a significant other(s) and originates as an Other to itself." Whether or not this is the case, religious texts by men and women necessarily represent a mediated "I" and therefore cannot represent ontologically independent subjects. Responding to theorists such as Mason, Nancy K. Miller ("Representing Others: Gender and the Subject of Autobiography," *differences: A Journal of Feminist Cultural Studies* 6 (1994): 4) wonders whether "we might not more usefully *expand* the vision of the autobiographical self as connected to a significant other and bound to a community rather than restrict it through mutually exclusive models."

[9] Kavanaugh, *Book*, p. 39.

[10] Carol Slade, *St. Teresa of Ávila. Author of a Heroic Life* (Berkeley: University of California Press, 1995), pp. 11-13, cites studies which qualify Teresa'a *Book* as all of these types; she herself labels it a judicial confession with elements of multiple other genres, secular and religious.

[11] Sonja Herpoel, "Los auditorios de Isabel de Jesús," Lou Charnon-Deutsch, ed., *Estudios sobre escritoras hispánicas en honor de Georgina Sabat-Rivers* (Madrid: Castalia, 1992), pp. 130-1, denominates as "autobiography" the spiritual life story of the seventeenth-century Augustinian nun Isabel de Jesús, but also observes how it resists the same category: plagued with long digressions, it turns into an apology for Christianity, then becomes a moral treatise. Antonio Carreño, "Las paradojas del 'yo' autobiográfico: El *Libro de la vida de*

Deciding exactly what to call women's spiritual life stores is perhaps a question best reserved for such time when confessional documents, most of which are the property of religious orders, are better known and understood than they are now, archival investigations which have advanced a great deal in recent years.[12] In the mean time, the book's title merits more immediate attention. Consideration of how Teresa's first-person account of God's mercies came to be called her *Life* and consequently read as autobiography, what elements of the text are obfuscated by the same label, and what interests are served by its continued employ, speaks directly to what is in a name.

Teresa was only 47 when she completed the first polished draft of what is now called her *Vida* and was just warming up, not cooling down, her reformist engines. In fact, her so-called "autobiography" ends precisely when her public life was beginning. The text supplies a probationary map of her early inner geography which leaves her mature inner contours and active pursuits virtually uncharted. She died a long and full twenty years later, by which time she "had personally founded fourteen more convents for women [after San José], directed another two at a distance, and played a crucial role in the establishment of the first two Discalced Carmelite houses for men."[13] By the time she died, she had written three other long prose works, poetry, accounts of conscience, instructions for monastic administrators, monastic constitutions, personal recollections and left 476 extant letters.

Santa Teresa de Jesús," in Manuel Griado de Val, ed., *Santa Teresa y la literatura mística hispánica* (Madrid: Edi-6, 1984), p. 264, points to the same features in Teresa's *Book*, calling attention to the several names Tersa uses in the text to refer to it, but reverts himself to *Vida* and reads the work in light of critical standards of autobiography (thus, "El trazado de su 'yo' viene a ser, a lo largo de la *Vida*, metáfora del ausente" ["The outline of her 'I' becomes, through the course of the *Life*, a metaphor of the absent"]). His argument reinforces Paul de Man's "Autobiography as Defacement," *MLN* 94 (1979): 919-30.

[12] Arenal and Schlau's pioneering work in the field has inspired results such as Poutrin's (*La voile*) catalogue and Slade's investigations into confessional procedures with visionary women (*Teresa*). Studies such as Jodi Bilinkoff, *The Ávila of St. Teresa: Religious Reform in a Sixteenth-Century City* (Ithaca, New York: Cornell University Press, 1989), on the political and religious ambiance that nurtured Teresa, also move Teresa's *Book* away from the single-handed feat by pointing to evidence of community support and pressures that helped produce it.

[13] Jodi Bilinkoff, "Woman with a Mission: Teresa of Ávila and the Apostolic Model," in *Modelli di Santité e modelli di comportamento: Constrasti, intersezioni complementiria*, ed. Guila Barone et al. (Turin: Rosenberg and Sellier, 1994), p. 300.

None of these activities are recorded in what is now called her *Vida*.[14] Naming the text her *Life*, and subsequently reading it through the lens of autobiography, effectively canonizes Teresa's life for posterity devoid of almost all of her public activity and without any of her other writings in it. The synecdoche implicit in any autobiography forges a direct relationship between Teresa herself and her most tentative text, written under pressing and threatening conditions when she was at the threshold, not culmination, of her relationship with God and the world. Autobiographical readings of her book, then, reinscribe the Council of Trent's injunction against women's apostolic activity, as well as its emphasis on women as humble vessels of supernatural expression. Indeed, Karen Scott describes similar transformations effected in records of Catherine of Siena's life during the sixteenth century: "During the Renaissance [Raymond of Capua's hagiographic portrait of Catherine] provided an important basis for her canonization (1461), and her political and ecclesiastical activities were mostly forgotten. . . . The increasing emphasis on inner spiritual experience, as well as the Catholic church's renewed insistence on monastic enclosure for all religious women . . . meant that the only relevant aspects of Catherine's life for others could be the ascetic and mystical ones."[15]

Teresa's intentions of reform constituted one of the reasons her piety was scrutinized with particular intensity, and her *Book* is a mainstay in that scrutiny. The text itself records that examination, as Luis de León noted in the dedication to his 1588 edition of it: "Porque no cuenta desnudamente las [revelaciones] que Dios comunicó a la Madre Teresa, sino dice también las diligencias que ella hizo para examinarlas" ["For it does not nakedly reveal the revelations that God communicated to Mother Teresa, rather tells as well the diligence she practiced in examining them".][16] The first version of Teresa's *Book*, most unlike an autobiography, was produced under the aegis of an official inquiry. That inquiry was initiated when its author, who was reporting messages from God of suspicious authenticity, had discovered a way to carry out an apostolic mission in a Church that did not want female apostles.[17] Her first book-length manuscript is evidence of official resistance to her enterprise,

---

[14] The first complete version, now lost, did not contain the account of her struggles to found the convent of San José (1562). Upon specific request from her confessor, Teresa added that section, completing what was to be the final version in 1565.

[15] Karen Scott, "St. Catherine of Siena, 'Apostola,'" *Church History* 61 (1992): 35-6.

[16] "Carta-dedicatoria a las madres y religiosas carmelitas descalzas del monasterio de Madrid, Priora Ana de Jesús [1588]," in Félix García, ed., *Obras completas castellanas de Fray Luis de León*, 4th ed. (Madrid: Editorial Católica, 1957), vol. 1, p. 911.

[17] Compare Bilinkoff, "Woman," who indicates that Teresa nonetheless managed to create a formula for a female apostolate, alhtough heavily conditioned by limitations on women's activities.

resistance which the same manuscript helped mitigate by producing an image of its author as obedient and submissive.

Teresa referred to the work produced by her carrying out her confessor's orders as *mi libro* ("my book,") and, much later in a 1581 letter, she referred to it saying, "intitulé ese libro 'De las misericordias de Dios'" ["I entitled that book 'On God's mercies'"] (OC 1,986), in consonance with the definition of what she was writing that opens her prologue. Thus, the simple term "book" is the most suitable to refer to Teresa of Ávila's first long narration; its nondescript meaning points with precision to the text's lack of place within canonical narrative categories and also adheres to early modern usage more closely than any other. It was standard sixteenth- and seventeenth-century practice to refer to written material beyond the length of a folio as a "book," as Sebastión de Covarrubias's 1611 dictionary indicates: "llamamos libro cualquier volumen de hojas, o de papel o pergamino ligado en cuadernos y cubierto" ["we call a book any volume of sheets, either paper or parchment, tied in quartos and covered"].[18] The generic denomination *libro* was modified with a clause describing the main business of the document. Thus books of chivalry were called *libros de caballería*, accounting books were called *libros de cuentas*, the official list of professions made at a convent was called the *libro de profesiones*, and a book describing God's mercies, *un libro de las mercedes de Dios*.

The *Book*'s first readers approached the text as did its author. Juan de Ávila, to whom Teresa sent her manuscript, referred to it only as "*el libro*" when writing back to her with comments.[19] Similarly, in the evaluation he wrote of the same manuscript, Domingo Bañez described the work as "este libro en que Teresa de Jesús, monja carmelita y fundadora de las Descalzas Carmelitas, da relación de todo lo que por su alma pasa, a fin de ser enseñada y guiada por sus confesores" ["this book in which Teresa of Jesus, Carmelite nun and foundress of the Discalced Carmelites, accounts for all which passes through her soul, so as to be taught and guided by her confessors"] (OC 230).[20] The initial function of Teresa's *Book* was to satisfy ecclesiastical authorities that the supernatural experiences of its author were divinely inspired, and the very

---

[18] *Tesoro de la lengua castellana o española* [1611; 1617]; ed. Martín de Riquer (Barcelona: Castalia, 1987), p. 765.

[19] *Obras completas*, eds Luis Sala Balust and Francisco Martín Hernéndez, V (Madrid: Editorial Católica, 1971), pp. 573-6.

[20] The phrase *dar relación* has juridical connotations which underscore the official nature of the inquiry into Teresa's piety. It means "aquel breve y sucinto informe que por persona pública se hace en voz o por escrito, al Juez, del hecho de un proceso" 'that short and succinct report which is made public by a person orally or in writing, in relationship to a trial' (see Sebastián de Covarrubias, *Tesoro de la lengua castellana o española*, ed. Martín de Riquer [Barcelona: Castalia, 1987], p. 556).

exercise of writing it constituted part of her manifest orthodoxy: it is obedience inscribed.

The term "book" and Teresa's reference to its contents as "the mercies of God" also appeals to a rich textual tradition of women's revelations which were exalted as exemplary female piety in sixteenth- and seventeenth-century Spanish Catholicism, a title that naturalized the otherwise extraordinary effects of grace the author was experiencing. The word "libro" recalls the titles of books relating visions of heroic spiritual women such as Angela of Foligno, whose *Libro de la bienaventurada santa Ángela de Fulgino* [sic] "*Book of the Blessed Saint Angela of Foligno*" was among the texts Archbishop Francisco Ximénez de Cisneros had translated into Spanish in 1510 specifically for placement in convents as edifying reading material for nuns.[21] St. Mechtild von Hackeborn's *Liber spiritualis gratiae Sanctae [Mechtildis]"The Book of Spiritual Grace of Saint Matilda*" (Toledo 1505) was included in Cisneros's 1505 Latin edition of Angela of Foligno's *Book* and pertains to the same tradition.[22] The simple designation "libro" reflects the unclassified nature of manuscript and early print materials, a generic lacuna that frustrates modern textual categories.

The earliest of over fifty extant spiritual life stories by Spanish women written in first-person prose between 1550 and 1660, Teresa's *Book* was produced at the same moment in her life as were the many which follow: when her piety trespassed the boundaries of standard Catholic experience. Anxious confessors almost always demanded this type of document when their authors were between the age of 40 and 50, mature and developing intentions to act on their interpretations of God's will. Their spiritual life stories represent crisis points in their careers, responses to the indignant question of what made them deserving of divine favors in their lives and the subsequent query of exactly how God operated therein. These texts are not late-life reflections and the topics they address were not chosen by their authors. Teresa points directly to the dictated route she followed in her account, saying, "por no hacer más de lo que

---

[21] Pedro de Quintanilla y Mendoza, *Arquetipo de virtudes, espejo de prelados: El venerable padre y siervo de Dios F. Francisco Jiménez e Cisneros* (Palermo, 1653), p. 141.

[22] Angela's *Book* was adapted and published in 1596 as the *Libro de singular excelencia y provecho para el alma 'Book of Singular Excellence and Benefit for the Soul'* (Valencia). Melquíades Andrés, *La teologia española en el siglo XVI* (Madrid: Editorial Católica, 1976), vol. 1, pp. 390-91, repeats Quintanilla's assertion that St. Matilda's book was translated into Spanish and published with Angela's in 1510 (see Quintanilla, *Arquetipo*, p. 141), but I have been unable to locate an edition which contains it. Spiritual life stories, which focus on the individual's relationship with God (versus the world), were named "books" in other countries was well, as indicated by the *Book of Margery Kempe*, dictated around 1431; see Margery Kempe, *The Book of Margery Kempe*, ed. Lynn Staley. (Kalamazoo, Michigan: Medieval Institute Publications, 1996).

mandaron, en muchas cosas seré corta más de lo que quisiera, en otras más large que era menester" ["but also as to do no more than what they gave me the command to do, I will be briefer in many matters than I desire, more extensive in others than necessary"] (6.8). Her text, like others of its kind, was originally a probing extension of the general confession, in which a confessant accounted in writing for her or his entire life as part of the initiation ritual into advanced spirituality. This process was carefully guided by a spiritual master or a confessor and was usually accompanied by written documents of lesser dimensions, such as Teresa's *cuentas de consciencia* ["accounts of conscience"].[23]

Teresa describes one of the several pre-texts of her *Book* as precisely this confessional type of ecclesiastical record, describing how her first written account of God's interventions in her life, composed in 1555 and now lost, so alarmed its readers that they asked immediately for a fuller explanation. Of this fuller account (also lost) she says, "Comencé a tratar de mi confesión general y poner por escrito todos los males y bienes; un discurso de mi vida lo más claramente que yo entendí y supe sin dejar nada por decir" ["I began to prepare my general confession and put down in writing all the good and bad things—as clear an account of my life as I knew how to without leaving anything out"] (23.15). Although this document evidently satisfied the requirements for a general confession, it did not delve specifically or deeply enough into Teresa's intimacies with God, for she was ordered to pick up her pen again to render that material particularly and completely. This is the document generally referred to as her *Life*.

Although her subsequent canonization allows readers today to approach Teresa's writings as saintly, at the time she wrote her *Book* her reputation was very much in question and that text re-constitutes not her life, but her struggle for credibility, recalling moments such as the one when some authorities wanted her exorcised (29.4). Furthermore, Teresa herself continued to express dissatisfaction over the incompleteness of the manuscript she had handed over to authorities in 1565. In 1577, she wrote to her brother Lorenzo of her attempt to reclaim her copy of it from Bishop Álvaro de Mendoza so she could finish it, saying "Al obispo envié a pedir *el libro*, porque quizá se me antojará de acabarle" ["I wrote to the Bishop to ask for *the book*, because maybe I'll get the urge to finish it"] (OC 1553; emphasis mine).

The temporally and thematically limited rendition of Teresa's life contained in her *Book* resulted from the fact that once she produced the information she was charged to provide, no more was desired and her role in the inquest was complete. Subsequently, her manuscript was used to represent

---

[23] These accounts may be found in OC 999-1060.

her extraordinary experience of grace to experts in the discernment of spirits whose job was to determine whether it was the devil or God at work in her, nothing else. For this reason, she recalls how her confessors prohibited her from writing the type of text she wanted to compose, which she humbly claims would have been a narration of her great sins: "Quisiera yo que . . . me la dieran [larga licencia] para que muy por menudo y con claridad dijera mis grandes pecados . . . Mas no han querido" ["I wish they would also have allowed me to tell very clearly and minutely about my great sins . . . But they didn't want me to"] (Prólogo 1). Having Teresa (or any other female ecstatic) carry out this written exercise, specifically having her reveal what her confessors wanted to know rather than what she wanted to tell, facilitated the examination process. The exercise produced hard evidence in what was an official inquiry, and disencumbered the investigation, since paper was circulated more easily and safely than a problematic woman, who in any case should have been cloistered or otherwise restrained from circulation. Ironically, it was this document, written to satisfy her superiors, that the Princess of Eboli denounced to the Inquisition in 1570, and Teresa's close encounters with the Holy Office began because she had submitted to this act of obedience.[24]

Importantly, men were not probed in this manner: all extant spiritual life stories written for the purpose of discernment of spirits in Spain during this period are by women, presumably because their supposedly weak nature rendered them more susceptible to the wiles of the devil than men, whose individual intimacies with God are almost never recorded in first-person prose unveiled by allegory or metaphor.[25] The church hierarchy which demanded these documents of women was not interested in a self portrait; as Gregory observes, "Ecclesiastical authorities applied litmus tests for heresy; they did not

---

[24] Gillian Ahlgren, *Teresa of Ávila and the Politics of Sanctity* (Ithaca, New York: Cornell University Press, 1996), pp. 32-67 describes the *Book*'s history with the Inquisition.

[25] Male and female mystics were ordered to write accounts of their spiritual experiences for posterity, toward the end of their lives. Such was the case of the Carmelite ecstatic Juan de Jesús María, who worked on his over the last ten years of his life. It was never examined and was used by Manuel de San Jerónimo as a primary source ("Principios de la vida del extático Padre Fray Juan de Jesús María, hasta tomar nuestro santo hábito en Sevilla," *Reforma de los descalzos de Nuestra Señora del Carmen de la primitiva observancia hecha por Santa Teresa de Jesús en la antiquísima religión fundada por el gran profeta Elías*, VI: 53-119. Madrid, 1710). One of John of the Cross's spiritual daughters, María Machuca, was ordered to compose the same type of text, which she wrote at the remarkable age of 71 (see Stephen Ross, "Blood Poured Out on Behalf of Many: The *Vida* and Writings of María de la Cruz, OCD," Paper presented at the Kentucky Foreign Language Conference, Lexington, Kentucky, 19-20 April 1996.

extend invitations for self-generated confessions of faith."[26] Confessors wanted to know exactly what was going on with God in the privacy of a woman's soul, events which were unobservable and impossible to verify except by means of first-person narration by the individual. This is the process which produced the text now called Teresa's *Life*, which was simply called her "book" as long as it circulated in manuscript.

A radical alteration was made in the denominator affixed to Teresa of Ávila's spiritual life story by the first editor of her works, the erudite Augustinian Fray Luis de León, who published it in 1588 as *La vida de la madre Teresa de Jesús, y algunas de las mercedes que Dios le hizo, escritas por ella misma por mandado de su confesor* ["*The Life of Mother Teresa of Jesus, and Some of the Mercies which God Showed Her, Written by Herself by Order of Her Confessor*"]. It has never been the same text since. The transformation from "book" to "life" had been effected, not by the text's author or during her lifetime but by an admiring male colleague after her death. The import of this metamorphosis should not be underestimated, for its reverberations confirm Williamson's idea that, "Ultimately, the question of entitlement proves crucial, especially for works by women. . . . Their reception is partially prescribed by the title they bear" (109).

There is a direct correlation between the new title with which Luis de León endowed Teresa's *Book* and his editorial agenda, for it reinforces the enthusiasm for domesticated, enclosed, and receptive women that exudes from his prescriptive treatise *La perfecta casada* ["*The Perfect Wife*"]. His ideological interests, representative of what Sánchez Lora has called "the zeal of a masculine society in crisis,"[27] were served by using Teresa of Ávila's life of prayer to represent her life itself, by eliding her public works, and by exalting her submission to the Church's examination of her most inner experiences. Publication of Teresa's intimacies with God as her *Life* also served male fascination with female mystical experience, something from which men's professional and intellectual burdens increasingly tended to exclude them.[28] Teresa herself berates men who complain of their inability to attain spiritual graces like hers, saying, "Mas para siervos de Dios, hombres de tomo, de letras,

---

[26] Brad S. Gregory, "The Violent Rending of Christendom: Martyrdom in the Early Modern Period," Paper presented at the Early Modern European and British Studies Workshop, Harvard University, Cambridge, MA, April 30, 1996, p. 23.

[27] José L. Sánchez Lora, *Mujeres, conventos y formas de la religiosidad barroca* (Madrid: Fundación Universitaria Española, 1988), p. 30.

[28] John Coakley, "Gender and the Authority of Friars: The Significance of Holy Women for Thirteenth-century Franciscans and Dominicans," *Church History* 60 (1991): 445-60 describes this fascination in the context of thirteenth-century confessors and how it conditioned their relationships with their female visionary confessants.

de entendimiento, que veo hacer tanto caso de que Dios no los da devoción, que me hace disgusto oírlo. . . . que entiendan que no es menester, pues Su Majestad no la da, y anden señores de sí mismos" ["When I see servants of God, men of prominence, learning and high intelligence make so much fuss because God doesn't give them devotion, it annoys me to hear them. . . . They should understand that since His Majesty doesn't give it, it isn't necessary, and they should be masters of themselves"] (11.14).

Early readers of the 1588 edition were quick to point out that to name Teresa's book her *Life* was misleading. In his 1590 biography of the future saint, the Jesuit Francisco de Ribera says he had access to a large manuscript collection of her works:

> Entre ellos anda *uno que llaman de su vida* . . . pero no escribió allí la madre Teresa de Jesús su vida, sino solamente lo que la mandaron, que fue el camino por donde el Señor la llevó en las cosas espirituales y muchas de las mercedes que la hizo hasta fundar el monasterio de S. José de Ávila que fue el primero de todos. . . . Mas no puso allí sus virtudes ni lo mucho que hizo en servicio del Señor, sino lo que de su mano recibió hasta el año de 1562, que no pasa de allí la historia de ese libro, y ella vivió veinte años después.[29]

> Among which there is *one that is said to be about her life* . . . but there Mother Teresa did not write her life, rather only what they ordered her to, which was the path along which the Lord led her in spiritual things and many of the mercies God showed her until she founded the monastery of St. Joseph's of Ávila, which was the first one of all. . . . But she did not put there her virtues nor all she accomplished in the service of God, rather what she received from God's hand until the year 1562, for the history of that book does not go beyond that date, and she lived twenty years more.

In spite of such caveats, the text continued to be published as Teresa of Ávila's *Life*, the name by which it is known today.

The title Luis de León imposed on Teresa's *Book* not only opened the door to future autobiographic readings, but also called attention to its internal division: the first 20 per cent (the first nine chapters), which recounts her life before she embraced God as its source and end, and the following 80 per cent (Chapters 10-40), which describes her experiences after her union with God had

---

[29] Francisco de Ribera, *La vida de la madre Teresa de Jesús*, 7. Salamanca, 1590. Emphasis mine.

begun.[30] The overwhelming imbalance of this bi-part structure indicates clearly that the vast majority of the text is not about Teresa herself as a human subject, but rather about Teresa's experience of God, the subject of the inquiry that produced the document in the first place. Chapters 1 through 9, devoted primarily to narrative, are merely the prologue for its primary section, which is descriptive.

In the main body of her *Book*, Teresa uses her personal experience of God to illuminate a method of prayer which she is increasingly determined to proselytize as she proceeds in the text. Restricted by prohibitions against women preaching, Teresa takes recourse in testimonial narrative to move and convince her readers, and by chapter 18 she is declaring this broadened intention as clearly as she had pronounced her initial one: "sabe Su Majestad que después de obedecer, es mi intención engolosinar las almas de un bien tan alto" ["His Majesty knows that besides obeying, it is my intention to attract souls to so high a blessing"] (18.8). This pedagogical objective draws her narration closer to testimonial literature, whose didactic, exemplary purpose overrides all others, and distances the text from autobiography. She repeats her instructional mission in chapter 27, saying, "Pienso decir pocas de las [mercedes] que el Señor me ha hecho a mí—si no me mandaren otra cosa—, si no son algunas visiones que pueden para alguna cosa aprovechar . . . o para declararle el modo y camino por donde el Señor me ha llevado, que es lo que me mandan escribir" ["So I am thinking of speaking but little of the favors the Lord granted me—unless I'm ordered to do otherwise—except for certain visions that can do some good for others . . . or that I might explain the manner and path by which the Lord led me, which is what they commanded me to write about"] (27.9).

By means of the content she selects for her story and the narrative grammar she employs to tell it, Teresa reflects an ongoing movement toward God, not only to help her manifest a divine spirit at work in herself, but also to move others in the same direction. By chapter 10, God and Teresa are a team; the book is no more "about" Teresa than it is "about" God. Their union is precisely what she was striving to prove, and is the most delicate issue of the entire text. Only by convincing her superiors that she and God were working indivisibly could Teresa hope to be allowed to continue with her relationship with the divine, which had been cut off previously by confessors who found her prayer unorthodox. Teamwork, particularly with the supernatural, has little

---

[30] Herraíz Garcia and Kavanaugh's more detailed divisions of the text likewise recognize a categorical distinction between chapters 1-10 and its other sections (see Maximiliano Herraíz García, *Introducción al "Libro de la vida" de Santa Teresa* [Desierto de las Palmas, Castellón: Centro de Espiritualidad Santa Teresa, 1981], pp. 80-85; Kavanaugh, *Book*, p. 43).

space in traditionally defined literary categories. Yet Teresa's *Book* can only sustain its essential meaning if readers accommodate her conviction that her self was jointed seamlessly to God. Proponents of Teresa's text as autobiography focus on Teresa as its subject; those who stress its religious import find that God is its protagonist. Such forced separation of Teresa from her co-author, which must happen for autobiography to occur, is antonymous to her text's fundamental integrity. Divorcing Teresa from God in her narrative mutes the challenge she poses to standard representational categories while dismissing her assigned task, which was precisely to convince readers she was at one with the divine.

Teresa herself is the subject of the first nine chapters only because God had not yet become her intimate life partner during the years they describe; the contrast between the first 20 per cent of her text and the remainder is meant to be clear, because it reinforces the exemplary difference between the years in which God was waiting in the background of her life and those in which God was standing squarely beside her. Her narrative teamwork with the divinity is a far cry from Augustine's *Confessions*, to which it is often compared, in which God never manages to upstage Augustine and never makes a direct appearance.

The contrasts between the *Book* and the *Confessions* are particularly important, because Augustine's text is a cornerstone in the [male] autobiographic tradition and Teresa is careful to mention that her confessors gave her a translated version of it: "En este tiempo me dieron las *Confesiones de San Agustín*, que parece el Señor lo ordenó, porque yo no las procuré ni nunca las havía visto" ["At this time they gave me *The Confessions of St. Augustine*. It seems the Lord ordained this, because I had not tried to procure a copy, nor had I ever seen one"] (9.7).[31] After expressing admiration for this male model of sin followed by a lightening conversion, she immediately distances herself from the same model, pointing to her own prolonged and grueling effort to turn to God: "que a ellos [pecadores] sola una vez los havía el Señor llamado, y no tornaban a caer, y a mí eran ya tantas, que esto me fatigaba" ["the Lord called them [sinners such as Augustine] only once, and

---

[31] To my knowledge, no one has studied the text of the *Confessions* that Teresa read, probably the 1554 Salamanca translation by Sebastión Toscano. That version differs substantially from the one used by scholars to compare it with Teresa's *Book*. Most notably, it ends after the first chapter of Book XI, because the commentaries in the remaining chapters were considered improper material for divulgation in the vulgar tongues (*Las confesiones de San Agustín, traducidas de latin en romance castellano por el padre maestro Fray Sebastión Toscano, de la orden de San Agustín*, 218^V. Salamanca, 1554). The idiosyncracies of the sixteenth-century Spanish translation read by Teresa suggest a need to reconsider similarities between her text and Augustine's.

they did not turn back and fall again; whereas in my case I had turned back so often that I was worn out from it"] (9.7).

Although she admits being moved by Augustine's conversion scene, Teresa describes herself as fundamentally different from him: "bien entendía yo —a mi parecer—le amaba, mas no entendía en qué estí el amar de veras a Dios" ["I clearly understood that I loved Him; but I did not understand as I should have what true love of God consists in"] (9.9). Teresa's halting path to God, contrasted overtly as it is with Augustine's abrupt turn from evil, reflects Weinstein and Bell's observation that in hagiographic models the pattern of women's lives evidences few ruptures and instead reflects a more slowly consolidated vocation.[32] Teresa's prolonged refinement of her spiritual life sustains Bynum's contention that "women tended to tell stories and develop personal models without crises or turning points."[33]

Teresa's own indication of the stark, if lamented, difference between her life story's text and Augustine's is reflective of other fundamental distinctions between them, one a difference in narrative grammar and another in gendered models of sin. As has been much observed, in the *Confessions* "God is the direct addressee of the discourse,"[34] in contrast to Teresa's multivalent receptors, who include her confessor, other male superiors, and asides to God articulated for the benefit of the same men. The *Confessions* display a conversational mode through which the narrator attempts to stimulate the conversion of his readers.[35] Augustine speaks at God; God, on the other hand, is remarkably silent. Throughout her *Book*, in contrast, Teresa speaks *with* God, whose interventions through visions and locutions are abundantly manifest. Her narrative grammar differs radically from Augustine's: she delivers not a monologue to a narratively absent divinity but rather delivers her intimate exchanges with God to her readers. Teresa and God do not stand in dialogic opposition but rather in union, and Teresa claims to be representing God's presence to Vuestra Merced, "Your Reverence," who is representative of the worldly authority that challenges Teresa's union with her narrative partner.

---

[32] Donald Weinstein and Rudolph M. Bell, *Saints and Society: The Two Worlds of Western Christendom, 1000-1700* (Chicago: University of Chicago Press, 1982), pp. 220-38.

[33] Caroline Bynum, *Holy Feast and Holy Fast. The Religious Significance of Food to Medieval Women* (Berkeley: University of California Press, 1987), p. 25. The *Confessions* have been used repeatedly as a measure of Teresa's text. For example, the question of how many Augustine-like "conversions" she had has been a matter of considerable discussion; the exact number is still under debate (see Enrique Llamas Martínez, "San Agustín y la 'conversión' de santa Teresa," *Augustinus* 32 [1987]: 385-415). Bynum's research indicates that the hunt for conversions is inappropriate in itself.

[34] Jean Starobinski, "The Style of Autobiography," Seymour Chatman, ed., *Literary Style: A Symposium* (Oxford: Oxford University Press, 1971), p. 288.

[35] Fernández, "La *Vida*," p. 293.

Throughout the main body of the *Book*, Teresa proffers dialogue with her co-protagonist in vivid exclamations, has her narrative voice speak to God as if in conversation, and represents God's interventions right beside her own: "porque yo no le veo, Señor, ni sí cómo es estrecho el camino que lleva a Vos" ["For I don't see, Lord, nor do I know how the road that leads to you is narrow"] (35.13); "Habiendo un día comulgado, mandóme mucho Su Majestad lo procurase [la fundación de San José] con todas mis fuerzas . . . y que se llamase San José" ["One day after Communion, His Majesty earnestly commanded me to strive for this new monastery with all my powers . . . He said it should be called St. Joseph"] (32.11).

Teresa's inclusive narrative grammar blends first-person singular with the plural and accommodates her self as subject, indistinguishable from her self as divine object. God is beside her and her first-person plural verbs include the divinity: "¿Qué es esto, Señor mío? ¿En tan peligrosa vida hemos de vivir? Que escribiendo esto estoy y me parece que con vuestro favor puedo decir lo que san Pablo . . . que no vivo yo ya, sino que Vos, Criador mío, vivís en mí [Gal. 2:20] . . . ¡No sí como queremos vivir, pues es todo tan incierto! Parecíame a mí, Señor mío, ya imposible dejaros tan del todo a Vos" ["What is this, my Lord! Must we live in so dangerous a life? . . . For in writing this it seems to me that with your favor and through Your mercy I can say what St. Paul said . . . that I no longer live but that You, my Creator, live in me. . . . I don't know why we desire to live since everything is so uncertain. It seemed to me impossible, my Lord, to abandon You so completely"] (6.9). Such grammatical maneuvers assisted Teresa in meeting her objective to represent herself at one with God. To the extent that she portrays herself as the human co-operator of divine will, orthodox and trustworthy, she accomplished her mission successfully. Had she composed an autobiography, a narrative account of a human being's life on earth, she would have failed in her task, been charged with false sanctity or meddling with the devil, and silenced immediately. Had Teresa of Ávila responded to her confessors with an autobiography, we would not have her text today.

Teresa's distanced narrative position from her own sins was dictated by her gender and moves her further from the Augustinian model of iniquity/conversion, and so further from relying on her historical self for her subject. The male image is fortified by the conversion model, which represents the hero moving from sin to holiness, because it provides essential proof of the subject's virility and strength of character, even if the direction in which those qualities are exercised is ultimately reversed. Thus it may be that in the *Confessions*, the vital narrative exists only in function of sin and transgression.[36]

---

[36] Fernández, "La *Vida*," p. 292.

A woman's life of sin, however, only confirms patriarchal suppositions of her inherent weakness and imperfection, and for Teresa to recount specific incidents of her morally reprehensible behavior would have rendered impossible her mission of proving her unity with God. Her superiors' prohibition of her writing about her sins reinforced the cultural requisite of inherent goodness in virtuous women, and to represent herself as otherwise would have cost her all of her credibility. The same prohibition, which kept her from delivering the specifics of her own human experience, rendered the autobiographic enterprise inaccessible to her.

As Weber has indicated, Teresa's evasion of the truly sinful episodes of her life is evident throughout her text.[37] For example, she deftly drops only the most remote and tantalizing hints about the adolescent behavior that provoked her father to enclose her in a convent, leaving readers ever after perplexed about what exactly happened: "Me atrevía a muchas cosas bien contra ella [honra] y contra Dios. . . . estaba en la mano el peligro, y ponía en él a mi padre y hermanos" ["I dared to do many things truly against my honor and against God . . . the danger was at hand, and my father's and brothers' reputation was in jeopardy as well"] (2.5-6). Precisely the specification of those "many things" constitutes the narrative intrigue of the *Confessions* and serves to individuate Augustine as a human being. They are precisely the things Teresa cannot tell. Treating evasively what few sins of her own she recounts, she represents herself instead as inherently rather than specifically sinful, on the one hand an effective rhetorical strategy,[38] and on the other a generalizing theological statement which offset the inquiry into her individual experience by representing herself as Catholic theology defined everyone. Thus, in composing her spiritual life story, Teresa knowingly avoided the Augustinian model of the confession/conversion, which would have necessitated representing herself as a grave sinner if not a heretic. This male model, although acceptable for the mythical Magdalene, in sixteenth-century Spain would have compromised any woman's suitability as a credible vessel of the divine. The model life pattern had to be slow but sure growth in virtue and power, of the type found in the *vitae* of virgin brides of Christ.

Luis de León's presentation of Teresa's manuscript as a "life" invokes the important presence of hagiography in her story, particularly in its first nine chapters, an influence which any early modern reader would have recognized. The text's hagiographic echoes serve to distance it from the individual life of Teresa and channel the text's representational energies into less direct vehicles of meaning. If chapters 10 through 40 deal with "the supernatural (infused or

---

[37] Weber, *Teresa*, pp. 42-76.
[38] Weber, *Teresa*, p. 76.

mystical) realities of the interior life,"[39] then the first section had to present an individual deserving of such intimacies. The hagiographic model was indispensable for this enterprise, and Teresa's account of "her" life follows the contours of the female saint's life quite faithfully, with specific details emphasized in harmony with a particular type of female *vita*.

Instead of the converted sinner, Teresa shaped her narrative persona in accordance with the hallowed textual tradition of the virgin bride of Christ, eminently suitable for her monastic ambitions and appropriate for her petition as a lover of God. Her primary models, then, were the activist holy virgins like St. Catherine of Siena, Angela of Foligno, and fellow foundresses St. Clare and St. Birgitta of Sweden, the latter of whom was known for her book of revelations.[40] Teresa's first biographers, who wrote before her canonization, all invoke these female models in their prologues to further embed her in the Catholic hagiographic tradition, signaling their understanding that Teresa had fashioned herself after them. Francisco de Ribera says, "Y como se leen las [visiones y revelaciones] de Santa Brígida y Santa Gertrudis, y Santa Catalina de Sena, y Santa Ángela de Folgino, y de otras santas con edificación y provecho de los que las leen, así las de la madre Teresa de Jesús, que en todo son semejantes a las de estas santas como de un mismo espíritu, harán sin duda el mismo efecto" ["And as one reads with edification and benefit the visions and revelations of St. Birgitta and St. Gertrude, and St. Catherine of Siena and St. Angela of Foligno and other saints, so those of Teresa of Jesus, which are completely similar to those of said saints as if from a single spirit, will work the same effect"].[41] Although several critics have invoked the neologism "autohagiography" to describe Teresa's *Book*, they employ the term to hypothesize Teresa's awareness of herself as saintly ("estaba segura de ser

---

[39] Kavanaugh, *Book*, p. 37.

[40] Teresa's Jesuit advisors at the time she was writing her *Book*, among whom was her confessor Baltasar Álvarez, were trained at colleges where Catherine of Siena's *Vita* and *Epistolae* were read at meal time (see Pedro de Leturia, "Lecturas ascéticas y lecturas místicas entre los jesuitas del siglo XVI," in Ignacio Iparraguirre, ed., *Estudios ignacianos* [Rome: Institutum Historicum, 1957], vol. 2, p. 300). It is probable that their familiarity with these texts shaped their guidance and expectations of Teresa. It bears mention that all these texts by or about women were mediated by men; see Catherine M. Mooney, "The Authorial Role of Brother A. in the Composition of Angela of Foligno's Revelations," Ann Matter and John Coakley, eds, *Creative Women in Medieval and Early Modern Italy* (Philadelphia: University of Pennsylvania Press, 1994), pp. 34-63.

[41] Ribera, *La vida*, p. 9. Blessed Angela of Foligno (d. 1309) was never canonized, although she was widely referred to as a saint in the early modern period.

santa" ["she was sure of being a saint,"] says Nepaulsingh), and the text's explicit alliance with concrete hagiographic models has passed unnoticed.[42]

Teresa's rendition of her own experience follows the broad-stroke patterns of her female models closely enough to call into question the validity of the self-portrait contained in her *Book* as human history, and points instead to its pertinence as spiritual history. As historian of her own prayer, she confirms the Catholic tradition by emphasizing or creating episodes of her own life to echo well-known, acceptable models: "Personhood in the *vita* is not (as moderns are wont to see) that highly particular self which history and society shape but the 'spiritual substance' which is realized through the love of God, the observance of His precepts, and the aid of divine grace."[43] At the outset of her *Book*, Teresa affirms her familiarity with these stories, describing her earliest reading activity as being of saints' lives (1.4, also 22.7, 30.17), a detail often passed over in favor of the more salacious one regarding her devoted consumption of chivalric literature (2.1).[44]

Hagiography flowered in early modern Spain, in collections which expanded and multiplied across the sixteenth and seventeenth centuries. Throughout the period, nonetheless, the protocol for an exemplary life remained essentially fixed, particularly for the virgin bride of Christ model.[45] Teresa's decision to cut the cloth of her self-representation from these saints' lives when writing her own account, particularly in the first section of her *Book*,

---

[42] Colbert I. Nepaulsingh, "El 'Libro de la vida' de Santa Teresa de Ávila," in Julio Fernández-Sevilla, et al., eds, *Philologica hispaniensia in honorem Manuel Alvar* (Madrid: Gredos, 1986), vol. 3, p. 300. In her study of female readers of early modern Spain, Sonja Herpoel, "El lector femenino en el Siglo de Oro español," in Rina Walthaus, ed., *La mujer en la literatura hispánica de la Edad Media y el Siglo de Oro* (Amsterdam: Rodopi, 1993), p. 92, mentions without elaboration "la enorme influencia de las vidas de santos, que no solamente proponen la trama de la autobiografía . . . sino que además imponen una estructura formal bastante rígida" ["the enormous influence of saints' lives, which not only provide the plot of the autobiography . . . but also impose a rather rigid formal structure upon them"].

[43] Resil B. Mojares, "The Life of Miguel Ayatumo: A Sixteenth-century Boholano," *Philippine Studies* 41 (1993): 449.

[44] Compare Paul Julian Smith, "Writing Women," p. 229, for example: "The other influence on the young Teresa is literature: chivalric romance and (later) devotional works." Senebre suggests that whether Teresa actually read books of chivalry or not is irrelevant, since the function of her mentioning it was to mention an innocuous sin; see Ricardo Senabre, "Forma y función del *Libro de la vida*," in Victor García de la Concha, et al., eds, *Actas del Congreso Internacional Teresiano. Salamanca, 4-7 Oct. 1982* (Salamanca: Université de Salamanca, 1983), vol. 2, p. 771.

[45] The major hagiographic texts of the period in Spanish were the anonymous *Leyenda de los santos* (?1497) a version of Jacobus de Voragine's *Golden Legend*; Pedro de la Vega's *Flos sanctorum* (published 1521-80); Alonso de Villegas's *Flos sanctorum* (published 1578-1603); Pedro de Ribadeneira's of the same title (published 1599-1643).

served to disarm the inquisitorial, detail-seeking process of her examination by engaging a category of representation decidedly disinterested in the circumstantial, a category which celebrates "modes of behavior which exist as cultural symbols and not as autonomous *sui generis* acts."[46] Hagiography's universalizing and delocalizing strategies allowed her to manifest her familiarity with the patterns of orthodoxy and also to signify her life in a context much broader than her own individual and problematic experience, since "what the *vita* seeks to narrate is not so much history as theophany."[47]

The bride of Christ, like the male saint and, before him, the archetypal hero, has a singular quality, often signaled at birth. In holy virgins, this is often an extraordinarily agreeable nature that moves those around her and indirectly teaches girls the importance of pleasing others: "era la más querida de mi padre," says Teresa, ". . . y parece tenía alguna razón" "I was the most loved of my father . . . And it seemed he was right" (1.4). Similarly, one reads in Catherine of Siena's *vita*, another translation patronized by Cardinal Cisneros for the edification of nuns: "y Caterina fue de su madre Lapa . . . amada sobre todos los otros hijos y hijas" ["and Catherine was loved by her mother Lapa over all her other sons and daughters"].[48] Like the model virgin bride, Teresa lays claim to a childhood vocation at an age too young to be explained by reason, therefore providing evidence of divine destiny: she describes her pre-adolescent tendencies to piety in 1:4-8 ("Pues mis hermanos ninguna cosa me desayudaban a servir a Dios . . ." ["My brothers and sisters did not in any way hold me back from the service of God . . ."] [1.5; English 1.4]).

The bride of Christ has at least one problematic parent or family member, whose moral inferiority serves to highlight the young woman's own holiness. This figure is Teresa's mother, reader of the titillating books of chivalry that were regularly censored by male moralists of Teresa's day and disapproved of by Teresa's father: "Era aficionada a libros de caballería. . . . desenvolvíamonos para leer en ellos" ["She loved books of chivalry. . . . we used to read them together in our spare time"] (2.1). The mildly evil influence of Teresa's mother is amplified in the unidentified female whom Teresa calls a "relative," whose devotion to frivolous behavior and bad moral example she says almost led her down the path to ruin (2.3). Teresa represents herself

---

[46] Thomas J. Heffernan, *Sacred Biography: Saints and Their Biographers in the Middle Ages* (New York: Oxford University Press, 1988), p. 151.

[47] Mojares, "Miguel Ayatumo," p. 449.

[48] Raymond, *Catherine*, 1ᵛ. Scott, "Catherine," pp. 37-46, points out that whereas Capua emphasized Catherine's extraordinary features and experiences, which supported his case for her canonization, she herself did not stress them in her own writings. Requiring women to compose written accounts of their supernatural encounters similarly forced them into a representational mode which rarified them.

superseding these women, eventually rejecting all such unworthy pleasures, since the pattern demands that God's design for the holy woman overcome all problematic family members.

According to the virgin-saint model, a period of conflict ensues after the woman is established in the reader's mind as a child marked by God, culminating in a vocation which meets with male resistance, usually from a father or a suitor, who represents worldly interests. This is Teresa's moving description of abandoning her father's house in 1535, disobeying his request that she not take vows yet: "Acuérdaseme — a todo mi parecer y con verdad — que, cuando salí de casa de mi padre, no creo será más el sentimiento cuando me muera" ["I remember clearly and truly, that when I left my father's house I felt that separation so keenly that the feeling will not be greater, I think, when I die"] (4.1). Importantly, Teresa records no attempt on her father's part to extract her from the convent, suggesting that her mention of his resistance to her profession may meet more formal than historical exigencies, particularly since hagiographic descriptions of Christ's brides running away from their fathers were especially dramatic. Of St. Clare, for example, Lilio's 1558 *Flos sanctorum* says, "Mandóle San Francisco . . . saliese a la noche secretamente de casa del padre," and subsequently falls into a colorful symbolic elaboration: "No salió por la puerta acostumbrada mas abrió con sus manos con maravillosa fortaleza una que estaba cerrada con piedras y con mucha madera . . ." ["St. Francis ordered her to secretly depart at night from the house of her father; She left not through the normal door rather opened with her hands, with wondrous strength, one that was closed with rocks and much wood . . ."].[49]

Since her vocation was exercised under such traumatic conditions, the holy woman becomes ill, a debilitated state which crescendos in a brush with death. The brush with death episode, like the archetypal hero's descent to the underworld, takes the woman to the portals of life, from which she returns to human existence enriched beyond mortal limitations. Teresa's description of her own four-day coma (which official historians record as *three*, replacing mundane reality with a symbolic one[50]) includes her recollection of almost being buried alive: "Teníanme a veces por tan muerta, que hasta la cera me hallé después en los ojos" ["At times they were so certain I was dead that afterward I

---

[49] Martín de Lilio, *Segunda parte del Flor sanctorum ahora nuevamente corregido y de muchos errores alimpiado*, 351^V. Alcalá, 1558. Lilio revised Pedro de la Vega's 1521 *Flos sanctorum* and it was often his revision that was published under de la Vega's name from 1556 to 1580.

[50] Efrén de la Madre de Dios and Otger Steggink, "Introducción general," in *Santa Teresa de Jesús: Obras completas* (Madrid: Editorial Católica, 1986), p. 20, refer to her three-day collapse, as do many others, although Teresa herself reaffirms that it was four in 6.1.

even found the wax on my eyes"] (5.9). Riveting though this passage is, it has peculiar resonance with episodes such as Julian of Norwich's remembrance of a similar moment in her own life. Immediately following her debilitating empathetic experience of Christ's passion, the key moment in her *Revelations*, she says, "My mother, who was standing there with the others, held up her hand in front of my face to close my eyes, for she thought that I was already dead or had that moment died."[51] Like Julian, Teresa recovered miraculously and just in time, recalling the event as a veritable Lazarus, for obvious reasons: she says, "parece me resucitó el Señor" ["apparently the Lord raised me from the dead"] (5.11).[52]

Although Cooney[53] points convincingly to uncanny similarities between Julian and Teresa's theology, there is no evidence of an early modern Spanish translation of the *Revelations* in Julian's name that Teresa could have seen. It may have circulated under another name or in a miscellany. But the correspondence between the two proffers even more compelling evidence of prototypical visionary experience if the textual corroboration is imprecise. The episode is standard in the bride of Christ's life pattern and Teresa surely knew the protocol; the 1511 Spanish *vita* of Catherine of Siena refers to Catherine's own brush with death, which forced her mother to release control over her, as an intense illness typically suffered during late youth: "la santa virgen cayó muy enferma de gran enfermedad corporal, de la cual suelen comunmente enfermar las personas en la juventud antes que vengan a edad mayor" ["the holy virgin fell very ill of a great bodily sickness, with which individuals in youth sicken before arriving at maturity"].[54] This description aptly tags the brush with death

---

[51] Julian of Norwich, *Showings*, trans. Edmund Colledge and James Walsh (New York: Paulist Press, 1978), p. 142.

[52] Male saints of an ecstatic nature are also described as experiencing the brush with death. For example, as Ribera, *La vide*, p. 35, says of Ignatius of Loyola, "tuvo un arrobamiento tan extraño y nunca oído que duró ocho días enteros, viéndole muchas personas porque era en una iglesia y quedando tan privado de los sentidos, que sin duda la enterraran si uno de los que allí estaban tocándole el pulso y poniéndole la mano sobre el corazón no echara de ver que estaba vivo" ["he had a rapture so strange and never before heard of that it lasted for eight solid days, with many people seeing him because it was in a church, and being so out of his senses that they would have buried him without a doubt if some of the people who were there, touching his pulse points and putting their hands on his heart, hadn't made it clear that he was alive"].

[53] Adrian James Cooney, "Dame Julian of Norwich and St. Teresa of Jesus: Some of their Complementary Teachings, pp. 172-218 in John Sullivan, ed., *Carmelite Studies IV: Teresian Culture* (Washington, DC: Institute of Carmelite Studies, 1987).

[54] Raymond, *Catherine*, f. 12^r.

as a rite of passage into adulthood which in heroic figures is extreme enough to certify their extraordinary merits.[55]

The brush with death and the subsequent ongoing physical debility with which the Catholic holy woman is marked literally reflects "a consequence of the mystical state, which overpowers the human frame,"[56] as well as the results of intense physical mortification. However, whereas a weakening in physical stature is an entrenched feature of the female visionary by the fourteenth century, it disappears from the male visionary's portrait by the same time,[57] and bears social as well as physiological meaning, reflective of increasing demands for female enclosure. The less physically active women were expected to be, the more illness became them.

In the dominant social economy of Teresa's day, infirmity served the important function of erasing the woman's significance in the sexual market, her defining commodity in a culture which increasingly esteemed her as a reproductive (versus productive) agent, most worthy in proportion to her value to the dominant male class. Only by nullifying her meaning as a compelling physical piece, by entering the symbolic order as "mère ou vierge sans identité de femme" ["mother or virgin without the identity of a woman,"] could she signify herself as a spiritual creature, at odds with the Aristotelian understanding of woman as body, and thereby be acknowledged as a locus of divine intervention on earth.[58]

Since her gender suggested that the religious woman's physical state be represented as consumed, she is rendered as perpetually ill, providing the paradigmatic skeleton for the consumptive, enclosed heroines of later periods. A 1558 *Flos sanctorum* describes St. Clare, for example, referring to "su cuerpo muy flaco y debilitado por grandes abstinencias" ["her very thin body weakened by great abstinence"].[59] A representational screen of physical debility, whether accomplished in self-representation or in a biography, greatly reduced the woman's threat to the dominant society upon whose approval her continued activity depended.

---

[55] The Catholic faith supports another explanation for such similarities: the Holy Spirit works in like ways across time. Hence Ribera, *La vida*, p. 9, mentions "un mismo espíritu" ["a same spirit"] at work in Teresa and her female models.

[56] Jean Leclercq, "Prologue," in Colledge and Walsh, *Showings*, pp. 1-14.

[57] Weinstein and Bell, *Two Worlds*, p. 234.

[58] Luce Irigaray, *Éthique de la Différence Sexuelle* (Paris: Les Éditions de Minuit, 1984), p. 110. Interestingly, Margery Kempe's *Book*, which did not pass through the hands of patriarchal editing, does not resort to the topos of physical debility. On the history of Kempe's text, see Clarissa Atkinson, *Mystic and Pilgrim: The Book and the World of Margery Kempe* (Ithaca, New York: Cornell University Press, 1983), pp. 192-9.

[59] Lilio, *Segunda parte*, f. 352^r.

The endurance of prolonged infirmity also provided a means to prove female heroic stature in a way that did not threaten societal norms, since unlike the active woman, the sick woman did not contradict the mandate that women be enclosed, passive, and submissive. Hence illness became a showcase for female heroics in a religious context, and the female body was employed as a metaphorical space in which physiological reality was contradicted so that sickness could signify God's positive attention. Lilio says Clare was ill "porque la que fuera enriquecida de merecimientos en el tiempo que estuvo sana fuese mucho más enriquecida por los trabajos de la enfermedad" ["in order that the one who was enriched with merits during the time she was healthy would be much more enriched with merits by means of the trials of illness"]. St. Francis, in contrast, was not rewarded with illness but rather punished with it by God for his youthful sins: "fue castigado de fuera con grave y prolija enfermedad" ["he was chastised from without with a grave and enduring illness"].[60]

St. Jerome, whose *Epistles* Teresa found inspirational (3.7), describes the good woman as the one whose physical bounty has been lacerated by penance, she who is "amarilla y flaca de los ayunos" ["yellow and weak from fasting"] (150 r). He points to an inverse relationship between female spiritual authenticity and physical bloom: "El cuerpo de fuera muy reluciente testigo es del alma muy sucia" ["The resplendent outer body is evidence of a very dirty soul".][61] Logically, Raymond of Capua stresses Catherine of Siena's illness, which functioned as an antidote to her political potency, illness which was so extreme "que parecía estar muerta" ["that she appeared to be dead".][62] He also supports a direct relationship between female physical disability and spiritual power, a relationship which Teresa means to invoke as well: "llegó en tan alto estado que como quier que su cuerpo fuese grandemente sujeto a muchas y graves enfermedades y pasase dolores y trabajos a otras personas insoportables, no había lugar la consunción del húmedo radical" ["she arrived at such an elevated state that regardless of her body being greatly subjected to many and grave infirmities, and although she endured pains and trials which would be unbearable to others, the radical humor was not consumed"].[63] On all counts, as Dixon suggests, "a sick woman was also a safe woman."[64]

---

[60] Lilio, *Segunda parte*, ff.387^V; 419^V.

[61] Jerome [Eusebius Hieronymus], *Epístolas de San Jerónimo*, trans. Juan de Molina, 178^V. Valencia, 1520.

[62] Raymond, *Catherine*, f. 11^r. It is important to recall that St. Catherine starved herself to death. Holy women's actual physical debility affirms the important role that illness plays in patterns of female piety.

[63] Raymond, *Catherine*, f. 9^V.

[64] Laurinda S. Dixon, *Perilous Chastity. Women and Illness in Pre-Enlightenment Art and Medicine* (Ithaca, New York: Cornell University Press, 1995), p. 220.

Like her models, Teresa does not dwell relentlessly on her illnesses in her *Book*, but her weakened physical condition fills the background of her narrative canvas. Chapter 5 is devoted to "las grandes enfermedades que tuvo" ("the great illnesses she had" 5.subtitle) and she punctuates her text with references to herself as perpetually sick: "casi nunca estoy—a mi parecer—sin grandes enfermedades, y algunas veces bien graves"; "como soy tan enferma"; "por ser tan grandes mis enfermedades"; "Pasaba grandes enfermedades" ["I am almost never, in my opinion, without many pains, and sometimes very severe ones"; "since I am so ill"; "because my illnesses are so great"; "on account of the severity of my illnesses" (7.11; 7.19; 13.7; 24.2; also 7.12; 7.14; 32.7 32.8; 32.10). Only by understanding physical infirmity as a representational requisite for the acceptable holy woman can we reconcile the blatant contradiction between Teresa's apparently endless physical woes and her equally bountiful physical energy, which sufficed to motor her over wide reaches of Spain and reform two branches of an important religious order, with those seventeen convents to her credit. The saintly paradigm for women required that she be ill; national Catholic reform required that she be well, and both find representation in her *Book*. Without underestimating Teresa's physical difficulties, which became increasingly acute as she aged, it is important to underscore the narrative larger than her own which shaped her self-description, a narrative of symbolic, not literal, self-representation. That narrative disallowed representation of her physical vigor and not only provided ample room for her to represent her bodily ailments, but required that she do so. Reading the text naively as a positivist account of her physical condition makes it appear inconsistent, flattens its deep Catholic texture, and also reinforces the alliance between female weakness and spiritual strength which Teresa undercuts by making it clear that she was well enough to take Spanish Catholicism by storm.

Similarly, there is an evident conflict between the enduring stomach pains and daily vomiting to which Teresa lays claim in her *Book* (7.11) and her chubby physique, to which many who knew her attested.[65] The endurance of bodily pain and the induction of vomiting by means of a plant stem or feather were standard female ascetic practices; the Spanish version of Catherine of Siena's *vita* describes that saint's recourse to the latter procedure in graphic terms, recording how she regurgitated anything more substantial than liquid, and sometimes even water, "metiendo [por la garganta] una varilla de hinojo o de otro ramo cualquiera que fuese delgado" ["inserting [down her throat] a

---

[65] Efrén de la Madre de Dios and Steggink, *Tiempo y vida de Santa Teresa* 2nd ed. (Madrid: Editorial Católica, 1972), p. 26.

stem of fennel or any other thin branch"].⁶⁶ The behavior (its representation or its practice) may constitute a symbolic distancing from sexuality, since, as Bynum points out, "Ever since Jerome, male writers had warned religious women that food was dangerous because it excited lust."⁶⁷ In early modern Spain, severe ascetic practices of eating, sleeping and dressing were considered the stuff of beginners in spiritual life, particularly for women, whose bodies supplied the field upon which their religious heroism was displayed. Teresa's story without such practices would have been a house without a foundation, and the contrasting hues of her dietary mortification and her robust stature are resolved on the palette of female religious representation, where they indeed capture better than more straightforward methods the paradoxes inherent in her status of an orthodox, active, and articulate woman.

All this is not to say that Teresa fabricated the experiences she sets forth in her *Book*; the question is not if it is "true" or not, but what sort of truth it upholds. Positing a scale of moral truth versus empirical historicity may be more appropriate for religious texts in general and Teresa's in particular, because it signifies outside the realm of "fact" or "fiction."⁶⁸ Evaluation of how Tersea presents herself in her *Book* is enhanced by two considerations. First, whatever her experiences were, her decision of what to include and embellish and what to silence was deeply conditioned by a textual tradition which was so formative of her self-representation as to make it most meaningful only from within that tradition. Furthermore, it is likely that early modern Catholic women were so conscious of the protocols of female piety that the same protocol actually determined their experiences of the divine, in harmony with the tradition they were upholding and the spiritual understanding to which they had been exposed since childhood. The mystical experience traces the silhouette of the familiar; just as Buddhists do not have visions of the Virgin Mary, so the Catholic mystic's experience of the divine is deeply shaped by the Catholic tradition. To read Teresa's *Book* without that tradition is to discard a large portion of its meaning, attributing to Teresa's self that which signifies much more than her personal identity.

---

⁶⁶ Raymond, *Catherine*, f. 39ʳ; also f. 36ʳ.
⁶⁷ Bynum, *Holy Feast*, p. 214.
⁶⁸ Carreño, "Las paradojas," p. 257, observes that Teresa's *Book* frequently borders on "fiction." María Ornella Marotti, "Memory and Absence: Toward a Typology of Women's Autobiography," in A. L. Accardo, et al., eds, *Identité e scrittura. Studi sull' Autobiografia Nord-Americana* (Rome: Bulzoni Editore, 1988), p. 177, suggests that women's autobiography is "a form of writing shaped both by the voluntary and involuntary procesess of memory, as well as the fusion of fact and fiction." I suggest that the dichotomy itself is inappropriate in reference to religious texts.

Teresa of Ávila's spiritual life story, with the many like it, forms part of an ecclesiastical inquiry into problematic spiritual experiences. It is an answer to a question, not spontaneous discourse. It is the text which made possible, but does not contain, the author's most energetic pursuit of the holy. Accepting Teresa's *Book* as her *Life* places its author specifically, and women in general, in autobiographic jeopardy. If "compared to tragedy, or epic, or lyric poetry, autobiography always looks slightly disreputable and self-indulgent,"[69] then interpreting this exclusively female genre as such sustains a relationship between disrepute, self-indulgence, and the many extant female spiritual life stories of which Teresa's is the model. If autobiography is "ultimately an assertion of arrival and embeddedness in the phallic order,"[70] then reading the *Book* as such misdirects the text's substantial energies away from its many challenges to that order, not the least of which is its lack of a quintessential, ontologically independent individual at its core.

More specifically, interpreting Teresa's *Book* as a historical account of her life exhibits and exalts as representative, even saintly, her most vulnerable years, reducing her career to its most threatened period and celebrating the text used to evidence the threat. Composed under a triple dose of prescribed self-denigration, it displays her own rhetoric of humility invoked to disarm her readers,[71] the rhetoric of humility required of all writers and speakers discussing themselves for superiors, and the humble discourse demanded of a woman treading on the male terrain of knowledge. To canonize a humbling style employed under these constraints as representative of a woman's life is to inflect female discourse and selfhood with humility, self-doubt, and deprecation.

The authority that issues forth from Teresa of Ávila's *Book* differs substantially from that of autobiography, and is rooted in methods through which individuals ally themselves with ongoing traditions as a means to ultimately alter the course of those same traditions. Only by locating her self deeply within Catholic monasticism could this remarkable woman hope to reform it. To cite Gilmore's term, Teresa's *Book* is at most an autobiographic, "in the discourses of truth and identity, those textual places where women's self-representation interrupts (or is interrupted by) the regulatory laws of gender and genre."[72] Read as her *Life*, Teresa's book renders women as submissive and incomplete, muddling the important distinction between selfhood and self-

---

[69] De Man, "Autobiography," p. 919.

[70] Sidonie Smith, *A Poetics of Women's Autobiography. Marginality and the Fictions of Self-Representation* (Bloomington, Indiana: University of Indiana Press, 1987), p. 40.

[71] Weber, *Teresa*.

[72] Leigh Gilmore, *Autobiographics: A Feminist Theory of Women's Self-Representation* (Ithaca, New York: Cornell University Press, 1994), p. 45.

representation. As a remarkable piece of writing crafted to engineer a legitimate place for its author in a long-standing spiritual tradition, the text is released from autobiographical constraints. Recognizing Teresa of Ávila's *Book* as a link in a vital chain of Catholic culture unmasks a provocative re-creation of a woman whose life was just beginning.

7 Teresa and Her Sisters

Jane Ackerman

Teresa of Ávila sought to involve only herself, a few outside supporters, four novices and a handful of like-minded sisters in her first Discalced convent. It was to be dedicated to rigorous observance of the 1247 Rule of St. Albert in a way that expressed ancient ideals of her Order. News of her project set off a brushfire of gossip among the inhabitants of the Incarnation Convent in which she lived:

> They said I was insulting them; that in my own monastery I could also serve God since there were others in it better than I; that I had no love for the house; that it would be better to procure income for this place than for some other. Several of them said I should be thrown into the prison cell; others—very few—defended me somewhat.[1]

Thereafter everything that Teresa did was subject to scrutiny. For years, doubts and challenges about her monastic foundations were voiced as her reform attracted followers. Her spiritual life never ceased to be subject to opinion.

Teresa continues to invite examination from various angles. Some, for instance, now think of her as a resourceful woman who accomplished her most desired ends despite the limitations placed on her by her male-oriented culture. Much has been written about the impact of men on the foundress. Gillian Ahlgren has probed the effect on Teresa of "complex and conflicting notions of female sanctity" afoot in her day largely because men promoted them. Jodi Bilinkoff shifted her gaze to Ávila, the feudal city in which Teresa began her life, discovering, among other things, that Ávilan women were sometimes admired if they acted like heroic men. Alison Weber and co-authors Electa Arenal and Stacey Schlau have examined the strategies Teresa learned to use when she wanted to maneuver past the censorship of confessors, superiors, and

---

[1] St. Teresa of Ávila, *The Book of Her Life* in *The Collected Works of St. Teresa of Ávila*, trans. K. Kavanaugh, O.C.D., and O. Rodriguez, O.C.D., vol. 1 (Washington, D.C.: ICS, 1985), p. 285. All quotations from Teresa's writing except those drawn from letters will be taken from this three-volume English translation. Excerpts from letters will be translated from Spanish and taken from Santa Teresa de Jesus, *Obras completas* (11th ed., Madrid: Aguilar, 1970).

inquisitors in order to communicate with her sisters in writing.[2] This, however, is only one of many lines of thinking concerning the charismatic foundress who will surely continue to attract academic attention, just as she has always attracted readers moved by many elements of her religious life.[3]

Bilinkoff's book and the introduction to Mary Giles's article, "Reflections on Suffering in a Mystical-Feminist Key," encouraged the present investigation.[4] Both authors employ the presumption that individuals learn habits of mind from people who surround them. Giles considers issues that confront present-day women reading about saints from earlier ages whose personal actions are strange or even repellant to them. Underlying her study of bodily suffering reported by medieval nuns is her belief that women in a later age can learn beneficial attitudes from women in the past by reading about them in certain ways. For Giles, women are a friendly cohort—or could be—even if they are not alike culturally. Bilinkoff's inquiry into the history of Teresa's city of birth strongly suggests that some of the foundress' habits were learned from citizens of Ávila. Those from whom Teresa could have learned attitudes or strategies in this case were Ávilan women, men, relatives, neighbors and citizens known through legend or report.

The following discussion also uses the presumption that individuals develop attitudes and habits as they interact with others. It will turn away from the men whose influence on the saint has been examined so thoughtfully of late to examine historical details concerning companions of Teresa's own gender. The saint developed spiritually while in contact with women as well as men. This study intends to show that her female companions were important to her success in reinstituting the original charism of her Order in community life. While individuals in it such as Ana de Jesús and Ana de San Bartolomé have

---

[2] Gillian T. W. Ahlgren, *Teresa of Ávila and the Politics of Sanctity* (Ithaca, New York: Cornell University Press, 1996); Electa Arenal and Stacey Schlau, *Untold Sisters: Hispanic Nuns in Their Own Works* (Albuquerque: University of New Mexico Press, 1989); Jodi Bilinkoff, *The Ávila of Saint Teresa: Religious Reform in a Sixteenth-Century City* (Ithaca, New York: Cornell University Press, 1989); Jodi Bilinkoff, "St. Teresa of Ávila and the Ávila of St. Teresa," in *Carmelite Studies 3*, J. Sullivan, O.C.D., ed. (Washington: ICS Publications, 1984), pp. 53-68; Alison Weber, *Teresa of Ávila and the Rhetoric of Femininity* (Princeton: Princeton University Press, 1990). Others as well have noted the influence of male cultures on the life of the saint. See, for example, Kieran Kavanaugh's remarks in his introductory essays to each volume of the *Collected Works*.

[3] For an examination of Teresa's writing strategies oriented to theological issues but unconcerned with issues of gender, see Terrance G. Walsh, "Writing Anxiety in Teresa's 'Interior Castle,'" *Theological Studies* 56 (1996): 251-76. Many studies have been written concerning Teresa's theology, teachings on prayer, and teachings on human relationships. Inquiries into the details of her life and into the national and ecclesiastical politics swirling around her reform efforts have also been made.

[4] Mary Giles, "Reflections on Suffering in a Mystical-Feminist Key," *Journal of Spiritual Formation* 15 (1994): 137-47. Bilinkoff's book has been cited.

been the subject of occasional study (Arenal and Schlau's book examines the writing style of the latter, for example), the first Carmelite women who committed themselves to the reform have not received much attention as a group. This study assembles historical details needed to address the question, with what kinds of women did Teresa share her developing vision?

Teresa's relationship with the Virgin Mary will be examined first. A case will be made that Carmelite traditions concerning the patroness of the Carmelite Order encouraged several of her habits of mind. Teresa also maintained important connections with several unprofessed women. The widow Doña Guiomar de Ulloa, a supporter of the first Discalced women's foundation in Ávila, is chosen from this group for discussion. The community living at St. Joseph's in Ávila will receive attention, since the convent became Teresa's earthly home (to the extent to which she had one), and its members her special spiritual sisters. Documentary details about some of these important woman companions at St. Joseph's are few, but other companions can be described well enough to allow thought about their effects on Teresa and vice versa. Details from the life of Bl. Ana de San Bartolomé, a Carmelite laysister who eventually rose to govern several communities, and from the life of three of the earliest choir nuns committed to the reform, María Bautista, Antonia del Espíritu Santo and Isabel de Santo Domingo, will be described below. Ana's life will receive more extensive comment because more remains about her in documents and because she was especially close to the Spanish saint. A full description of the foundress' woman companions will not be achieved, but several themes of relationship will emerge from the study.

Mary, Teresa's Lady and Mother

Teresa chose to join a religious order committed to important spiritual models. As is highly visible in her writing, Teresa's greatest model was Jesus Christ. There was no more influential being in her life. Her writing constantly recalls Christ's deeds and virtues. Meditating especially on his generous love, she found Christ in every part of her existence. Keith Egan observes that for Teresa the Church, meaning for her the whole Church that she had known, was Christ to her.[5] Her Lord was especially present to her in the Eucharist. She frequently experienced his presence in visions and locutions, as well as in more unitive spiritual events. Decisions in her exterior life were guided by her Lord's instructions. Her mystical relationship with him matured, especially after she was able to depend on him fullheartedly. Teresa constantly wrote to her sisters that their whole life's work was to imitate and love Christ.

---

[5] Keith Egan, "Teresa of Jesus: Daughter of the Church, Woman of the Reformation" in *Carmelite Studies 3*, ed. John Sullivan O.C.D. (Washington, DC: ICS, 1984), p. 79.

The foundress' second spiritual model was the Virgin Mary, whom the Carmelite Order had long claimed as its patroness.[6] Carmelite reverence for the Virgin included, of course, devotion to her purity, to her relationship with her Son and to her beauty, general responses to her in an era of Marian devotion. The Order also had its own ways of responding to its patroness. For example, due to their especially strong commitment to their patroness, Carmelites supplemented Marian feasts celebrated by the whole Church. Thus throughout the year, Teresa celebrated the Purification of the Virgin, the Annunciation (the earliest date in which a particular Carmelite celebration is mentioned in a constitution or appears in a missal is 1362), the Visitation (celebrated in Carmel after 1391), the Feast of Our Lady of Mount Carmel (1386), the Assumption (14th century), the Nativity (14th century) and the Conception (made a solemn feast among Carmelites in 1306).[7] The Feast of Our Lady of Mount Carmel offered thanks to the Virgin for all that she had done for the Carmelite Order.[8] The feast of the Purification was celebrated with great fanfare in Ávila during Teresa's lifetime.[9] The Spanish nun most likely also heard a daily morning Mass of her Lady, since the practice continued in the Order between 1324 and 1584.[10] Carmelites often added hymns to Mary to liturgies. Beginning in the thirteenth century, the *Salve regina* was sung every night after Compline. In 1324, the custom was extended to every Mass and every Hour of the Office.[11] The *Regina coeli* was added to Easter liturgy in 1584, the *Ave Maria* was added to canonical hours in 1462, and the hymn dear to Carmelites that their tradition attributed to St. Simon Stock, *Ave stella matutina*, became an antiphon to the *Magnificat*.[12] Teresa and her sisters lived in an environment deeply imbued with Marian ideals.

---

[6] Spiritual reading offered Teresa the mental company of other feminine models, as well. One may have been Bl. Frances d'Amboise (1427-1485), a married noblewoman who founded the first Carmelite women's communities in France and entered Carmel after her husband's death. Frances's *Exhortations* were widely read. If Teresa knew the work, the noblewoman's devotion to Christ and her insistence that Carmelite nuns relinquish class distinctions in their community life surely impressed the Spanish nun. St. Clare of Assisi (*circa* 1193-1253), foundress of the Franciscan Poor Clares, had a place in Teresa's life. She knew Clare's writing and once reported contact with her in a vision. Teresa also dedicated one of the hermitages in the garden at St. Joseph's convent in Ávila to Clare.

[7] Archdale A. King, *Liturgies of the Religious Orders* (London: Longmans, 1954), pp. 271-8.

[8] Gabriel Barry, O.C.D., *Historical Notes on the Carmelite Order* (n.p.: n.p., 1980), p. 75.

[9] Balbino Velasco Bayón, O. Carm., *Los carmelitas: Historia de la órden del Cármen. IV. El Carmelo español (1260-1980)* (Madrid: BAC, 1993), p. 118.

[10] King, *Liturgies*, pp. 278; see also Velasco Bayón, *Los carmelitas*, p. 143.

[11] Redemptus Maria Valabek, O. Carm., "Prayer Among Carmelites of the Ancient Observance," *Carmelus* 28 (1981): 90.

[12] King, *Liturgies*, pp. 278-9.

It is perhaps not a surprise, then, that she reports having received special graces during or after Marian liturgies (special knowledge of her Lord often came to her after the Eucharist, as well). In 1572, the Mother of God and a multitude of angels appeared to Teresa as the *Salve regina* was begun.[13] Three years later, on the feast of the Nativity of the Virgin, the day Teresa chose to renew her vows, she received another vision, in which "the Blessed Virgin, our Lady, appeared to me through an illuminative vision; and it seems to me I renewed them in her hands, and that they were pleasing to her. This vision remained with me for some days, as though she were next to me at my left."[14] Some of Teresa's attitudes concerning Mary are perhaps visible in this experience. First, since the patroness was a great exemplar of the very vows to which the Carmelite was re-committing herself, including dependence on God, chastity, obedience and (symbolically in Mary's immaculate state) the cloister, the Spanish nun observed herself in the vision re-committing herself to imitating the excellences of her great feminine model. Second, Teresa's remark that Mary seemed to remain near her "for some days, as though she were next to me at my left" suggests that she was aware that the Virgin supported her. Third, Teresa witnessed herself reenacting a very old Carmelite gesture of fealty to the patroness of the Order.

Carmelite veneration of Mary originally followed feudal custom. The 1207 formula of life which, with a few additions, became the 1247 monastic rule that Teresa followed, required the hermits who had requested it to construct an oratory "in the midst of the cells as conveniently as possible, where you are to gather each day in the morning to hear Mass . . ."[15] Reports of pilgrims to the Holy Land indicate that the hermits had accomplished this by 1270, and had dedicated their church to Mary. The latter gesture signified a particular relationship:

> The members of a religious community were "mancipati," that is, bound to the service of a titulus or church. To the feudal mind this meant being the "vassals" of the saint to whom the church was dedicated. Just as a secular vassal bound himself by oath to the service, "servitium obsequium" of his liege lord, so the religious bound himself by his profession to the service of the patron saint of his church who was in turn, with all his or her liegemen, bound to the service of Our Lord.

---

[13] *Spiritual Testimonies* 21 in *Collected Works*, 1:395.
[14] *Spiritual Testimonies* 43 in *Collected Works*, 1:411.
[15] Chapter 10, *Rule of St. Albert* in *Albert's Way: The First North American Congress on the Carmelite Rule*, ed. M. Mulhall, O.Carm. (Rome: Institutum Carmelitanum, 1989). All quotations from the Carmelite Rule will be drawn from this source.

Service of Mary was inseparable from the service of Christ to which the 1207 and 1247 Rules called Carmelites:

> The free choice of Our Lady as titular of the oratory on Mount Carmel, meant nothing less than a conscious and deliberate dedication of the institute and each of its members to her service. Our Lady was, of course, her Son's principal vassal, so that there was complete accord between her service and the "obsequium Jesu Christi" enjoined by the Carmelite Rule on these dwellers in His own feudal territory, the Holy Land. It is interesting to recall in this connection, that the earliest extant Carmelite profession formula promises in the first place "obedience to God and blessed Mary."[16]

Thus when she saw herself renewing her vows in Mary's hands in her vision, Teresa saw herself reenacting a very old Carmelite act of commitment to service to the Order and to the service of God and Mary.[17] Given the number of times that she calls her sisters to hasten to serve Mary and Christ, and the frequency with which she examined her own efforts at such service, it is obvious that Teresa was imprinted with this characteristic Carmelite response to Mary as a feudal lady deserving fealty.

Affiliation with Mary as patroness in centuries predating Teresa's life meant that Carmelites gave themselves to their Lady's service but also, according to feudal custom, knew that she would protect them.[18] Teresa seems to have explored this traditional dimension of her relationship with her patroness. It seems from her comments that she especially pondered and tried to imitate her Lady's maternal care. Carmelite belief in Mary's protection is demonstrated, for example, in their traditions about garments that the Virgin either gives members of the Order or extends over them.[19] The legend grew up

---

[16] Barry draws these details from a study by Ludovico Saggi, O.Carm. (Barry, *Historical Notes*, pp. 74-5).

[17] Teresa was acquainted with early traditions of the order. The Incarnation Convent where she led the first twenty years of her religious life possessed a Latin-Spanish copy of a collection of medieval documents of the the Order during her stay. Her correspondence also reveals that she discussed the beginnings of the Order and its traditions with several whom she felt were knowledgeable about such issues. It is furthermore possible that Teresa learned the old habit of swearing obedience to God and Mary from constitutions. Adrian Staring reports that Spanish women's constitutions were closely modeled on those of fifteenth-century women's houses in the Low Countries. These contain profession formulas which lead sisters to promise "obedience to God and blessed Mary, Mother of God" ("The Carmelite Sisters in the Netherlands," *Carmelus* 10 [1963]: 88-9).

[18] Emanuele Boaga, *A Senhora do lugar: Maria na historia e na vida do Carmelo*, trans. Sr. Augusta de Castro Cotta (Paranavai: Editoria Grafica a Paranavai, 1994), p. 227.

[19] The gesture is ancient. In the Bible donning or being covered by garments often signifies that a person is able to care for another or is the recipient of protection. Ruth, for

among Carmelites by the second half of the fourteenth century that their first European prior general, St. Simon Stock, asked the Virgin to give the Order a special favor. She appeared to him in a vision, holding in her hand a scapular (originally, the sleeveless outer garment of the habit) and declared, "whoever dies in this will achieve salvation."[20] Surviving paintings belonging to the Order, including a fifteenth-century one located in Convent of the Incarnation in which Teresa resided for twenty years, also depict the Virgin stretching a cloak over those who pray to her. In the picture that Teresa may have often seen, Mary is wearing the white cloak which the order adopted in 1287 to honor her purity.[21] She extends it as a loving canopy over Carmelites ranged on her right and left. The often-repeated image merges Mary's protection with the protection that the Order itself provides its members.[22]

Teresa's belief in Mary's loving care began when she was a child. She relates that her mother taught her to pray to the Virgin when she was six or seven, and when her mother died several years later, Teresa, then twelve, asked Mary to become her mother. "It seems that though I did this in simplicity it helped me," she wrote in her autobiography, "For I have found favor with this sovereign Virgin in everything I have asked of her, and in the end she has drawn me to herself.[23] Given these features of her childhood, Teresa's understanding of Mary's protection was possibly more that of a mother for her children than

---

instance, asks her dead husband's distant kinsman Boaz to cover her with his garment, which he does, symbolically drawing her under the protection of the family.

[20] Joachim Smet, O. Carm., *The Carmelites: A History of the Brothers of Our Lady of Mount Carmel*, volume 1 (Rev. ed., Darien, Illinois: Carmelite Spiritual Center, 1988), p. 23. See also Barry, *Historical Notes*, pp. 73-5. Although the tradition is particularly Carmelite, other medieval orders developed similar legends in which the Virgin promised protection to wearers of one religious habit or another. In the fifteenth century, Arnold Bostius, a great devotee of the patroness, "orientated the tradition of the Scapular vision toward the actual practice of the Scapular devotion through imitation of Mary" (Christian Ceroke, O. Carm., "The Credibility of the Scapular Promise," *Carmelus* 11 [1964]: 81-123). The sixteenth-century prior general, John Baptist Rossi, who became a supporter of Teresa's reform after meeting her increased the popularity of the scapular legend along with its corollary, the "Sabbatine Privilege," which claimed that wearing the scapular would insure release from purgatory the Saturday after one died (Barry, *Historical Notes*, p. 76). Rossi promoted the devotion with great success during a month-long stay in Seville in 1566 (Velasco Bayón, *Los carmelitas*, p. 195).

[21] A photograph of the picture is included as an appendix in Velasco Bayón's history.

[22] Concerning the detail that Mary is wearing a Carmelite garment, Boaga remarks that "reflection on [Mary as] 'Sister' developed into the affirmation that not only does Carmel totally belong to Mary, she also belonged to Carmel: this idea is explicitly expressed in the title, 'Carmelite Virgin,' as if Mary were effectively a member of the Order" (Boaga, *Senhora*, p. 231).

[23] Chapter 1, *Life* in *Collected Works*, 1:54-6.

that of a feudal lady for her vassals, but both kinds of relationship seem to be suggested in her words.

Mary became in Teresa's mind a great protectress of the new convents founded to follow the "primitive" Rule of the Order. Teresa several times recorded her memory of the moment in which God told her set her doubts aside and to found St. Joseph's in Ávila: "He said it should be called St. Joseph and that this saint would keep watch over us at one door, and our Lady at the other, that Christ would remain with us, and that it would be a star shining with great splendor."[24] Adrian Staring reports that beguinages in the Low Countries (communities of pious women such as Teresa's original convent of the Incarnation was, until some years before her profession) customarily placed statues of their patron saints in niches over entrances to their houses as a sign of their protection.[25]

Mary offered Teresa spiritual aid during difficult days in 1561 when criticisms of the new foundation of St. Joseph's were mounting and funds to complete it were in short supply. During Mass on the feast of the Assumption, Teresa saw Mary and Joseph, the two future protectors of the convent, vest her with a white robe, a biblical sign of Teresa's purity but also, as has been shown, a sign of the Carmelite Order and of Mary herself:

> It seemed to me then that our Lady took me by the hands. She told me I made her very happy in serving the glorious St. Joseph, that I should believe that what I was striving for in regard to the monastery would be accomplished, that the Lord and those two would be greatly served in it, that I shouldn't fear there would ever be any failure in this matter even though the obedience which was to be given was not to my liking, because they would watch over us, and that her Son had already promised us He would be with us, that as a sign that this was true she was give me a jewel.

In the vision Mary then placed a golden crucifix around Teresa's neck.[26] The investiture symbolically drew her under the protection of all associated with the white garment and the crucifix.

It is possible to think that Teresa's conception of how she should act in the leadership roles of foundress, prioress and teacher of prioresses was shaped by Carmelite devotion to Mary as a feudal lady. The Spanish saint's often-demonstrated concern for her sisters and expectation of their prompt, humble obedience at least generally parallel the motifs of service and protection that the Order strongly associated with the Virgin. Teresa's descriptions of Mary's care

---

[24] Chapter 32, *Life* in *Collected Works*, 1:280.
[25] Staring, "Carmelite Sisters," p. 77.
[26] Chapter 33, *Life* in *Collected Works*, 1:291.

especially incline to examples of generous, motherly support, a feature of her own leadership, as well.

One of her gestures as the contested prioress of the Incarnation Convent reveals as much belief in the ability of her Lady to resolve the situation as it does Teresa's skill as a leader. María Bautista, whose relationship with the foundress will be described later, told inquirers at beatification proceedings that Teresa won many of the hostile members of the convent to her cause by declining to sit in the prioress' choir stall. Instead she placed a small altar on the seat and on it a statue of the Virgin of Clemency. Every night Teresa brought the keys to the convent door to the statue, remarking how consoled she was to have such a prioress. The physical demonstration of who really governed the convent, on the spiritual level, and to whom the nuns in the convent owed fealty could not have been clearer. María Bautista reported that Teresa received confirmation that the Virgin accepted the gesture. She appeared to her in a vision, surrounded by a host of angels, and sat in the prioress' stall, saying "You did well in placing me here. I will be a witness to all the praises sung to my Son, and I will present them to him."[27]

Finally, in the centuries before Teresa's lifetime, members of the Order began to add to their service of Mary and trust in her protection their response to her in relationships "marked by affection, cordiality, tenderness, intimacy and familiarity."[28] Allusions to her as sister and mother increased.[29] Legends emphasizing familial relationships or intimate cordiality began to appear. An early fifteenth-century document of the Order retold the legend, for example, that the Virgin and other chaste women had sometimes come to visit Carmelite ancestors living on Mount Carmel in Israel.[30] There is also support for intimacy with Mary in the rule of the order, which, although it calls Carmelites to obey their priors or prioresses as if they were obeying Christ himself (as do other monastic rules), often encourages members of the order to act as

---

[27] "Dicho de María Bautista, C.D.," in Silverio de Santa Teresa, O.C.D., *Procesos de beatificación y canonización de Santa Teresa de Jesus*, vol. 1 (Burgos: El Monte Carmelo, 1934), p. 42. All excerpts from the beatification and canonization proceedings will be drawn from this three-volume source. María Bautista's report of the content of the vision is closely modeled on Teresa's account of it.

[28] Boaga, *Senhora*, p. 228.

[29] Eamon Carroll, O.Carm., remarks that a "developed theology of Mary as spiritual mother in the sense that Catholics have come to appreciate it did not arise until the high middle ages" ("Revolution in Mariology 1949-1989" in *The Land of Carmel: Essays in Honor of Joachim Smet, O. Carm.* [Rome: Institutum Carmelitanum, 1991], p. 451).

[30] In his *Viridarium* (circa 1410), Jean Grossi writes that the "glorious Virgin Mary often visited the sons of the prophets as if they were her own sons and brothers and they were the first to build a chapel in her honor and choose her as their patron" (Rudolf Hendriks, "La Succession héréditaire [1280-1451]" in *Élie le prophète*, vol. 2, Études Carmélitaines [Paris: Desclée de Brower, 1956], p. 68).

siblings—brothers, the original document repeatedly says—a relationship of equals, and remands many of the community's decisions to the discretion of the entire group. What results is an ethos of family whose parent is divine and whose members are brothers and sisters.

Teresa's affection for her Lady is obvious, as is her trust in her generous support, but her writing provides no evidence that she thought of Mary as her sister. She instead places Mary and her Son far above her, offering them the love of a vassal, of a humble daughter, and, in Christ's case, of a spouse whose adored bridegroom is more noble than she. Teresa did once remark on one thing that she saw she shared with Mary, however partially. Christians have meditated on the Virgin's spiritual participation in the Passion and her sorrow at her Son's death. Teresa's soul was once pierced with a similar wound. After undergoing the harrowing pain, she wrote to a confessor: "I have understood better what our Lady experienced, for until today—as I say—I did not understand the nature of this transpiercing." She wrote that Jesus then appeared to her, telling her more about his mother's suffering: "He told me that immediately after his resurrection, he went to see our Lady because she then had great need and that the pain she experienced so absorbed and transpierced her soul that she did not return immediately to herself to rejoice in that joy." Many things converged in Teresa's experience. She wrote that she not only better understood the depths of Mary's suffering by means of her own but was also united with God by means of it:

> Even this morning I felt the pain, for while in prayer I experienced a great rapture. And it seemed that our Lord brought my spirit next to His Father and said to Him; "This soul You have given to Me, I give to You." And it seemed the Father took me to himself. . . . One day [shortly after Teresa's transpiercing] Christ appeared to her, saying "see me here, daughter, for it is I; give me your hands." And it seemed he took them and placed them on his side and said: "Behold my wounds. You are not without me. This short life is passing away."[31]

Intimacy with Mary's sorrow was either an introduction to closer contact with Father and Son, or was concordant with it, in Teresa's experience.

Doña Guiomar de Ulloa

Teresa sought to imitate the Virgin's perfections. She seemed, in contrast, to have maintained a friendship with Doña Guiomar de Ulloa in spite of the latter's

---

[31] *Spiritual Testimonies,* 12 in *Collected Works,* 1:390.

human limitations. The devout widow, of varying reputation among her Ávilan observers, was an important mediating figure for the small community of women who first occupied the Convent of St. Joseph. References to the noblewoman in letters written to others in later years indicate that Teresa remained faithful to the nuns after circumstances of her life took her away from Ávila.

Doña Guiomar's well-to-do husband Francisco Dávila died when she was twenty-five, leaving her with four children and the resources to maintain a gracious lifestyle in a palace in Ávila. Opinions of the noblewoman retrieved from contemporary documents by Efrén de la Madre de Dios and Otger Steggink conflict on some points, but the impression emerges that Doña Guiomar was strongheaded, devout and somewhat frivolous. A priest, Juan de Orellana, remembered her as a laughing stock, saying "she was well-known throughout Ávila for her flightiness and lack of judgment."[32] Domingo Báñez's remark that the noblewoman "has become saintly because her habits [before] didn't have much to do with sainthood given the generally poor opinion of her stubbornness and expenditures" suggests a change of heart which Frs. Efrén and Steggink believe was due to Teresa's influence. Pedro de Alcántara, who became Doña Guiomar's confessor, is also a candidate for having produced her abrupt assumption of humility and poor clothing, given what is known of his views on poverty. At 12,000 inhabitants, Ávila was certainly small enough to gossip about its public figures. Guiomar was said to be "good looking and fond of dressing well" but on the other hand was criticized for going overboard in dressing poorly, carrying her own seating to church and acting so humbly that people commented and even laughed. Her relatives thought her behavior unbecoming to her station.[33]

Doña Guiomar's palace was across the street from a community of Jesuits through which she met Teresa. She drew many devout people around her in her home. One frequent participant in spiritual conversations there was the young Jesuit Juan de Prádanos assigned to the household as a confessor for three years. He confessed Teresa for a while, as well. Another was the already-mentioned Franciscan Pedro de Alcántara, whom Doña Guiomar introduced to Teresa, beginning a profound spiritual friendship. According to Jodi Bilinkoff, Doña Guiomar also arranged a meeting between Alcántara, Teresa and Mari Díaz, a peasant woman in her service who was famous for her devotion. Remarks of Teresa's niece Beatriz de Jesus suggest that women in Ahumada family often visited the noblewoman. Juana de Ahumada, who was

---

[32] *Informe dirigido a la Inquisición*, quoted in Efrén de la Madre de Dios, O.C.D. and Otger Steggink, O.Carm., *Santa Teresa y su tiempo*, volume 1 (Salamanca: Biblioteca de la Caja de Ahorros, 1982), p. 355. (Hereafter, this three-volume work will be cited by "Efrén," and volume number 1, 2.1 or 2.2)

[33] Efrén, 1:354-5.

Teresa's sister and Beatriz's mother, once entered a chapel in the palace when Teresa was at prayer.[34] One of Doña Guiomar's daughters entered St. Joseph's in Ávila when the noblewoman refused to accept her choice of husband.[35]

Bilinkoff has demonstrated that sixteenth-century Ávila possessed stereotypes of feminine behavior. Some of these are in play in what is known of Doña Guiomar de Ulloa. The city possessed a tradition of forceful women which Bilinkoff traces to the medieval legend of Jimena Blásquez, a governor's wife said to have rallied Ávila's women to defend its ramparts when its men were away at battle.[36] Widows and daughters of influential men were active in urban affairs of the city. Displaying considerable independence of spirit in other matters, Doña Guiomar joins a group of women who endowed and supported new religious houses. It is reasonable to think she was acquainted with the deeds of at least some of the group of these on whom Bilinkoff comments. Doña Catalina Guiera, daughter of a French knight and widow of a wealthy landowner, founded a house for pious laywomen in 1478. Twice-widowed Doña María Dávila, who was responsible for several foundations, including a shrine to the Virgin, also became a *beata* and eventually the abbess of a convent of Poor Clares which she founded in 1502. In 1479, Doña Elvira González de Medina founded the *beaterio* which became the Carmelite Convent of the Incarnation in which Teresa made her vows. Doña Mencía López, widow of a wealthy silversmith, established a *beaterio* in her own home. Doña María de Herrera, daughter and widow of powerful men, and, as Bilinkoff notes, "a woman of forceful character," established a chapel and a hospital for the poor and elderly.[37]

Doña Guiomar partially followed this pattern of behavior acceptable for well-to-do Ávilan widows. She pursued a program of highly visible personal devotion and supported a religious foundation. She diverges in one particular from some of the women mentioned above whom Bilinkoff studied. While most of these eventually chose to enter vowed life, whether as *beatas* or as cloistered nuns, as was the case with María Dávila, who became an abbess, Doña Guiomar pursued her piety on her own terms, apparently electing to seek spiritual contacts in her own home with visitors such as St. Teresa or St. Pedro de Alcántara, instead of casting in her lot with a group of women under the authority of a provincial and bishop. Perhaps some who thought her flighty or stubborn came to that conclusion because she declined to end her life in enclosure, as Ávila seems to have expected pious widows to do.

For a time at least, Doña Guiomar was a trusted conversation partner. In a letter written to her brother in 1561, Teresa called her "very spiritual": "For

---

[34] *Procesos*, 3:114-15.
[35] Efrén,1:221.
[36] Bilinkoff, *The Ávila of St. Teresa*, pp. 2-3. See also Efrén, 1:209-12.
[37] Bilinkoff, *The Ávila of St. Teresa*, pp. 39-50.

four years we have had the closest friendship that I could have with a sister."[38] More than a decade later, Teresa commented in a letter to María Bautista, "Anything that you may do for Doña Guiomar will be well done, for she is more saintly than is thought, and carries heavy burdens."[39] It is reported that when she entered Teresa's cell at Incarnation in 1560 to join the group chatting about how wonderful it would be to found an austere convent modeled after the life of "our holy fathers of old," Doña Guiomar promptly volunteered to support such a foundation, a gesture which Teresa later reported encouraged her to move beyond thinking about the project as an abstraction.[40] Doña Guiomar's monetary support of St. Joseph's was slight (and in any event, Teresa wanted to begin the foundation without endowments). It is perhaps most important that she lent her name as the proposed convent's foundress on two occasions and was willing to intercede for it. The noblewoman approached the Carmelite provincial of Castile, convincing him to support the project, although he subsequently backed down under the criticisms of it by municipal authorities. The noble widow again accepted the role of the initiator of the project in the document Teresa wrote to Rome seeking support for it.[41] Efrén de la Madre de Dios and Steggink report that Teresa's assessment of "such a strange woman" was that she was "a widowed noblewoman of great quality and prayer life, full of spirit."[42] Doña Guiomar was one of many devout women of firm will with whom Teresa surrounded herself as she began her efforts to recapture what she saw was the original charism of her Order.

The Women of St. Joseph's Convent

Members of the first Discalced convent were carefully chosen. Teresa led the decision-making, but Pedro de Alcántara, Doña Guiomar, Julián de Ávila, who became the convent's confessor, and Gaspar Daza also made proposals concerning membership of the initial community. It was decided that St. Joseph would be founded with four novices. The move is not too surprising, given that monastic reforms have often been introduced first among new recruits.[43] The

---

[38] "A Don Lorenzo de Cepeda" in *Obras*, p. 732.
[39] "A la Madre María Bautista" in *Obras*, p. 797.
[40] Joachim Smet, O.Carm., *Cloistered Carmel. A Brief History of the Carmelite Nuns* (Rome: Institutum Carmelitanum, 1986), p. 49.
[41] Smet, *Cloistered*, p. 50. Teresa's sister Juana de Ahumada was involved in the petitions, as well (*Procesos*, 3:115).
[42] Efrén, 1:355.
[43] In the following century the Touraine Reform of the Carmelite Ancient Observance sprang from the efforts of those whose professions were relatively new. Prior general Bl. Jean Soreth's fifteenth-century creation of the Second Order (which formally accepted professed women as members of the Carmelite Order) may also be interpreted as

novices were to be poor or to be otherwise less than usually attached to class and family expectations.[44] Three were women considerably older than the usual postulancy age range of 16 to 20. All are remembered as being virtuous women of resolute purpose.

Three months after St. Joseph was founded, Teresa returned to serve as prioress, bringing with her four nuns from Incarnation. More novices were added to the group in the following years. Teresa lived at St. Joseph's for four years which she later remembered as the most tranquil in her vowed life. She remained close to the community at St. Joseph despite her obliged return to Incarnation as its prioress and her journeys to make other new Discalced foundations. She recorded her feelings about the group as she returned to Ávila in 1568 after a long absence: "And to leave my daughters and Sisters when going from one place to another, was not the smallest cross, I tell you, since I love them so much; especially when I thought I was not going to return to see them again and I saw their great sadness and tears." As she wrote, Teresa did not separate her own emotions from those of her sisters: "Even though they are detached from other things, God has not given them the gift to be detached from me, perhaps so that it might be a greater torment to me, for I am not detached from them either, even though I forced myself as much as I could so as not to show it and I reprimanded them. But this was of little help since their love for me is great, and in many ways it is obvious that this love is true."[45]

Teresa's relationship with the group rested on more than ties of affection. In her *Life* first redacted in 1562, the year of the St. Joseph's foundation, she said:

> It is the most wonderful consolation for me to be able to live with souls so detached. Their conversation is about how they can make progress in the service of God. Solitude is their comfort, and the thought of seeing others (when doing so is not a help toward an enkindling within them of a greater love of their Spouse) is a burden to them even though these others may be relatives. As a result no one comes to this house save those who speak about this love, for otherwise neither are the nuns satisfied nor are their visitors. Their language allows them to speak only of God, and so they only understand one who speaks the

---

involving new recruits in his effort to spread reform by instituting the measures among them that he was seeking to implant in the Order.

[44] Efrén, 1:423. Isabel de Santo Domingo remarked that in later years she heard Teresa express particular satisfaction if she could admit women to her new foundations who could not enter other houses because they lacked a dowry (*Procesos*, 1:85).

[45] Chapter 27, *Foundations* in *Collected Works*, 3:248. Efrén de la Madre de Dios and Otger Steggink's conclusion that Teresa is referring to the community at St. Joseph's in Ávila community is reasonable, since it remained the base to which she returned between journeys.

same language; nor would they in turn be understood by anyone who doesn't.[46]

A decade later, Teresa commented about the group:

> It was a delight to me to be among souls so holy and pure, whose only concern was to serve and praise our Lord . . . With respect to the virtue of obedience, to which I am very devoted (although I didn't know how to practice it until those servants of God so taught me that I couldn't be ignorant as to whether or not I possessed it), I could mention many things that I saw there . . .[47]

It appears that the Spanish saint deliberately constituted the community at St. Joseph's in Ávila with novices and seasoned nuns whose previous lives demonstrated their inclination to the ideals of her reform. The sisters' love and zeal for the service of God must have gratified Teresa very much.

She also must have been delighted that in the practice of daily life the first Discalced community showed a sincere inclination to the solitude which she believed was part of the original charism of the Order:

> Well, now, this wretched one was among these angelic souls. They didn't seem to me to be anything else, for there was no fault they hid from me, even if interior. And the favors, and ardent desires, and detachment the Lord gave them were great. Their consolation was their solitude. . . . The one who had the greater opportunity to remain in a hermitage considered herself the luckiest. In considering the real value of these souls and the courage God gave them to serve and suffer for Him, certainly not a characteristic of women, I often though that the riches God placed in them were meant for some great purpose . . . . Whoever conversed with them was always edified.[48]

Teresa's occasional observations such as the one just cited, in which she asserts stereotypes of feminine weakness, have drawn attention recently. Alison Weber comments that such comments are often deliberately ironic:

> In these passages (and in many others) Teresa concedes to woman's weakness, timidity, powerlessness, and intellectual inferiority but uses the concessions ironically to defend, respectively, the legitimacy of her own spiritual favors, her disobedience of *letrados*, her administrative

---

[46] Chapter 36, *Life* in *Collected Works*, 1:321.
[47] Chapter 1, *Foundations* in *Collected Works*, 3:99-100.
[48] Chapter 1, *Foundations* in *Collected Works*, p. 101.

initiative, her right to "teach" in the Pauline sense, and her unmediated access to scriptures.[49]

Details in the present study confirm Weber's conclusion that Teresa's life often did not match her disclaimers. When details about the women with whom she actually interacted are examined, the fact emerges that, regardless of what Teresa said about her gender, she chose effective, often confident female companions for herself.

This suggests much about Teresa. The admirable sisters with whom she lived during her four years at St. Joseph's and in between her journeys gave her important confirmation of her own ways of being and of the validity of the reform she sought. When she saw that they, as she, prospered when they embraced poverty and advanced in prayer with courage, Teresa must have been reassured about the pattern of her own life. When she found members of the St. Joseph group to exceed her in virtue, as she did on penning the passages just cited, the St. Joseph group, or perhaps one or another member of it, became a human model for imitation. Contact with these women, in particular, must have been a source of strength for Teresa as she expanded her reform.

The four initial novices were Antonia del Espíritu Santo (Antonia de Henao), twenty-six, remembered as possessing a "great spirit and an inclination to penitence and mortification"; María de la Cruz (María de Paz), a maid in Doña Guiomar's household who spent many hours in Teresa's company before becoming a novice; Ursula de los Santos, forty-one, who Gerardo de San Juan de la Cruz remarked was "very much a woman in her own house and born to lead" and whose strong will Teresa apparently felt compelled to soften; and María de San José (María de Ávila), thirty-seven, a sister of Teresa's confessor and companion in reform Julián de Ávila, who became chaplain of St. Joseph.[50] Isabel de Santo Domingo (Isabel Ortega) was proposed by Teresa's Franciscan spiritual guide Pedro de Alcántara, but she did not enter St. Joseph's until its second year. The nuns from Incarnation who first transferred to the community were Ana de San Juan (Ana Dávila), Ana de los Angeles (Ana Gómez), María Isabel (María Isabel Ordóñez, sister of Ana Gómez) and Isabel de San Pablo (Isabel de la Peña). Family relations at times drew relatives into the same community. María Bautista, one of the earliest novices, was Teresa's second cousin. Another cousin, María de San Jerónimo, professed in St. Joseph's in 1563.[51]

Teresa recalled her hopes for the novices at the outset. They were to be the foundation of the renewed Carmelite life she sought:

---

[49] Weber, *Teresa*, pp. 39-40. See the details of Weber's discussion of the politics of Teresa's apologies for her gender on pp. 36-49.
[50] Efrén, 1:424.
[51] *Procesos*, 1:158.

> Well, with me it was like being in glory to see the Blessed Sacrament reserved and that four poor orphans (for they didn't bring in any dowry) and four great servants of God (for this is what I had in mind from the beginning, that persons would enter who by their example of prayer and a very perfect life would be a foundation upon which we could achieve our goal) would give each other support; and to see a work accomplished that I knew was for the service of the Lord and to the honor of the habit of His glorious Mother—for these were my concerns.[52]

As it turns out, Antonia del Espíritu Santo, María Bautista and several others, including the laywoman Ana de San Bartolomé who entered St. Joseph's shortly thereafter, repaid Teresa's hopes by becoming leaders in their own right.

The first four recruits are remembered for a collective gesture. Notice of the planned foundation of St. Joseph's got out, perhaps as Teresa was securing the approval of superiors for the project. The Carmelite provincial at first indicated he would support the foundation, but withdrew support when criticism of it surfaced. The local bishop provided the authorization for the foundation, and approval also came from Rome, facts that were apparently not widely known until later. Criticism of the project spilled out of the walls of Incarnation into the surrounding town. The town council of Ávila opposed the venture when it became known that Teresa planned to found the community without an endowment income that would cover its ordinary expenses. As opposition was mounting, Teresa engaged her brother-in-law to purchase a house and prepare it for the new community. Construction was completed surreptitiously in 1562. An altar was set up and adorned. Teresa and the novices entered the house. The Mass inaugurating the community was celebrated. Gaspar Daza accepted the novices into the community.

Bells ringing the Hours the following morning alerted the residents of the neighborhood that the house had been occupied, and by midday the town was in an uproar. Julián de Ávila, who was present at the inauguration, reported that townspeople and men of religious position in Ávila wanted to turn the four novices out. Teresa's prioress, at the command of the provincial, ordered her to return to Incarnation Convent. She obeyed, leaving Ursula de los Santos (remembered for her strong will) in charge. The situation became more intense. The *corregidor* of Ávila pounded on the door, telling the novices to come out or the doors would be broken down, "but the novices responded that they would not unless it was at the hands of the one who put them there. If the *corregidor* wanted to break the doors down, let him do it, but to consider

---

[52] Chapter 36, *Life* in *Collected Works*, 1:311. Kavanaugh remarks that it was not strictly true that the four entered without a dowry: "[H]istorians point out that Ursula de los Santos, for example, brought in three hundred ducats" (*Collected Works*, 1:487).

well what he was doing." The official did not carry out his threat, since the Sacrament had been placed in the house, but the four novices were determined to stay at all costs.[53] Isabel Bautista, an early recruit, remarked later that the four had barricaded the doors.[54] The town fathers were placated and the situation calmed when it was learned that the bishop had approved the foundation. For a moment, however, institution of unmitigated Carmelite life among women hinged on the courage of the four.

Antonia del Espíritu Santo

Three of the first novices, Ursula de los Santos, María de San José and María de la Cruz, have left behind few traces. Slightly more known about another, Antonia del Espíritu Santo. She is remembered as having been committed to prayer in spite of the hunger the community at St. Joseph's often suffered. María de Salazar, who later entered the reform, remembered that Antonia bore difficulties of religious life with openness and joy.[55] Teresa at times took Antonia along as a traveling companion. She, Antonia and Ana de los Angeles journeyed to Medina and Malagón to make foundations in 1567 and 1568.[56] Antonia and María de la Cruz collaborated with Teresa in the foundation at Valladolid in 1568.[57] Teresa preserves a remark made by Antonia suggestive of her discretion. On their return from Valladolid to Toledo, the party stopped by Duruelo to inspect the house destined for the first Discalced men's community. Teresa remarked that Antonia, on seeing the house in shambles, reacted negatively in spite of her own habit of bearing difficulty well, saying: "Mother, there is nobody, no matter how good, who could tolerate this," an accurate assessment, as it turns out, since the community soon decamped to a healthier location.[58] Antonia served as subprioress at Valladolid between 1568 and 1569.[59] She was elected prioress of St. Joseph's in Ávila in 1574.[60]

---

[53] *Procesos*, 2:206. See also Efrén, 1:426-32.
[54] Efrén, 1:431.
[55] Efrén, 2.1:22.
[56] *Procesos*, 1:84.
[57] Efrén, 2.1:230, 239.
[58] Chapter 11, *Foundations* in *Complete Works*, 3:162
[59] Efren, 2.1:205.
[60] "A Doña Ana Enríquez" in *Obras*, p. 808.

María Bautista (1543-1603)[61]

María Bautista testified in support of Teresa's beatification in 1595. Examiners turned to her because of her lengthy relationship with the saint. A second cousin of the foundress, María knew Teresa from the time she was a child. She lived with her at the Convent of the Incarnation for two years. Sharing living quarters with Teresa allowed María to witness the saint's ecstasies and to hear the content of her prayer. She participated in the conversation in Teresa's cell in which the convent at St. Joseph's moved from being a dream to a concrete project. María reports that she encouraged Teresa to attempt the foundation.[62] She made her profession at St. Joseph's in 1564.[63]

Teresa's involvement of her second cousin in her reform opens a window on the saint's administrative habits and demonstrates how much she relied on some of the first women who became Discalced nuns. The foundress governed her new convents by appointing their prioresses, an act technically at variance with the Carmelite Rule, which tells members of a community, "The first thing we require is that one of you is to be the Prior[ess], who is to be chosen for that office by the consent of all, or the greater and maturer part of you," but apparently conforming to the practice in Spain at the time.[64] Teresa herself was assigned to the Incarnation Convent as prioress over the protests of its members, who surely felt that their prerogative stated in the Rule was being violated. What is noteworthy, of course, is that Teresa, being a woman, was able to place and move her Discalced prioresses. Given her commitment to obedience and her efforts to secure institutional approval for her foundations,

---

[61] Documentary details relating to María Bautista's identity are not easy to untangle. There were, apparently, two María Bautistas in the early reform. Efrén de la Madre de Dios and Otger Steggink identify one in prior life as María Ocampo, daughter of Diego de Cepeda, Teresa's brother. They say that this María, Teresa's niece, came to live with her at Incarnation and was present at the formative conversation in Teresa's cell, taking the name of María Bautista after profession. However, they assign most of Teresa's correspondence, testimony at Teresa's beatification hearings, and service as prioress at Valladolid to María Bautista Méndez (see their index on 2.1:877). Kieran Kavanaugh and Otilio Rodriguez identify María de Cepeda y Ocampo as a daughter of Teresa's cousin who took the name of María Bautista and professed at St. Joseph's in Ávila: "This Sister, María Bautista (de Ocampo) (1543-1603), later became prioress of Valladolid. She was one of Teresa's most frequent correspondents" (*Collected Works*, 1:472, 1:483 and 3:415). The present study depends on the research and conclusions of Kavanaugh and Rodriguez, since they are most consistent with the details given by "la Madre María Bautista" who identifies herself as a "prima segunda de la dicha madre" in a deposition made in Valladolid in 1595 (see *Procesos*, 1:37-44).

[62] *Procesos*, 1:39.
[63] *Procesos*, 1:37.
[64] Chapter 1, *Rule*.

she most likely also secured official support for her habit of naming key members of new communities.

Teresa relied on her prioresses to put the ideals of her reform into practice in the new communities. She also asked them to inform her about the life of their convents, to carry out tasks for her in the community or locally, and to relay messages to the group or to individual members in it. María Bautista's relationship with the foundress in that capacity contrasted with that of Ana de Jesús, at least during one unhappy period. Teresa had expressed less than full confidence about Ana in a letter she wrote to María Bautista in 1574 in which she said that she was going to place Ana as the first prioress in Beas:

> I propose Ana de Jesús as prioress, whom we accepted in St. Joseph's of Plasencia. She has been and now is in Salamanca. I can see no other who is adequate for the position. One of the noblewomen founding the house says wonderful things about her saintliness and humility. Both are good qualities. It is important not to choose someone thought to be imperfect, for that house must be the beginning of much good.[65]

Teresa later named Ana de Jesús prioress of the foundation made in Granada on January 20, 1582. A letter that Teresa wrote to her from Burgos on May 30 of the same year reveals that Ana had committed a number of indiscretions, including not complying with the patents for the foundation, requiring more nuns to transfer to Granada from Beas than the resources and space of the house could apparently tolerate, and, most seriously, breaking communication with Teresa and operating on her own. Teresa put the full weight of her authority, that of their provincial (saying, "for everything that has to do with the Discalced sisters I have the support of the Father provincial") and that of God himself in her reproving words to Ana:

> I have given this matter to Our Lord during these days (for I didn't want to respond to the letters hastily), and I find that His Majesty will be served [in what I tell you]; because any type of attachment, even if it is to one's subprioress, is far from the spirit of the Discalced sisters, and it will not ever profit their spirit. God wants his spouses free, clinging only to him. I don't want this house to begin to go the way that Beas went. I will never forget a letter written to me from there, when your reverence left the office [of prioress]. Not even a Calced sister would write such a thing. It is the beginning of factions and

---

[65] "A la Madre María Bautista" in *Obras*, p. 806.

> other unhappy misfortunes . . . This time do not follow your opinion but mine, for charity's sake.[66]

Teresa worried that she had lost connection with the lives of the women at Granada: "I really don't know who [the nuns transferred from Beas to Granada] are, for they have been kept very secret from me and our Father provincial. I never dreamed you would take so many from [Beas]."[67]

In contrast, Teresa trusted María Bautista as an intimate on whom she could rely without thinking. When the foundation was made at Valladolid 1568, Teresa insured that it would conform to the ideals she was implanting by placing two of the first members of St. Joseph's in leadership positions. As has been mentioned, she named Antonia del Espíritu Santo subprioress in 1568. The following year, she replaced her with María Bautista, and in 1571 appointed her second cousin as prioress, a position that the latter held for eight years.[68] Because Teresa often drew on the St. Joseph's community in this way it can be said that the first generation of Discalced Carmelite nuns contributed substantially to the success of the reform among women. Although their roles in it were different from those of male confessors, advisors, superiors and lay financial backers who fostered the initiative, the Discalced women Teresa placed in governance positions were no less important. Teresa relied on her sisters' spiritual integrity and, in some cases, leadership skills. Gerardo de San Juan de la Cruz remarks "María Bautista was among the primitive Discalced nuns possessing the greatest talent and virtue, and greatest ability to lead."[69]

She and María Bautista corresponded frequently. From Teresa's letters it appears that the pair had the habit of writing to each other freely and with affection. When in 1575 Teresa was told that she should find a house and stay put, she wrote María Bautista, saying that, if it came to pass, she would like to end up in Valladolid so that she could be close to her and to Domingo Báñez, with whom she was also fast friends.[70] The extent to which Teresa thought of María Bautista as an extension of herself is visible in a letter written in May of 1574:

> Father Domingo [Báñez] will tell you what is happening [concerning secret support for the Discalced foundations] and about some papers I am sending him. Whatever you write to me do not send it here [to Segovia] but to a certain person . . . Give an important message to Doña María de Samago on my behalf, that in this world we can only trust God . . . . Send a message to the prioress of the Mother of God [a

---

[66] "A la Madre Ana de Jesús" in *Obras*, pp. 1266-7.
[67] "A la Madre Ana de Jesús" in *Obras*, , p. 1267.
[68] Efrén 2.1: 207 and 328.
[69] *Procesos*, 1:37.
[70] "A la Madre María Bautista" in *Obras*, p. 834.

Dominican convent] that thanks to them we are being treated with great charity, and since my eyesight is not good now may she pardon me if I don't write to her. Please care for her health.[71]

She trusted María Bautista's discretion well enough to ask her to write to Bishop Alvaro de Mendoza on her account.[72]

Isabel de Santo Domingo (1538?-1624?)

A native of Ávila, Isabel de Santo Domingo entered the novitiate in St. Joseph's in 1563. She had been under the spiritual guidance of Pedro de Alcántara, who recommended her to Teresa. Isabel made her profession in 1565. A sign of her standing in Teresa's eyes, she served the reform as prioress of the new convent in Toledo for several months in 1569, after a difficult foundation. Isabel also was prioress in several other houses, including a five-year term at Pastrana and sixteen years at Segovia. While Isabel was at Pastrana, Teresa commented to a nobleman that the sisters there "are very good souls who would please you if you could converse with them, especially the prioress."[73] She finally returned to Ávila, where she died at the age of eighty-six.

Isabel met Teresa shortly after the four first novices at St. Joseph's were chosen. The interview occurred in the principal church in Ávila, when Teresa was on leave from Incarnation to care for a relative who was ill (possibly the brother-in-law who bought the house in which St. Joseph's would be established, and whose illness she later remarked miraculously coincided with construction on the house). Isabel testifies that the saint spoke to her openly about the goals that she hoped to accomplish at St. Joseph's, and told her of the ecclesiastical support which the project had then received. She says that Teresa offered her the opportunity to be among the first group of novices but that she entered the following year, after clearing up family matters. Teresa was Isabel's prioress at St. Joseph's for four years. After that they corresponded.[74] Isabel's two depositions in Teresa's beatification hearings are lengthy. The last, made when Isabel was seventy-three, is more self-asserting than most of the other depositions made by women.

Ana de San Bartolomé (1549-1626)

Teresa sought to surround herself with able women in the early years of her reform. She also at times sought to recruit women from the lower economic

---

[71] "A la Madre María Bautista" in *Obras*, pp. 793-4.
[72] "A Don Alvaro de Mendoza" in *Obras*, p. 791.
[73] "A Don Teutonio de Braganza" in *Obras*, p. 791.
[74] *Procesos*, 1:75-102 and 457-518.

reaches of her society. Many conjectures concerning her motives for the gestures are possible. Carmel in Spain certainly needed members of firm commitment at that juncture in its history. Women who were of modest means possibly were seen as having fewer ties of social obligation to complicate their religious life. Bilinkoff furthermore has shown that Teresa came from a city where women of forceful personality were admired if they pursued certain activities. It is possible that the foundress saw that she benefitted from working on a common cause with those whose temperaments were somewhere near the size of her own, and whose attitudes toward possessions would accommodate the poverty she planned for her convents. Whatever Teresa's motives for assembling such a group, Ana de San Bartolomé stands out for her dedication to Teresa and her causes. Facts assembled by the co-authors Efrén de la Madre de Dios and Otger Steggink, and more recently by the co-authors Electa Arenal and Stacey Schlau make it difficult to warm to her, but the lay Carmelite can easily be appreciated. She was her own person. Although rigid and at times short-sighted, she was honest, loyal and committed to God. Teresa valued her highly.

Ana de San Bartolomé's early life has some interesting parallels with that of Mari Díaz, a saintly woman in Ávila whom Teresa once met.[75] Mari Díaz was born into a well-to-do peasant family from Vita, a town outside of Ávila. She refused to marry for religious reasons. When she was around forty, she moved to Ávila because it had more churches and "because she had heard it said that there were sermons in the city of Ávila."[76] Thereafter her devotion, her asceticism and her spiritual teachings attracted admirers. Bilinkoff concludes that respect for her spiritual life allowed Mari Díaz to escape the strictures of her economic class, but it is worth noting that the devout woman's confessors solved the problem of what to do with a woman who chose to live alone to fulfill her religious convictions by sending her to live in Doña Guiomar's household as a servant.[77] Ana de San Bartolomé's life ran parallel to Mari Díaz's at first. She also was the child of a prosperous peasant family living

---

[75] In the late 1550s, Doña Guiomar introduced the peasant woman to the locally revered Franciscan spiritual master Pedro de Alcántara and to the future foundress. The two women conversed about spiritual matters. Bilinkoff translates the following exchange between the two from *Santa Teresa y su tiempo* by Efrén de la Madre de Dios and Otger Steggink (1:356): "Teresa, who often visited the house, once asked the old woman, 'Mother, do you not have a great desire to die?... Because I do, in order to see my [celestial] husband.' The *beata* replied, 'No, daughter, I do not desire to die, but rather to live longer, in order to suffer for Christ, which I won't be able to do after death, and then there will be plenty of time to enjoy Him'" (Bilinkoff, *The Ávila of Saint Teresa*, p. 100).

[76] Quoted in Bilinkoff, *The Ávila of St. Teresa*, p. 98.

[77] Bilinkoff, *The Ávila of Saint Teresa*, pp. 99-100. As Bilinkoff describes them, Mari Díaz's freedoms were proscribed by the desires of members of the comfortable class, who summoned her when they wanted her advice.

in a neighboring town. Like Mari Díaz, she also rejected marriage, opting instead for a religious life, and like Mari Díaz she went to Ávila because of its religious opportunities.

Her writings and comments made about her suggest that Ana de San Bartolomé's life was often fraught with tension. She especially seems to have worried over her strength to endure opposition and her sinfulness. One receives the impression from her autobiography that while she proceeded resolutely throughout her life, Ana was often compelled to muster all of her psychic resources to surmount the obstacles that never ceased to loom. She reports a life of great effort with few quiet interludes.

Ana's fortitude manifested itself in her childhood. She was mistreated more than once, but pursued her own course regardless of what was done to her.[78] When she refused to marry, Ana underwent a long period of disfavor in her family. Her brothers seem to have been particularly rough with her, assigning her manual labor hard even for a man to accomplish: "My brothers threatened me with tests and made me do the work of laborers, carrying things for which a man's strength was needed. The servants in the house said that two of them together couldn't do what I was doing. I laughed, because the weight they asked me to lift was like a straw." She attributes her success at these tasks to divine help: "I was filled with the strength of the Spirit."[79] Feelings ran so high in her family over her insistence on religious life that her brother once drew his sword on her. After years of family squabbles over the matter, Ana triumphed and entered St. Joseph's in Ávila around 1570 or 1571, when she was in her twenties.

Arenal and Schlau report that Ana joined the community of women as a "lay servant nun."[80] The transcriber of her autobiography, Fortunato Antolín, calls her the first Discalced "*freila*, laysister or sister of the white veil."[81] Her monastic role had some similarities to that of *conversi* or laybrothers in Benedictine abbeys in earlier centuries. *Conversi* were usually illiterate peasants who, as Ana did, took vows and joined a monastic community. Where in older monasteries male *conversi* often performed farm work, Carmelite lay, or "*non inclusae*," sisters served in various domestic capacities. If the habits of Carmelite laysisters in the Netherlands in the fifteenth and sixteenth centuries describe those of laysisters in Spain, Ana and other lay women at St. Joseph's went out in pairs, wearing a white cloak, sometimes to visit the sick and at other times on errands. In 1574, the Dutch convent at Vilvoorde depended on

---

[78] Arenal and Schlau, *Untold Sisters*, p. 22.
[79] Ana de San Bartolomé, *Autobiografía* (Madrid: Editorial de Espiritualidad, 1969), p. 33.
[80] Arenal and Schlau, *Untold Sisters*, pp. 22-3.
[81] Fortunato Antolín, Introduction to Ana de San Bartolomé, *Autobiografía*, p. 17.

seven laysisters and seven women servants to aid twenty choir nuns.[82] Teresa's foundations began with fewer women in these supporting roles. Ana often served as a nurse of those who were ill. For a time which Arenal and Schlau have shown was formative in her life, she was Teresa's personal assistant and nurse. She developed a touching preoccupation with Teresa's physical person, worrying deeply during her Mother's infirmities and agonizing when Teresa would not eat, or when there was nothing she could find to give her to eat. After Teresa died, Ana was assigned to Teresa's cousin, María de San Jerónimo, by then a prioress, as a personal assistant. Around the age of fifty-five, she was sent to France to become a prioress herself.

Ana's early vowed life resembled that of Benedictine *conversi* in the important particular of illiteracy. Religious who could read participated fully in all liturgies, a very important part of Carmelite prayer life that is inseparable from personal devotion. Literate community members regularly gathered in the oratory to read or chant the liturgies of the Hours or the Eucharist. *Conversi* said some of their prayers at their work location. Even if she entered the oratory at the usual times, given the fact that she could not read when she entered St. Joseph's, Ana probably gave her praise to God according to the provision of the Carmelite Rule that "Those who do not know how [to read] are to say the *Our Father* twenty-five times for the night offices, except on Sundays and solemnities when we command that the stated number be doubled, so that the *Our Father* be said fifty times. The same prayer is to be said seven times for morning praise."[83]

The pattern of the laywoman's religious life shows that while she did not entirely shed her peasant beginnings, many parts of her life changed. Indeed, in her old age, she must have marveled at how far she had come. She related that she miraculously learned to write in one afternoon, after Teresa remarked that she wished Ana could help her with her correspondence. What Arenal and Schlau report makes one wonder how much of the event could be called a miracle and how much of it was due to Ana's intelligence and iron will:

> Madre Ana was anxious to please, but she insisted that she could
> learn only from Madre Teresa's handwriting. After she refused
> to imitate a sample of an unknown nun's beautiful handwriting,
> Saint Teresa gave her follower two lines in her own handwriting,
> and Madre Ana learned to write that same afternoon.[84]

Ana later reported in her deposition for Teresa's sainthood that that afternoon she composed a letter to send to another community, which suggests that she

---

[82] Staring, "Carmelite Sisters," pp. 60, 76, 77.
[83] Chapter 8, *Rule*.
[84] Arenal and Schlau, *Untold Sisters*, p. 23.

had acquired the ability to read as well as copy in Spanish. Arenal and Schlau indicate that at first she could only take dictation, but six years later she composed a history of the last year of Teresa's life.[85] She wrote her own autobiography between 1615 and 1624.

Literacy continued to be an issue in her life. After she was sent to Paris in 1605 to make a foundation, she was sorely troubled because she could not read the Hours in Latin. She anguished over what her French novices thought of her a Prioress "who could not read the breviary but who was forced to pray it as if she knew it":

> This afflicted me very much. It seemed to be the greatest humiliation that I had had. Everything oppressed me . . . One time I wanted to put the breviary away, and as I was doing this the Lord spoke to me, saying "Don't put it down. Mortify yourself and say what you can. I want it thus." This he said to me in prayer. I took heart at this and did it, and that night after everyone had retired, I spent hours looking at the book, poring over what I was to recite the next day. And what I had prayed in the choir came out well.[86]

Once again Ana's extraordinary will power converged with divine favor to help her overcome an obstacle. Even so, she continued to worry so much about her inability to read her prayers in Latin that she reported saying the breviary in her dreams.

Ana's attachment to Teresa was very strong. (In a foreword to her autobiography, A. Barrientos calls her a "beneficial shadow" of Teresa "who neither wanted nor could separate herself from her."[87]) In the transcript of her testimony on behalf of her Mother's sainthood, it is recorded that the laywoman said simply, "when Mother Teresa of Jesus was separated from her she didn't feel the happiness and consolation that she did when Mother was present." Ana attributed this to the fact that God gave consolations to others through Teresa.[88] She studied the great foundress closely, coming to rather firm conclusions concerning her Mother's intentions. Her clashes with others after Teresa's death often can be traced to her unshakable belief that she (and sometimes only she) knew what the foundress meant the Order to be. The positions she took in these later disagreements suggest that Ana was literalistic, strict, preoccupied with hierarchy and obedience, and, after Teresa's death, especially fixed on the past.

---

[85] Arenal and Schlau, *Untold Sisters*, p. 20.
[86] Ana de San Bartolomé, *Autobiografía*, p. 133.
[87] A. Barrientos, foreword to Ana de San Bartolomé, p. 10.
[88] *Procesos*, 2:168.

One situation in which these responses came into play involved Bl. Ana de Jesús, another close confidante of Teresa, and an important figure in the reform but one who, as has been seen, had had a serious *contretemps* with the foundress. The fledgling Discalced Carmelite reform divided painfully over whether or not women could choose their own confessors, a matter of considerable importance to contemplative prayer. In earlier periods of the order, women had at times enjoyed this privilege.[89] The freedom with which Teresa sought her own confessors must have been well known. One Discalced group, including Juan de la Cruz and Ana de Jesús, took exception to Discalced Superior General Nicolás Doria's modification of the constitution which took that right away. "Although she too had grave doubts about Doria's new Rules [*sic*], Ana de San Bartolomé was equally horrified by the brief [signed by those who were opposed to them] because she saw in it a violation of her Mother's strict emphasis on obedience to one's superiors."[90] Ana de San Bartolomé never relinquished her support of Doria's decision. With extremely few exceptions, once she made a decision she did not change her mind.

She also became increasingly bitter about Ana de Jesús, about whom she had additional complaints. A preoccupation with weakness and strength is suggested by many of the details of Ana's life. One of her greatest complaints about Ana de Jesús was that she was weak for having abandoned foundational work in Brussels. She vigorously opposed efforts to have Ana de Jesús beatified some some thirty years later, saying that she knew no reason why her Discalced sister should be considered for distinction. Ana often thought those with whom she had disagreements were fainthearted, untrustworthy or just plain wrong. Arenal and Schlau record that Ana wrote to Leonor de San Bernardo, "God has given us the gift of being daughters of the Order, for all the rest have turned out a waste."[91] Her judgmental rigidity often visible in the reports of encounters in her later life is somewhat difficult to reconcile with the tenderness she expresses for the sisters in her community when she speaks of them in general and her maternal affection for Teresa of Ávila.

Ana's upbringing perhaps provides clues to inconsistencies in her behavior once she achieved the status of Mother Superior and became involved in new foundations in France and the Low Countries, a period that lasted from about 1602 to 1629. In spite of her apparently strong sense of herself and her literacy in Spanish whose miraculous acquisition in her eyes surely was an indication of divine favor, Ana as a prioress in France stubbornly refused the orders of her male superiors to take the black veil of a choir nun. Even in

---

[89] In Spain, for example, in 1506, the prior general permitted the Carmelite Convent of Valencia to choose its confessor. The Convent of the Incarnation in Ávila enjoyed the privilege at times as well (see Velasco Bayón, *Los carmelitas*, pp. 153 and 158).

[90] Arenal and Schlau, *Untold Sisters*, p. 24.

[91] Arenal and Schlau, *Untold Sisters*, pp. 24-5.

Teresa's more egalitarian convents the veil must have been seen as a symbol of full inclusion into Carmelite life, so Ana was refusing something important when she declined to take it. Teresa herself had asked Ana several times to take the veil, but Ana seems to have wanted to retain the markers and habits of who she had been in the beginning of religious life, a laysister of peasant stock who served the convent domestically. She says that she told Teresa, "I would be unhappy to leave my vocation."[92] In one of the few recorded instances in which she changed her mind, Ana accepted the veil around 1605 under great pressure, which in her report, included nine days of Masses said by a community of Jesuits petitioning God to give Ana light in the matter, an apparition of her Lord telling her to take the veil and the threat of sinning if she didn't. "I finally obeyed," Ana wrote, "my spirit greatly perplexed and not assuring me of anything in the matter."[93]

Teresa had had great appreciation for obedience as a feature of vowed religious life. Those who testified concerning her sainthood indicate that her humble obedience was one of her most visible personal attributes. She left behind in writing an insistence that Carmelite sisters should place their will in the hands of their superiors as part of their spiritual maturation. Ana became a doughty champion of monastic obedience, especially as it was given to male superiors, and continued to battle against the right of nuns to choose their confessors. In conflict with this position, and with perhaps a Spanish peasant's anti-foreigner chauvinism, she fought against Pierre de Bérulle, her superior in France, who sought to institute French confessors in the new Discalced convents there.[94] Ana passionately believed that Bérulle was reneging on an agreement to bring male Carmelites from Spain for the task, and resented the fact that no male Discalced foundations were being made in France. Struggles between the two soon spread to other matters. Characterizing France as a country full of heretics, Ana did not want anyone other than a Spaniard to hear her confession. She complained to her countryman Tomás de Jesús that the French superior was abusing his power and resolutely refused to do what Bérulle and other French "*Prelados*" ordered, recording the confused threat about them in hindsight, "They have done much good in France and God has a crown reserved for them, but they have lost much of the prize because of what they did concerning the governance of the nuns. In this they most surely have erred. It will come to pass soon that they are neither Carmelites nor will things

---

[92] Ana de San Bartolomé, *Autobiografia*, p. 117.

[93] Ana de San Bartolomé, *Autobiografia*, p. 119.

[94] Kavanaugh remarks that hatred of foreigners and suspicion of "those who deviated from the common norm" was endemic in sixteenth-century Spain (Introduction to *The Book of Her Life* in *Collected Works*, 1:25).

remain according to the Rule and Constitutions the way that Holy Mother left them for her daughters."[95]

Ana also had enough courage to speak to Bérulle directly. He was her confessor, a role that could only have amplified the issues of authority in play between the two to an impossible pitch: "Speaking directly to him of his interference with her convent in Paris and of his meanness, she compares him to the devil: . . .'it is not God's way to sow discord among friends, . . . to take to hating me and to afflict me, with no one to shed light on the matter for me is not God, or his way, but quite the contrary.'"[96] Typically, Ana did not resolve the impasse. It mattered less to her that she was, as a religious woman, disobeying a male superior or that her position was in direct conflict with her campaign against allowing women to choose their confessors than it did that she believed she was right. Tomás de Jesús broke the deadlock when he was named Superior General of the Discalced Carmelites in the Low Countries by calling her to Flanders.[97]

Those who pursue spiritual life are never plaster saints, no matter what later hagiography does to them. Ana de San Bartolomé combined a rigorous, often prickly exterior life with an admirable dedication to prayer. She remembers her first vision occurring when she was small enough that she was not yet able to speak. She said that she saw God in his majesty "and that he was the one who would judge me, and I was afraid that I might sin . . . ."[98] The same fear caused her to begin to pray to many saints when she was seven, the age at which her sisters told her that children began to sin. She asked her saints to protect her from sinning and to give her chastity. Fear of God's judgment continued to affect her religious life. Sometime after professing at St. Joseph's Ana had a vision in which Christ angrily prepared to chastise her with switches covered with blood, but was stopped from doing so by the Virgin's entreaties.[99] Her many visions throughout her life inspired fear of sin but also gave her strength to endure. Often they inflamed her love or gave her consolation. Sometimes she seems to have struggled against their content.

If her reporting can be taken literally, she was capable of wrestling even with God when she did not want to do something. When she was unwilling to go to France, her Lord came to her saying, "olives and grapes must pass through the press of martyrdom to offer their liquid."[100] "This awakened new courage in me, for I was downcast, and taking heart, I offered myself again to whatever God wanted of me." The vision would seem to have resolved the

---

[95] Ana de San Bartolomé, *Autobiografia*, p. 162.
[96] Arenal and Schlau, *Untold Sisters*, pp. 25-6.
[97] Arenal and Schlau, *Untold Sisters.*, p. 26.
[98] Ana de San Bartolomé, *Autobiografica*, p. 22.
[99] Ana de San Bartolomé, *Autobiografica*, p. 96.
[100] Ana de San Bartolomé, *Autobiografica*, p. 111.

question of whether or not she would go to France, but "[a]nother day after communion I was thinking of something a priest had said to me, that perhaps it was neither good nor necessary for nuns to go to France, among so many heretics, without being able to preach to them, and I concluded that this was true. And the Lord appeared to me and said 'Don't involve yourself in that. You will attract souls just as flies are drawn to a honeycomb.'"[101] This did not resolve the question either. "God made war on me, showing me how to be faithful to him and to do what I had promised him at other times. The interior and exterior struggle was no small cross." God appeared to her a fourth time, this time directly commanding: "Do not fail to go, for if you don't go nothing will be done there, for all the rest will return once they arrive."[102] This is not the only time in her life that Ana reports having struggled with what her visions told her to do. As she reports them in her autobiography, she did not resolve these dilemmas by accepting the opinions of other humans, and several times disobeyed her confessors. Her habit of reserving final decision making to herself left her at these times in the painful situation of having no outside reference point to help her decide how comply with what she believed was divine communication.

Although worry and struggle are often present in her reports of the circumstance of her special spiritual experiences, Ana also wrote of interior experiences of love and mercy. One of the most loving visions she reports involved her dear Mother Teresa after the latter's death:

> Our Holy Mother appeared to me as if alive, showing me grace and love. This happened three times. And wanting to awaken from the ecstasy I was in, I opened my eyes and there she was, and she embraced me, and I her. She remained with me awhile and then disappeared."[103]

Teresa's supernatural care of Ana in visions such as this one extended the spiritual guidance the foundress gave her when they lived together at St. Joseph's in Ávila or traveled to found new convents. Gathered together, the details concerning Teresa's earthly interaction with Ana on spiritual matters open a further vista on the saint's ways of being.

While alive, Teresa seems to have guided the laywoman gently but firmly away from excesses. One Good Friday, wishing to humble herself, Ana was moved to try to have someone slap her as Jesus had been buffeted during the Passion. She told an errand boy at St. Joseph's that she was a woman of ill repute, and that he should have one of the nearby workmen hit her, which he

---

[101] Ana de San Bartolomé, *Autobiografica*, p. 112.

[102] Ana de San Bartolomé, *Autobiografica*, p. 114.

[103] Ana de San Bartolomé, *Autobiografica*, pp. 180-1.

did. Ana's confessor severely chastised her for what he saw as stupidity, as he had at other times. Teresa, however, said nothing to her, but required that henceforth no member of the house should go to the door alone.[104] On another occasion she consoled the laywoman that her frequent ecstasies were usual in a beginner, and once told her it was no sin to stop praying in order to go to sleep at the ordinary time, words of a mother guiding a child. Once Ana had a dream of being in purgatory, submerged in a painful river of fire before Christ her judge. When she told her dream to Teresa, the latter simply said, "Oh, daughter, you won't go to purgatory." Ana almost never disagreed with Teresa, but this time decided that her Mother was joking with her: "I think I will be in purgatory a long time, and that God in his mercy will put me there and not somewhere worse, for the life that I've lived."[105]

Ana of San Bartolomé was a very obviously human counterpoint in Teresa's life to the Virgin Mary. Her religious horizon was often occupied with fear, rules and judgment of others. She was particularly limited in her ability to come to sound conclusions about spiritual matters. She seemed to prefer to be what she had been when she entered Carmel, a laysister dedicated to nursing and domestic work. In a particularly poignant interlude, she once was criticized while in France for the way she was handling the sisters under her. Although prioress, she abandoned (or was taken out of) her administrative duties, busied herself with menial tasks, and only resumed the role of prioress in the oratory. Regardless of her frailties, Ana's touching love for Teresa, her will to continue to try do to what she understood was right and her commitment to the reform more than earn her a place in history as a companion-in-arms of the foundress. Teresa's treatment of her suggests how wise and gentle the foundress was with her sisters.

In Summary

In her insightful study of the stereotypes and politics of Ávila, the city in which Teresa was raised and began her reform, Jodi Bilinkoff remarks that certain of Teresa's actions were motivated by her understanding that the ties that bound her and her sisters to their larger culture were very strong indeed, but needed to be severed if a life truly dedicated to Christ were to be accomplished:

> For Teresa, the key to the proper observance of the religious life lay in one's total indifference to the things of this world. She recognized that for many the most difficult aspect of "detachment" (*desasimiento*) involved severing ties with family members. In a society in which the concerns of kin and dynasty played a ubiquitous role in an individual's

---

[104] Ana de San Bartolomé, *Autobiografica*, pp. 44-5.
[105] Ana de San Bartolomé, *Autobiografica*, p. 94.

existence and even identity, this was a genuine sacrifice. After her conversion, Teresa, who herself shared strong bonds of affection with her numerous relatives, bitterly criticized the pervasive obsession with lineage. Her position as conversa may well have partly inspired her strong preference for merit above pedigree.[106]

At issue in Bilinkoff's remarks are two identities: the identity constructed by one's upbringing, with its tissue of obligatory social interactions, and the identity of the enclosed nun, which this study hopefully has suggested has its own characteristic ties with others. "Total indifference to things of this world" involved a transformation of human relationships for Teresa and her sisters, certainly not an abandonment of them. Substitution of contact with one's family of origin, neighbors and friends with contact with religious of one's own gender, and especially with those dedicated to one's own spiritual goals, meant that Teresa and her Discalced sisters could shape each other's ways of being and, to some degree, live as one.

Examining details concerning women living in her immediate vicinity confirms some generalizations made about Teresa of Ávila in the past and inspires new thoughts about her. Details of her interactions with her intimate Carmelite companions once again show that Teresa was a remarkable woman, not only for the depth of her personal prayer life but for her ability to open it out to others. Humility and obedience, qualities that Gillian Ahlgren has noted were believed to be especially female virtues, seem, in these reported relationships, more shared qualities that bound women to each other than ones reinforcing hierarchical separations then usual between men and women. As Alison Weber has shown, Teresa was strongly pressed by male suspicion of women's reports of spiritual favors to demonstrate that she was humble by remaining mute about her spiritual life, a problem that Weber says she addressed by developing a complex rhetoric.[107] Weber also has insightfully noted the distinctions Teresa drew between true humility and the false humilities of trying too hard to please authorities, abandoning virtuous effort due to lack of self-confidence, or accepting inaccurate assessments of oneself.[108] Teresa often exemplified true humility among her sisters. Able to shift her words and actions up and down a range of social registers according to whom she contacted, Teresa was most herself and most at home in unpretentious communion with Discalced women. She often wrote to her nuns that true spiritual humility was a divine state of communion which, far from weakening the spiritual person, drew her into the core of Jesus' identity in relationship to

---

[106] Bilinkoff, *The Ávila of St. Teresa*, p.128.
[107] Weber, *Teresa*, 47-8.
[108] Weber, *Teresa*, 72-5.

his Father, and far from impoverishing the person, filled her with gifts to give others.

Teresa's spiritual identity most resided in her love of Christ and God but also partially resided in the lives of particular women whose company she sought and kept. This fact has up to the present been somewhat overlooked. Even in strongly patriarchal networks such as the Church in sixteenth-century Spain most certainly was, women are never only the sum of their responses to male influences. Teresa and her sisters gave and received, inspired and imitated each other. Like the composer of a symphony or a general, the foundress was able to draw able women companions around her, teach them, send them forth and, remarkably, continue to convey her ways of being to them over great distance. This she did through many letters, but also through placing trusted women companions in varying connections to her and to each other. She also drew inspiration and consolation from these companions.

The upsetting events in Granada that involved Ana de Jesús occurred in the last year of Teresa's life. The foundress' passionate care for the nuns who were being crowded together at Granada and shuttled from Beas to the new foundation, disturbing their spiritual life unnecessarily, is obvious in the letter she wrote to Ana de Jesús. She penned it when she was sixty-seven, weakened by ill health and the rigors of travel, and mere days after enduring a terrible flood in Burgos that nearly brought down the building in which she and her nuns had huddled. One has a sense on reading the 1562 letter of overhearing the words of a spiritual chieftain—the term, "mother" is better, if it is given nuances of capability and courage—mustering strength once again to rally the followers in whose life she partially lived her own. Like Jesus in the Gospels or like the Virgin Mary in her Order's iconography, the affectionate spiritual leader cared about the chicks under her wings. The chicks also cared for their mother, living in her, as well.

8 Demonizing Ecstasy: Alonso de la Fuente and the *Alumbrados* of Extremadura

Alison Weber

> They indulged in all kinds of ferocious concupiscence and impure acts which I will not relate to avoid offending the ears of my readers, if only for reasons of aesthetics and good taste.
>
> Marcelino Menéndez Pelayo[1]

There is perhaps no more confusing term in Spanish historiography than *alumbradismo*. It has been used to designate evangelicals with vaguely protestant leanings, eucharistic enthusiasts, contemplatives, orgiasts, religious hypocrites, and deluded visionaries and stigmatics.[2] Although in the sixteenth and seventeenth centuries the Inquisition made several attempts to find a common thread that might link divergent manifestations of heterodox behavior into an over-arching heresy, *alumbradismo* remained a widely used but inconsistently defined appellation for a variety of suspect religious practices and beliefs.[3]

Nonetheless, it is generally accepted that the earliest manifestation of *alumbradismo* in the sixteenth century differed fundamentally from the "outbreaks" later in the century. The first group designated *alumbrados* was active in the region around Toledo in the 1520s. The Inquisition's 1525 edict of

---

[1] Marcelino Meníndez Pelayo, *Historia de los heterodoxos españoles*, vol. 4, *Sectas místicas. Alumbrados. Quietistas. Miguel de Molinos. Embustes y milagrerías* (1880-1882; rpt. Mexico City: Porría, 1982), p. 322. All translations from the Spanish are my own.

[2] Spain's most famous sixteenth-century saints—Ignacio de Loyola, Teresa of Ávila, and Juan de la Cruz—were at various times accused of *alumbradismo* because of their practice of contemplative prayer.

[3] On the indiscriminate use of the term, see José Luis Sánchez Lora, *Mujeres, conventos y formas de la religiosidad barroca* (Madrid: Fundación Universitaria Española, 1988), p. 349. *Alumbradismo* is sometimes translated as "Illuminism" in English; however, I have retained the Spanish term to avoid the implication of connections with earlier mystical sects.

condemnation focused largely on such "protestant" errors as disdain for ceremonies and sacraments and the belief in divine inspiration from reading the Scriptures. By 1579, however, a list of *alumbrado* errors drawn up for an *auto de fe* celebrated in Extremadura emphasized primarily irregularities in eucharistic or confessional practices, and sexual activity between priests and penitents.[4] Although the early Toledo *alumbrados* have been the subject of revisionist studies, scholars have assumed that the later group, the *alumbrados* of Llerena, Extremadura, were indeed an orgiastic sect of licentious priests and their female devotees. In other words, we are still reading the story of the Llerena *alumbrados* in the terms defined by the nineteenth-century historian Marcelino Menéndez y Pelayo in his influential *Historia de los heterodoxos*—as a particularly embarrassing chapter in Spanish religious history, of prurient interest at best.[5]

This essay will explore how Alonso de la Fuente, the Dominican friar who claimed he had discovered the Llerena *alumbrados*, came to define,

---

[4] For the history of the Toledo *alumbrados*, see Antonio Márquez, *Los alumbrados. Orígenes y filosofía, 1525-1559*, rev. ed. (Madrid: Taurus, 1980). Although the 1525 edict on *alumbradismo* errors makes no charges of sexual activity among the alumbrados, Francisca Hernández, an estranged associate of the Toledo *alumbrados*, was twice arrested and charged with scandalous relationships with her male devotees. See Mary E. Giles, "Francisca Hernández and the Sexuality of Religious Dissent," in *Women in the Inquisition. Spain and the New World*, ed. Mary E. Giles (Baltimore: Johns Hopkins, 1999), pp. 75-97. The degree to which the Toledo *alumbrados* represent a native protestant movement is still a matter of debate among modern historians. See Melquíades Andrés, "Alumbrados, erasmistas, 'luteranos' y místicos, y su común denominador: el riesgo de una espiritualidad más 'intimista,'" *Inquisición Española y mentalidad inquisitorial*, ed. Angel Alcalá et al. (Barcelona: Ariel, 1984), pp. 373-409. Alastair Hamilton, in *Heresy and Mysticism in Sixteenth-Century Spain* (Toronto: University of Toronto Press, 1992), examines various manifestations of *alumbradismo* within the context of variations of orthodox and heterodox mysticism. Alvaro Huerga has transcribed key documents from late sixteenth- and seventeenth-century cases in his massive *Historia de los Alumbrados (1570-1630)*, 5 vols. (Madrid: Fundación Universitaria Española, 1978-1994).

[5] Menéndez y Pelayo's fascinated abhorrence with the *alumbrados* deserves a study of its own. Although he expresses distaste for Fray Alonso's rhetoric, his own language is at times as unbridled as the Dominican's: "The name of sect or heresy seems too mild for such a band of villains, who really only wanted to wallow in pleasure like brute beasts" (*Historia de los heterodoxos* 4: 322). Similarly, the Jesuit historian Bernardino Llorca concedes that La Fuente may have exaggerated the dangers of the *alumbrados* of Llerena, but does not doubt the reality of their "perversions"; *La inquisición Española y los alumbrados (1509-1667)*, rev. ed. (Salamanca: Universidad Pontificia, 1980), esp. pp. 108 and 120. The view that the *alumbrados* of Extremadura engaged in lascivious acts is also shared by Alvaro Huerga and most recently by Alastair Hamilton. María Palacios Alcalde, without commenting directing on the *alumbradas* of Extremadura, proposes that the *beatas* of the late sixteenth century fell into a kind of sexual decadence characterized by "sexual self-satisfaction, either through masturbation or intense imagining of sexual encounters, leading to the somatic experience of orgasm"; "Las beatas ante la Inquisición," *Hispania Sacra* 40 (1988): 107-31.

propagandize, and adapt his own version of the *alumbrado* heresy. As we shall see, his conception was a dynamic one. Furthermore, the list of heresies and errors he originally communicated to the Inquisition does not in the end coincide with the one the Inquisition applied in the *auto de fe* of 1579. Eventually, his persecutory zeal and over-reaching definition of heresy would bring about his downfall. The story of the rise and fall of this inquisitorial preacher not only allows us to follow the process by which the Inquisition fashioned its notions of heresy, it also illustrates the ambivalence of the sixteenth-century Spanish church toward religious ecstasy. This area of inquiry has been been charted, more than any other scholar, by Mary E. Giles, who has eloquently argued for a more sympathetic and nuanced reading of the embodied "texts" of women's religious experience.[6]

In the 1560s, Extremadura and western Andalucia had proven to be fertile ground for various movements of lay piety. The teachings of the reformer Juan de Ávila had attracted a school of followers at the University of Baeza. Luis de Granada, the author of the extraordinarily popular guidebook to contemplative prayer, *Libro de la oración*, and many Jesuits had been actively preaching in the region. Two successive bishops of Badajoz were supporters of *beatas*, lay women who dedicated their lives to prayer and pious works. But by 1570, Juan de Ávila was dead, Luis de Granada had moved to Portugal, and the pro-*beata* bishops of Badajoz had been replaced.[7] It was at this time that Fray Alonso de la Fuente discovered what he believed to be a secret, deceptively pious, demonic sect.

His own account of the history of his discovery is preserved in a report he submitted to King Philip II on December 17, 1575. Fray Alonso recounts that at the end of 1570, he had been assigned to preach in his home town of La Fuente el Maestre. Here he found that a Theatine priest, Gaspar Sánchez, had gathered around him a group of pious female disciples. The devotees, whom Alonso called alternately *teatinas* and *beatas*, included married and unmarried

---

[6] See, for example, Mary E. Giles, *The Book of Prayer of Sor María of Santo Domingo: A Study and Translation* (Albany: State University of New York Press, 1990); Mary E. Giles, "The Discourse of Ecstasy: Late Medieval Spanish Women and Their Texts," in *Gender and Text in the Later Middle Ages*, ed. Jance Chance (Gainesville: University Press of Florida, 1996), pp. 306-30; and Giles, "Introduction," *Women in the Inquisition*, pp. 9-15.

[7] According to Luis Sala Balust, Juan de Ávila was alarmed over the Eucharistic enthusiasm of some of his followers in Extremadura, and warned them against the dangers of seeking out "sensible sweetness" in their devotions. See Sala Balust, "En torno al grupo de alumbrados de Llerena," in *Miscelanea Beltrán de Heredia* (Salamanca: Universidad de Salamanca, 1972), 3: pp. 509-23, quotation at pp. 512-13. The bishops who protected *beatas* were Cristóbal de Rojas and Juan de Ribera. In 1568, Ribera moved to Valencia, where, as archbishop, he continued to be a devotee of visionary women. On Ribera, see Benjamin A. Ehlers, "La esclava y el patriarca: las visiones de Catalina Muñoz en la Valencia de Juan de Ribera," *Estudis* 23 (1997): 101-16.

women, and widows, some of them slaves.[8] Fray Alonso's initial impression of Sánchez's coterie was favorable, but gradually the women began to confide in him that they practiced "contemplation" or mental prayer, and that during prayer they had experienced raptures. As he informed the king:

> This news [of contemplative prayer] offended me more than the news of the raptures, because there was among these women such ignorance of the law of God that they scarcely knew the common prayers of the church, and being subjects of this sort, they had all at once ascended to divine contemplation. I advised them, then, that they not practice contemplation, because they would be lost. They did not take this advice, but rather in my absence mocked and derided me.[9]

Preaching in Badajoz, Alonso heard stories of "devout men" who had "captivated maidens, caused married couples to separate, went into ecstasy and shouted and bellowed in church, clenched their teeth during communion, swore obedience to their teachers, hoisted the banner of their own sanctity and held all others to be sinners" (*Extremadura*, 332). On his return to La Fuente el Maestre, he found that one of his own nieces had become a *beata*: "I was astonished to see that a girl of sixteen years had suddenly cut off her hair, changed her style of dress and given up . . . ordinary behavior and conversation, so changed in appearance, yellow-skinned, dirty, thin, moaning, sighing, with bowed head" (*Extremadura*, 332). Fray Alonso recounts that when he gently persuaded his niece to tell him the effects of her method of prayer, he learned that it evoked in the girl "bad thoughts, filthy ideas, carnal impulses, . . . heresies, blasphemies against God, the saints, . . . and she endured all in

---

[8] *Beatas* in Spain were generally lower-class unmarried women or widows who, like beguines or members of third orders, took vows of chastity and wore religious habits but rarely followed the rule of any religious order. For discussion of *beatas* in early modern Spain, see Claire Guilhem, "La inquisición y la devaluacón del verbo femenino," *Inquisición Española: Poder político y control social*, ed. Bartolomé Bennassar et al., trans. Javier Alfaya (Barcelona: Crítica, 1984), pp. 171-207; Mary Elizabeth Perry, "Beatas and the Inquisition in Early Modern Seville," in *Inquisition and Society in Early Modern Europe*, ed. Stephen Haliczer (London and Sydney: Croom Helm, 1987), pp. 147-68; Mary Elizabeth Perry, *Gender and Disorder in Early Modern Seville* (Princeton: Princeton University Press, 1990); and Carmelo Lisón Tolosana, *Demonios y exorcismos en los siglos de oro* (Madrid: Akal, 1990), especially chapter 2, "Beatos y demonios." On the imprecise use of the term "Theatine" in sixteenth-century Spain to refer to Jesuits as well as advocates of lay piety in general, see A. D. Wright, *Catholicism and Spanish Society under the Reign of Philip II, 1555-1598, and Philip III, 1598-1621* (Lewiston, New York: Edwin Mellen Press, 1991), p. 164.

[9] Alvaro Huerga, *Historia de los Alumbrados*, vol. 1, *Los alumbrados de Extremadura (1570-1582)*, p. 331. All citations to Alonso's report to Philip II as well as inquisitorial documents related to the Llerena *alumbrados* are from his edition, cited hereafter as *Extremadura*.

patience, because her master told her that all that was a sign of perfection and the sure path to improvement" (*Extremadura*, 333). The Dominican concludes, "I did not need more information to convince me that there was the devil and a pact with Satan in that doctrine" (*Extremadura*, 333).

In Talaveruela, three leagues from Badajoz, he discovered another "flock" and "new rites" associated with the doctrine, in particular "great idleness": "Many of them had completely given up bodily work and passed the entire day in contemplation and at night asked God to sustain their bodies" (*Extremadura*, 334). Alonso was also disturbed by the eucharistic enthusiasm of the *teatinas*. One Mari Sánchez took communion every day, "for she had such hunger for the Host that on the days she did not take communion she took to bed ill and moaned and suffered cruel torments and acted like a woman afflicted with rabies, so much so that she amazed not only the simple people, but confused wise religious men" (*Extremadura*, 335). One day, just after Fray Alonso was finishing a sermon on the errors of the *beatas*, she rushed toward the stairs leading to the pulpit and "instantly" climbed it. Such dexterity, Fray Alonso deduced, "obviously was a work of Satan, since the stairs to the pulpit were very steep and one of the steps was broken, but she climbed with as much speed and agility as a cat" (*Extremadura*,336). From the pulpit, the enraged *beata* brandished a cross, broken in the rush up the stairs, and shouted to Fray Alonso, "Come back, you silly pedant."[10] "The justices of the peace," the friar relates, "tried to drag her down from the pulpit, but she offered such strong and powerful resistance that it was necessary for them to grab her shameful parts to make her come down, and in this way she gave up and they carried her down in a very unchaste way, upside down, with her legs in the air and her bare skin exposed" (*Extremadura*, 336). The town, however, did not unanimously share Alonso's interpretation of the events. In fact, a priest defended Mari Sánchez and argued that her remarkable agility and strength in pulpit were signs not of demonic but of divine assistance.[11]

Alonso continued to visit the towns of the region of Badajoz, preaching and collecting information on the *beatas*. He encountered a woman who had corporeal visions of Christ in the manger: one day she went into ecstasy in his presence and reported, upon regaining normal consciousness, that she had seen the riches of heaven and heard celestial music. One of the friars of his order remarked that the phenomenon he described was very similar to that of the

---

[10] In Spanish, she uses a derogatory diminutive: "¡Venid acá, bachillerejo!"

[11] As Alonso makes clear in section XLII of his report to Philip, he believed the *alumbrados* were not simply "possessed" (*endemoniados*), but had willingly entered into demonic pacts—a crucial legal distinction, since the possession could elicit compassionate treatment, whereas witchcraft was considered heretical. Alonso, significantly, declares no sympathy for a Sevillian *alumbrado* who "pretend[ed] to be possessed in order to flee . . . the blows of the Inquisition" (*Extremadura*, p. 371).

alumbrados of Toledo. At this point, fourteen months after his initial discovery, Alonso decided it was time to send a report to the Inquisition denouncing a new outbreak of *alumbradismo*.[12]

Much to Alonso's disappointment, the first report made little impression on the provincial inquisitors of Llerena "because in truth it contained things that were very new, obscure and never before seen by the Inquisition, and there was nothing clear that could be seized upon" (*Extremadura*, 341). The reaction to his subsequent reports was even more discouraging: "I was shocked to see what little effect my reports caused, since in them I had depicted the heresy, to my mind, as plain and clear as day, and this is why I made so much noise and was so importunate in this matter. I really saw the heresy clearly and openly, and I could not show it to the Holy Office nor could I make anyone see it, so much so that many times, I had doubts and feared that the evil spirit had deceived me" (*Extremadura*, 341).

Worse still, Alonso found himself the target of mockery: "One of the means the *alumbrados* had to discredit what I preached was to see the little effect I had on the Inquisition. They mocked me, seeing me coming and going from the Holy Office, and said that the inquisitors laughed at my reports and charges. And they were right . . . for when I presented a new report, which was very well written and stated very clearly the evil of this heresy, a secretary [of the Holy Office] laughed and mocked me saying that was of no importance" (*Extremadura*, 341). Rumors spread in the region that Alonso was "raving mad."[13] Sometime after Ascension Sunday of 1572, Alonso and another Dominican were reprimanded by the Holy Office and prohibited from making specific charges of heresy against specific persons. Alonso's *per diem* allowance for expenses was cut; the prior of his monastery turned against him and forbade him to preach in Fuente de Cantos, an order which nevertheless was overturned by the Inquisition (*Extremadura*, 346).

Meanwhile, Alonso expanded his list of the sect's social ills, errors and heresies: married women were lured away from their husbands, and daughters from their parents' homes; vocal prayer and the recitation of the rosary were rejected; priests attracted adherents through sorcery; mental prayer was a form of witchcraft invoking Satan; the ecstasies it produced were operations of the Antichrist (348).

---

[12] In a letter dated April 21, 1573, the Llerena tribunal reports to the Suprema in Madrid having received news of "a certain doctrine called 'de alumbrados'" in the area. AHN, Inq. Libro 578, f 82v.

[13] "Hombre loco y desvariado" (*Extremadura*, p. 342).

At this point, some of those he had attacked sought and found protection under the Archbishop of Seville and the Bishop of Badajoz.[14] The Discalced Franciscans, whom Alonso had also targeted as *alumbrados*, drew up a list of counter-charges: that Fray Alonso attempted to discourage women from partaking in the sacraments, that he condemned frequent confession and criticized the state of virginity (349).[15] The friar felt he was losing ground; many of the women he had converted returned to their confessors.

In spring of 1574 the Supreme Council of the Holy Office finally summoned Fray Alonso to Madrid, where he won over at least one member of the Council, the prosecutor Juan López de Montoya. The rest of the inquisitors, inexperienced neophytes "with fuzz on their cheeks," according to Alonso (362), were indifferent to his charges. Nonetheless, an order for Montoya to accompany Alonso to Extremadura was issued on June 28, 1574.[16]

Alonso returned to Extremadura to prepare the way for the Inquisitorial visit. He was reluctant to preach in Zafra, a town (at least according to Alonso) with a large *converso* population: "there are almost seventy priests, and sixty of them Jews" (*Extremadura*, 363).[17] There he began to preach on what he now believed to be "the heart" of the heresy: "how the *alumbrados* invoked the devil and passed him off as the Holy Spirit, how they robbed their confessional daughters of their inheritance and their honor, and *became lords of their bodies*, how they used magic to go into ecstasies, and how Satan showed them visions and revelations" (*Extremadura*, 365, my emphasis).

The Inquisitorial visit was initiated on July 28, 1574 with a public reading of the *edicto de la fe*, a list of heretical beliefs or practices, followed by exhortation to the faithful to report whether they knew of anyone, living or dead, guilty of such errors. Most of the errors of this edict recall the 1525 edict against the *alumbrados* of Toledo: disdain for oral prayer and exclusive dedication to mental prayer, rejection of the monastic vocation, confidence in having achieved a state of Grace, and "*dejamiento*" or passive surrender to God's will. Also of evident concern was the social and economic control the "masters of the doctrine" exerted over their devotees, who were said to cut

---

[14] Alonso complains that a bad precedent had been set by Don Juan de Ribera, the Bishop of Badajoz and Archbishop of Valencia, who gave alms, stipends (*salarios*) and other presents to those who experienced ecstasies and stigmata (*Extremadura*, p. 355).

[15] Frequent and daily communion was a topic of intense theological debate in sixteenth-century Spain. See Julión Zarco Cuevas, *Espala y la comunión frecuente y diaria en los siglos XVI y XVII* (El Escorial, 1912).

[16] *Extremadura*, p. 145.

[17] Although Alonso may have exaggerated the number of priests in Zafra who were *conversos* (descendants of converts from Judaism), they did in fact play an important role in pietistic movements inspired by Juan de Ávila. The fact that the Dominican refers to them as "Jews" indicates that he shared the racialist suspicions and prejudices of many Spaniards of this period regarding the piety of *conversos*.

their hair, reject marriage, and refrain from their labors out of sworn obedience to their confessors.[18] Novel eucharistic practices—such as receiving many forms during Communion or closing the eyes when the Host is elevated—are cited. Finally, the faithful are exhorted to report if they know of persons who secretly promise that the said practices will allow then to "see, taste and feel marvelous things."[19]

Surprisingly, the edict makes no mention of the visions or demonic sexuality that Fray Alonso claims to have discovered, but rather refers in much less precise terms to the belief that "certain burning, trembling, pain and swoons that they suffer are signs of the love of God" (*Extremadura*, 149). Although it is possible that the friar misrepresented the chronology of his allegations later in his report to Philip, it seems more likely that the edict represents the *Suprema*'s selective interpretation of Alonso's reports at that date. In other words, as Montoya began his visit, the *Suprema* was concerned primarily with vaguely protestant anti-ceremonialism and disturbances in traditional clerical and gender hierarchies; it had chosen to ignore Alonso's theory of a demonic heresy.

Initially, Montoya found nothing to condemn, a fact which dismayed Fray Alonso, who reconstructs the events in his report to Philip as follows:

> The only thing that could be discovered in said doctrine was fasting and discipline, prayer, contemplation, hair shirts, confessions, frequent communion, and if any grain of the bad and suspect doctrine was discovered, it was so veiled and confused with the language of God and the sacraments, and it did not stand out nor was the bad apparent as it was so much wrapped up in the good. And therefore many times I saw that the Inquisitor [Montoya] was sad and disconsolate and fearful, and he didn't know what to do, because all that was written of the *alumbrados* were holy and blessed things (*Extremadura*, 368).[20]

---

[18] The social insubordination caused by the *alumbrados* was a theme Alonso returned to repeatedly. In 1576 he wrote to the Portuguese inquisitor: "[They are] thieving wolves in sheep skins who usurp the obedience owed to the elders"; "even if their disciples are poor, busy women subject to their fathers and husbands, they are made to put aside all their obligations in order to dedicate two hours a day to contemplation" (*Extremadura*, pp. 411, 412).

[19] Archivo Histórico Nacional, Sección Inquisición (hereafter AHN, Inq.) libro 578, ff. 235v-236r. Huerga transcribes the text of the 1574 Edict in *Historia de los Alumbrados*, 1:148-9 (this citation at p. 149). Huerga also transcribes selections from the correspondence between the Llerena tribunal and the Suprema. In cases where I have verified his transcriptions, I provide the AHN document location, followed by the reference to Huerga's citation. AHN references without citation to Huerga refer to documents not included in *Historia de los alumbrados*.

[20] Fray Alonso uses the plural "confesiones" and "comuniones" which I take to mean frequent confession and communion.

In this time of need, the Dominican continues, "the usefulness of preaching became evident." Aided by a Franciscan friar,[21] he began to exhort the people to tell what they knew to the Inquisition:

> And coming down in particular on the many dirty and shameful sins, we put it to their conscience that they reveal all, since they would greatly aid in the direct knowledge of this new heresy. This was marvelous advice and necessary at such a time: to investigate the life and doctrine, because one was revealed through the other; and there were in this sect such obscure things, so difficult to understand, that *if they were not joined with the bad deeds*, it could not be known if it was God or the devil. And thus the Inquisitor [Montoya], very discretely, gradually combined the one with the other, and it turned out so well: . . . because seeing raptures and visions and stigmata, no one dared to condemn it as evil; but looking into the life and conversation of those who felt said effects, it became as clear as day that everything was . . . the work of Satan. (*Extremadura*, 368, my emphasis)

By the end of the summer of 1574, the sermons which included specific allegations of sexual misconduct and financial malfeasance were beginning to produce the desired results. As Fray Alonso's proclaims the triumphs that summer: "I alone and without company to help me, with only the virtue of my preaching, and although many giants turned against me—the *alumbrados*, the priests, the prelates and all those deemed saintly . . .—they could not resist me nor silence me, nor did they have strength against me, but rather they fell confounded and shamed and struck down by the hand of God" (*Extremadura*, 366). Alonso's estimation of the beneficial effects of preaching was probably accurate. It must be remembered that edicts of faith entailed punishments (fines or flogging) for failure to delate the publicized offenses. There was thus considerable pressure to comply with the exhortations of the edicts. But the inhabitants of the small towns in Extremadura may have been perplexed over the initial edict's emphasis on heretical "dejamiento" and had even less comprehension of what constituted "heterodox" Eucharistic piety. "Bad deeds" of a sexual nature or disobedience to one's parents must have constituted much less ambiguous categories for deviance. Alonso's preaching may well have provided clear and specific suggestions of what was expected in denunciations. It was only after an extensive preaching campaign in which, as Alonso himself admits, he and his colleague came down "in particular on the many dirty and shameful sins" that many came forward to denounce the abominations of the *beatas* and their confessors. Although the three most prestigious priests and two female leaders had been held in preventative detention since the end of

---

[21] Alonso does not name this Franciscan collaborator, a fact that suggests he may have been attempting to take sole credit for the discovery of a "new heresy."

1573,[22] a cascade of imprisonments followed the preaching campaign of the summer of 1574.[23]

Significantly, the list of questions to be put to prisoners makes no mention of demonic pacts; the emphasis is on specific carnal acts between the women and their confessors. Although Alonso is silent on the subject, we know from correspondence from the Suprema that the prisoners were subjected to torture. After torture, Crisbobal Chamizo, considered to be the "head of the sect" along with Alvarez, admitted to "deflowering many *beatas*, his penitential daughters, telling them that it was no sin to kiss, embrace and fondle them." Hernando Alvarez, having confessed to "kisses and lascivious fondling", endured five turns of the *cordel* and a round of water torture before the ordinary intervened because of the prisoner's advanced age and swollen legs.[24] Three turns of the rope and subjection to the rack did not, however, induce further confessions.[25] Fray Pedro de Santa María, aged sixty-three, persistently denied the accusations against him; he was spared torture because of his age and infirmity. Although Inquisitorial procedures expressly forbade repeated torture, a session could be "interrupted" and resumed at a further date. This appears to have been the case with Chamizo. In a letter dated July 7, 1577, the Suprema asks for clarification on the amount of water he was forced to drink during the *toca* or water torture, and advises waiting until he had regained his health before submitting him to "the complete torture."[26]

The *beatas* were tortured as well—the fifty-year-old widow Mari González endured the rack. Mari Sánchez, the woman who had interrupted Fray Alonso's sermon, proved to be the most obstinate of the *beatas*:

> She confessed some things and denied others; she was tortured regarding what she had testified, and she resisted; she proved to be hard, proud and presumptuous, regarding herself as perfect and

---

[22] *Extremadura*, p. 243

[23] AHN, Inq., libro 578, f. 207v, 208r.

[24] Relación de 1579, AHN, Inq., leg. 1988. Cited by Huerga, *Extremadura*, p. 495. The inquisitors reported to the Suprema in 1579 that all the clergy arrested for *alumbradismo* had been tortured and failed to confess, "though it must be said that since several of them are very old and also ill and infirm from their long confinement, it has not been possible to torture them with the required rigour" (cited by Henry Kamen, *Inquisition and Society in Spain in the Sixteenth and Seventeenth Centuries* (Bloomington, Indiana: Indiana University Press, 1985), p. 176.

[25] *Extremadura*, p. 497. Chamizo also apparently suffered from ill health.

[26] AHN, Inq., Libro 579, f. 86v. Correspondence from the Suprema authorized new rounds of torture in 1578 and 1579, in preparation for the *auto de fe* (AHN, Inq. libro 578, 184 r, and libro 579, 99r, 205v). For discussion of the Inquisition's regulations regarding torture, see Bartolomé Bennassar, "La Inquisición o la pedagogía del miedo," in *Inquisición Española: Poder político y control social*, pp. 94-125.

saintly, and she abused the ministers of the Holy Office in word and deed and shouted in her cell, for which she was flogged.[27]

The first confessions of sexual misconduct were obtained around August of 1575,[28] but it was not until 1579 that the *auto de fe* took place in Llerena. Nine women and ten men were tried and penanced as *alumbrados*. For the women, the average sentence was one hundred lashes and two to three years' reclusion. Mari Sánchez, who was also suspected of strangling her cell mate, was given the harshest sentence—four hundred lashes.[29] Several of the priests were defrocked and given sentences of from four to six years in the galleys.

The lesser sentences imposed on the *beatas* suggest that the judges, contrary to Fray Alonso's assessment, considered that the women had been relatively passive participants in the sexual liaisons. Of the women, only the "proud and presumptuous" Mari Sánchez was singled out for exceptionally harsh punishment.[30]

Although Alonso's role in the Llerena persecutions was over by late 1575, he carried his campaign westward. In early 1576, he sent a report to the Portuguese inquisitors alerting them to new incidents of *alumbradismo*, implicating the famous Dominican preacher Luis de Granada and the entire Jesuit order in the heresy. The Jesuits, he alleged, were necromancers and sorcerers; they engaged in "filthy acts" with their penitential daughters while "inflamed" with prayer; they adored Satan, believing him to be Christ. Alonso, however, had not taken into consideration that the Portuguese Inquisitor General, Cardinal Prince Enrique, was a devoted admirer of Jesuits.[31] Prince

---

[27] Llorca, *La inquisición*, p. 110.

[28] The first reference to a confession of solicitation among the Extremaduran *alumbradas* is found in AHN, Inq. libro 578, 327r. The undated letter immediately follows a letter of August 31, 1575.

[29] The death of Inés Alonso, the cell mate of María Sánchez, is reported in a letter dated August 6, 1578 (AHN, Inq. libro 579, f. 182v).

[30] Mari Sánchez's four hundred lashes represented an unusually severe punishment for a woman. The punishments given the other *beatas* (one hundred lashes and several years in reclusion or exile) are similar to those imposed on women convicted of selling love potions and charms (Olga Valbuena, personal communication). In her study of *beatas* accused of *alumbradismo* from early seventeenth-century Seville, Mary Elizabeth Perry finds that the Inquisition's records "concluded that they were merely weak and deluded women suffering from mental lapses or victims misled by heretical clerics"; "Beatas and the Inquisition," p. 158. Based on her study of seventeenth-century cases, Claire Guilhem observes that the more celebrated *beatas* were given harsher sentences; "La inquisición y la devaluación del verbo femenino," p. 180. The question of differences in treatment of the sexes regarding inquisitorial torture, sentencing, and punishments is a topic that has yet to be treated extensively.

[31] For the documents relating to Fray Alonso's attack on the Jesuits and the subsequent suit, see *Extremadura* pp. 444-65, 542-50, 608-37. Luis de Granada's *Libro de la oración* was the most widely printed vernacular book in Spain in sixteenth-century Spain.

Enrique wrote an irate letter to Philip II, as a consequence of which Alonso was convicted of libel and forced to retract his accusations. In 1576 the Inquisitor General Don Gaspar de Quiroga remanded him to monastic reclusion in the Sevillian monastery of Portaceli, and forbade him to preach further against *alumbradismo*. Alonso, however, proved to be irrepressible. As one of his Jesuit opponents protested, reclusion in Portaceli was not an especially harsh punishment, for good fish was more readily available in Seville than in Extremadura! Alonso also apparently ignored the Inquisitor General's mandate of silence; in 1577 the Tribunal of Seville was obliged to initiate a trial against him on the charges that he had once again slandered the Jesuits. The Suprema, however, halted the trial and Alonso was given conditional liberty while forbidding him to preach on "su tema." This expression is particularly revealing of the Suprema's attitude toward Alonso's character. "Tema" or "theme" refers—in early modern as well as in modern Spanish—to an obsessive preoccupation. In 1611, the lexicographer Sebastión de Covarrubias glossed the term by citing the proverb "Cada loco con su tema" ["every madman has his theme"], "because they always have some particular little obsession which is generally the reason why they lost their wits."[32] Irrepressible as ever, Alonso nonetheless flouted the Suprema's prohibition and continued to pen warnings on his "theme" from his cell that the priests and *beatas* of Llerena represented only one claw of the immense, invisible dragon of *alumbrado* heresy.[33]

Still, the Inquisition found it difficult to sever ties with Alonso completely, although they attempted to keep him at arms' length. He was consulted regarding a suspected outbreak of *alumbradismo* in Córdoba in 1586, although his opinions were received with skepticism. As one inquisitorial visitor wrote to the Suprema in 1587: "Fray Alonso de la Fuente . . . insists that there are Alumbrados here. . . . Perhaps this friar has the spirit of God in him, although I suspect that he is deceived."

In 1589, Alonso turned his ire against a Carmelite nun whose works had been published posthumously. His letter to the Suprema protests:

> Having read and considered the works of Mother Teresa de Jesús attentively, I find in them writings of the Masilian sect with signs of other sects, especially ecstatic heretics, *alumbrados* and *dejados* . . . The editor of said book sells it and recommends it as doctrine revealed by God and inspired by the Holy Spirit. If in fact it was the nun who wrote it, as the title proclaims, it is a preternatural business and

---

Enrique was the uncle of King Sebastión. For Granada's troubles with the Inquisition see, Alvaro Huerga, "Fray Luis de Granada entre mística, alumbrados e Inquisición," *Angelicum* 66 (1988): 540-64.

[32] *Extremadura*, pp. 210-15.

[33] *Tesoro de la lengua castellana o Española* (1611), ed. Felipe Maldonado and Manuel Camarero (Madrid: Castalia, 1995).

something taught by an angel, because it exceeds the capacity of a woman. But it is not possible that it was a good angel, but rather a bad angel, the same one who deceived Mohammed and Luther and the other heresiarchs.[34]

The Suprema failed to act on Alonso's warnings and the future saint's works were reprinted, uncensored. In October of 1590, Alonso was named "teólogo calificador" (an expert consultant on theological questions) to the Llerena tribunal. With an ambivalence that characterized their long association with the Dominican preacher, the Suprema wrote the Llerena inquisitors two months later, advising them to refrain using his services as much as possible.[35] Alonso died in 1592 at the age of fifty-nine.

Although Alonso's conspiracy theory was so wide-ranging that even the inquisitors considered him an extremist, others shared his views. The notions that mental prayer leads to demonic possession, that beatific visions are invariably of demonic origin, and that priests are far too sympathetic towards demoniacs—appear illustrated with shocking new anecdotes in an anonymous manuscript, *Suma de solícitos engaños* (*Compendium of Various Deceptions*). Although the ideas and vocabulary of the *Suma* coincide with those of Alonso, the fact that Jesuits figure prominently as exemplars of "good" spiritual directors makes it seem unlikely that Alonso was the sole author.[36] Leaving aside the question of authorship, the tract is significant in that it provides a fascinating compendium of what might be called the eroto-demonic theory of heresy. Too often, the author(s) repeatedly protest, inexperienced confessors have failed to perceive the devil's real and effective presence in the lives of their penitential daughters, and have consequently mistaken possession for ecstasy:

> There are persons given to [mental] prayer who, deceived by the devil, believed that they have arrived at that exalted state of the Spirit that is described in the Song of Songs . . . and thus the devil transfigured makes these persons believe that it is Jesus who wishes to have that closeness the bridegroom has with the bride and thus things happen

---

[34] The letter dated August 26, 1589 is transcribed in Enrique Llamas Martínez, *Santa Teresa De Jesús y la Inquisición Española* (Madrid: CSIC, 1972), pp. 396-7. Alonso also sent five reports to the Consejo between 1589-1591 denouncing Teresa's writing and doctrine. For an analysis of the posthumous debates on Teresa's orthodoxy in which Alonso participated, see Gillian T. W. Ahlgren, *Teresa of Ávila and the Politics of Sanctity* (Ithaca, New York: Cornell University Press, 1996), pp. 114-44.

[35] *Extremadura*, pp. 83-6.

[36] Sala Balust acknowledges that the first part of the manuscript consists of a "good extract from the memorials of Fray Alonso" but surmises that it was composed by a Jesuit (possibly Rodrigo Alvarez) sometime between 1576 and 1581 ("En torno al grupo de alumbrados," 520). Sala Balust's conclusion—that the *Suma* represents an adaptation of Alonso's theories designed to disassociate Jesuits from the *alumbrados*—seems plausible.

that are not fit to be put to paper, and these persons call this closeness 'the union of the soul with God' and since they use these terms they deceive their confessors.[37]

The *Suma* also deplores the penchant of other confessors to diagnose possession as melancholy or madness: "Such persons are clearly deceived, for experience clearly shows that such things are not melancholy or vehement imagination or madness or a particular humor as they say, but clearly the devil" (29v).

The case of the maiden from Baeza illustrates with particular clarity how the eroto-demonic model differed from the one Inquisition eventually followed in Llerena:

> One night when she was in her bed, the devil came to her in the form of her own fifty-year-old father, who urged her to give herself to him, and she responded, "How, are you not my father?" He answered, "That is of little importance" and said other such words in this tone, telling her that it was not a sin, or not important, and saying this he had his way with her, making her feel extraordinary delights. . . . Another time the devil took the form of her own brother, and she said, "How, are you not my brother?" and he answered as had her father *et habuet rem cum ea*. . . . Another time the devil took the form of her own sister and other times, the form of a neighbor woman . . . and both began to seduce her in the same way. The devil did the same thing many times with her taking the form of her own confessor, which is a very common problem . . . . (47v-48v)

The *Suma* goes on to attributes the large incidence of possession by incubi to a new doctrine popular among the many *beatas* of Baeza:

> These people believe that such possession and torment of the devil are permitted to test their virtue and since in our time there are no tyrants who persecute the good, in their stead God has permitted demons to possess these women, and torment them . . . because by resisting these carnal pleasures . . . they deserve the crown of martyrdom . . . . There are many vain silly women fond of being esteemed for their sanctity who are given to understand that having revelations and being possessed by the devil is a sign of great sanctity. (51r-v)

In spite of coming very close to a "picaresque" model for possession, the *Suma* rejects the notion that possession is simply consciously feigned, attention-getting behavior, much less unconscious "imaginings." The argument is rather

---

[37] *Suma de solícitos engaños en estos miserables tiempos*, Biblioteca de la Real Academia de Historia, Ms. 9 5793, 96v.

that the pernicious doctrine exalting demonic temptation as a sign of sanctity prepares the ground for the devil's success and delays his discovery.

The *Suma de solícitos engaños* was never published. It is impossible to say how widely it was circulated—two known manuscript copies survive—but it is evident that the theory of a vast conspiracy of mental prayer practitioners, ecstatics and demoniacs failed to produce what Alonso advocated—the persecution and eradication of all forms of embodied religious expression.

The limited success of the eroto-demonic heresy theory has several implications for our understanding of how Spanish society responded to the conceptual and legal enigmas presented by embodied religious expression. First, we must reconsider the notion that the ecclesiastical elites were unremittingly hostile to the varied forms of embodied piety in post-Tridentine Spain.[38] As we have seen, persons of influence—the Jesuits, the Archbishop of Seville, the Bishop of Badajoz, and later the Prince Cardinal Enrique and Inquisitor Quiroga—were sympathetic to mental prayer, and rejected Alonso's attempt to equate contemplation and possession.[39] The Inquisition itself was caught in something of a double bind, desiring to promote pious observances by the parish faithful—frequent communion and confession, fasting and vigils, affective responses to the Passion—while containing religious enthusiasm that was manifestly disruptive or anti-authoritarian. Consequently, it was reluctant to endorse Alonso's conviction that popular interior piety was inherently heretical. Nor did Alonso's 1576 memorandum to Philip II persuade the king to join his camp. As recent studies have shown, Philip's own piety was remarkably "popular"—he was a devoted admirer of ascetics, visionaries, and mystics.[40] In short, Alonso's view of *alumbradismo* failed because it was too inclusive; it

---

[38] For representative examples of revisionist historiography on the Spanish Inquisition, see Jean-Pierre Dedieu, "Los cuatro tiempos de la Inquisición," *Inquisición Española: Poder político y control social*, pp. 15-39; A. W. Lovett "The Inquisition under close scrutiny" (review essay), *The Historical Journal* 32 (1989): 709-12; E. William Monter, *Frontiers of Heresy: The Spanish Inquisition from the Basque Lands to Sicily* (New York: Cambridge University Press, 1990); E. William Monter, "The New Social History and the Spanish Inquisition" (review essay), *Journal of Social History* 17 (1984): 705-13; and Geoffrey Parker, "Some Recent Work on the Inquisition in Spain and Italy" (review essay), *Journal of Modern History* 54 (1982): 519-32.

[39] We might also note that the Inquisitor General Gaspar Quiroga read and approved the spiritual autobiography of Teresa de Jesús when it was sequestered by the Inquisition. The interest in interior piety among the royal family and highest aristocracy is a phenomenon that deserves much more attention. For example, several of Teresa of Ávila's principal supports were wealthy aristocrats, such as Doña Luisa de la Cerda and the Princess of Eboli.

[40] See, for example, Richard Kagan, *Lucrecia's Dreams: Politics and Prophecy in Sixteenth-Century Spain* (Berkeley: University of California Press, 1990). Philip was remarkably slow to move against the visionary dreamer Lucrecia de León, in spite of the fact that her dreams were extremely critical of his reign.

condemned forms of piety endorsed by elite and popular classes alike, including practices advocated by the post-Tridentine Church and favored by the king.

Secondly, Alonso's peripatetic career provides further evidence of the Inquisition's relative skepticism regarding witchcraft and demonic possession, and its reluctance to conflate ecstatic piety and possession. His initial hypothesis of *alumbradismo* as a diabolical pact simply did not coincide with the Inquisition's prevailing interpretive paradigm or with its current reform agenda. As Henry Kamen has observed, throughout the sixteenth and seventeenth centuries, the Inquisition manifested two parallel but contradictory attitudes toward witchcraft: on the one hand, the belief in the heretical nature of witchcraft, and on the other hand, growing skepticism regarding the reality of witchcraft, a skepticism reflected in relatively mild sentences.[41] Mary Elizabeth Perry has argued more recently that the Inquisition's social agenda necessitated the subordination of disorderly women within the traditional gender order, and that it was more effective to discredit them as *ilusas*—weak-minded, deluded women—or as sexual delinquents than to present them as powerful witches or sorceresses.[42] Whether or not this paradigm was consciously connected to a program of social control, it proved to be more plausible than witchcraft or possession theories in many tribunals.

Furthermore, the limited success of Alonso's version of heresy suggests that as an institution, the Inquisition was relatively unresponsive to theories that did not fit into its current agenda. By the 1570s the Inquisition had shifted its attention from uncovering crypto-Jews or Protestant heretics to reforming and correcting certain sexual practices and beliefs, particularly fornication, bigamy and sodomy.[43] Also at this time, reports of confessional solicitation had begun

---

[41] "Notas sobre brujería y sexualidad y la Inquisición," in *Inquisición Española y mentalidad inquisitorial*, 226-36. Kamen notes that in a meeting of inquisitors in Granada in 1526, six out of the ten held that accused witches confessed to illusory crimes; in 1550 an inquisitor in Barcelona was removed from office for condemning six persons as witches without sufficient proof (232-3). For a study concentrating on cases from the seventeenth century, see Gustav Henningsen, *The Witches' Advocate: Basque Witchcraft and the Spanish Inquisition* (Reno: University of Nevada Press, 1980).

[42] "Beatas and the Inquisition," p. 158; *Gender and Disorder*, p. 113. Perry's arguments are based on her study of *beatas* accused of *alumbradismo* in early seventeenth-century Seville. See also Claire Guilhem, "La inquisición," pp. 199-207.

[43] The extent to which the Inquisition was concerned with controlling sexual behavior as opposed to heretical ideas regarding sexual behavior is still a topic of debate. Bennassar argues that the Inquisition's post-Tridentine focus on sexual behavior was motivated in large part by the Inquisition's desire to promulgate Tridentine marriage doctrine and its tendency to identify "simple fornication" (the belief that consensual sexual intercourse between unmarried persons was not a mortal sin) and bigamy as potential "Lutheran" heresies. Thus, the number of cases related to sexual behavior began to rise after the Council of Trent; in the Toledo tribunal, bigamy cases peaked between 1566-1570, and fornication cases between 1576-1580. See Bartolomé Bennassar, "El modelo sexual: La defensa del

to reach the Supreme Council, and between December of 1573 and July 1576 five *acordadas* or memoranda were issued requiring local tribunals to punish such misdeeds with all due rigor.[44] We have seen that Alonso had little success until his theory of demonic possession until the obscure doctrine was "joined with bad deeds," that is, until he included specific charges of confessional solicitation. With a sexual delinquency agenda on the table, as it were, it was the erotic rather than the demonic component of Alonso's theory that spurred the inquisitors to action.

The inquisitors' demonological skepticism was, of course, relative, for they seldom failed to acknowledge the devil's capacity to induce human sinfulness. Thus, the 1578 list of propositions does refer to demonic visions that provoked "terrible carnal desires" in the *alumbradas*.[45] Nonetheless, the *beatas* and their confessors were clearly punished for the sexual commerce with each other, not for their union with the devil disguised as the angel of light.[46] The defensiveness expressed by the author(s) of the *Suma de solícitos engaños* further suggests that the eroto-demonic theory was losing ground against competing medical, psychological, and social deviance models. Put another way, while the Inquisition inclined toward a mind/body dualism, Alonso and the demonologists who authored the *Suma de solícitos engaños* were radical monists. For Alonso, the devil, the flesh and desire were one and the same. The

---

matrimonio cristiano," in *Inquisición Española: Poder político y control social*, pp. 270-94. Although in Castile the prosecution of sodomy was left to civil and ordinary ecclesiastical courts, in other districts such as Zaragoza and Valencia sodomy did fall under Inquisitorial jurisdiction, there is a significant rise in the prosecution of these cases between 1560 and 1580. See Bartolomé Bennassar, "El modelo sexual: la Inquisición de Aragón y la represión de los pecados 'abominables,'" in *Inquisición Española: Poder político y control social*, pp. 295-319.

[44] AHN, Inq. libro 578, f 137r, 149r, 338v, 375, 409r. On confessional solicitation see María Helena Sánchez, "Un sondeo en la historia de la sexualidad sobre fuentes inquisitoriales," *Inquisición Española: Nueva visión, nuevos horizontes*, ed. J. Pérez Villanueva (Madrid: Siglo XXI, 1980), p. 927, note 14 (inclusive pages 917-30). Basing her arguments on data from the Toledo Tribunal, Sánchez Ortega finds 19 solicitation cases in the sixteenth century, 39 in the seventeenth, and 40 in the eighteenth. See also by Sánchez Ortega, *La mujer y la sexualidad en el antiguo régimen: La perspectiva inquisitorial* (Madrid: Akal, 1992), and Stephen Haliczer, *Sexuality in the Confessional. A Sacrament Profaned* (New York: Oxford University Press, 1996). My point is not to deny the that acts of confessional solicitation took place, but to suggest that the Inquisition's concern over solicitation colored their interpretation of the events in Llerena.

[45] AHN, Inq. legajo 4443, expediente 24, 14r.

[46] The degree of demonological skepticism varied according to Inquisitorial district and the period of prosecution. Bartolomé Bennassar describes the case of a *beata* from Toledo who in 1654 was accused of having entered into "implicit or explicit pacts with the devil." The prosecutor asked that she be released, but the inquisitors ignored his recommendation, and instead turned the woman over to the care of physicians; "La Inquisición o la pedagogía del miedo," in *Inquisición Española: poder politico*, p. 102.

Inquisitors, however, as well as many lay priests, were operating under assumptions that attempted to discriminate between acts and desires, sin and temptation, fact and fantasy.

Alonso believed that he had failed to persuade his countrymen of the full extent of the *alumbrado* heresy. But for the men and women sentenced to the oar and the lash in the 1579 *auto de fe*, he was all too successful. Although today they are remembered as orgiasts rather than demoniacs, their "deviance" is widely accepted. Ironically, this prevailing view is based largely on the Inquisition's skeptical revision of a script created by a man they themselves considered to be a "madman with a theme."[47] We can never know with certainty whether the "filthy and obscene fondling" that the Llerena *alumbrados* confessed to were, in fact, a component of their embodied religious expression, or were as fantastical as the Baeza woman's serial seductions by her father, brother, sister, neighbor and confessor. As Mary Giles has reminded us, in assessing the sexuality of religious dissent, historians have been too willing to make categorical moral judgments on the basis of confessions exacted under torture by an institution prejudiced against the accused.[48] Given the problematic hermeneutics inherent in interpreting inquisitorial documents, we are more likely to find indications of sexual attitudes than evidence of sexual acts. In other words, it is time to re-read the story of the *alumbrados* of Llerena, not as a story of sexual deviance, but as a story of how narratives of deviance are engendered.

---

[47] As Alonso confesses in his letter to Philip II, many considered him "falta de juicio."

[48] "Francisca Hernández and the Sexuality of Religoius Dissent," 97.

9 The Beautiful Dove, the Body Divine: Luisa de Carvajal y Mendoza's Mystical Poetics

Michael Bradburn-Ruster

Luisa de Carvajal y Mendoza (1566-1614) achieves, in the sonnet "De inmenso amor,"[1] one of the most stunning images in baroque poetry, yet by the simplest means: depicting herself at the moment of taking communion, she offers not her own thoughts or affections; rather, we grasp her experience through hearing the voice of Christ address her; and this verbal mirror, so to speak, presents not the literal scene of Luisa opening her mouth to receive the bread, but instead the crucified Christ—-the visible God invisibly present within the host—his arms open to embrace her, inviting this soul he calls "little dove" to enter the door that is the open wound of his breast, where she will find a sacred bed of flowers and flame (vv. 1-6). While the mutual embrace is of course a spiritual event, it is figured in the most intensely corporeal terms: a reciprocal absorption, a communion that is a commingling of inmost flesh and utmost spirit. "See how I surrender to you," Christ tells her, "my whole being and exalted sublimity" (vv. 9-10). Within his arms she will be granted the "delight that no one deserves" (vv. 13-14). The poem culminates, then, in the gift of grace, especially appropriate when we recall that Eucharist (*efcharistó*) is precisely *gracias*, "Thanks," in Greek.

What I find initially striking us here is the strange beauty of this image: Luisa not simply being called a dove but changed into one and invited into the wound, so that the figure clearly derived from the Song of Songs is intensified through baroque *admiratio*: by combining the dove with both the Passion and the Sacrament, the amatory figure of two lovers becoming one flesh is

---

[1] *Tras el espejo la musa escribe: lírica femenina de los Siglos de Oro*, ed. Julián Olivares and Elizabeth S. Boyce (Madrid: Siglo Veintiuno, 1993), p. 485. All quotations are from this selection of Doña Luisa's poetry, on account of its convenience and availability. For a complete edition of Luisa de Carvajal's poetry, see María Luisa García-Nieto Onrubia, ed., *Poesías completas* (Badajoz: Clásicos extremeños, Disputación Provincial, 1990).

amalgamated with the idea of the communicant eating the flesh of God and thereby becoming a member of his body. It is in terms of grace freely given, and of the transformation of death into life through Incarnation, Crucifixion, and Resurrection that we need to view Carvajal's images of suffering and a desire for martyrdom that might be facilely dismissed as morbid. I intend first to explore some of these concrete images and second to show how they constellate to reveal an implicit mystical theology that is both particularly Jesuit in nature and at the same time of universal spiritual significance, since we find in many of the great traditions an emphasis on the divine body, the manifestation or avatar of God as the means of bridging the worlds of spirit and flesh, cosmos and individual.

These themes are made clear in a variety of images of flight, death, and union that recur frequently in Luisa's work. Another sonnet, "En el siniestro brazo recostada,"[2] presents her as a "Phoenix enflamed" (v. 13), a symbol expanded in the *romance* "Teniéndose en la memoria,"[3] where the wound in Christ's side is the door to the Royal Palace of his body: love grants her wings, and she flies into his breast, dying in the flames, a Phoenix renewed (vv. 27-34). Another *romance*, "Sintiendo Silva de amor,"[4] offers satirical passages worthy of Erasmus, as she leaves a will in verse bequeathing all the vanities, follies, lies, empty pomp, and chimerical illusions to her beneficiary, the world, which esteems such things (vv. 21-4). In the final verses, the Shepherd places her in the "glorious sepulcher" within his breast (vv. 76-7), where she lies hidden from the perfidious world, enfolded like the Phoenix in a thousand flames, blessed and happy (vv. 87-90).

The cumulative effect is emphatically not on death, but on the felicity that comes from transcendence of self, a transformation preceding union and rebirth, as evinced by the Phoenix, a Near Eastern symbol that appears in Christianity as early as Tertullian in the second century and Lactantius in the fourth. According to the mystical zoology of the influential *Physiologus* (ca. 200), the Phoenix that immolates itself on a pyre, only to appear as a worm among the ashes, becoming feathered on the second day and flying away on the third, is a figure of Christ's Resurrection.[5]

In the Lira "Al alma que te adora,"[6] love itself is winged and after stealing her willing heart, with which it soars aloft, conceals it within Christ's eyes, leaving her breast an altar where a fire burns in homage to divine love (vv. 61-70). Is this meant as a pentecostal flame, an image of the Holy Spirit? This

---

[2] Olivares and Boyce, *Tras el espejo*, p. 487.
[3] Olivares and Boyce, *Tras el espejo*, pp. 517-18.
[4] Olivares and Boyce, *Tras el espejo*, pp. 514-16.
[5] See Gerhart B. Ladner, *God, Cosmos, and Humankind: The World of Early Christian Symbolism* (Berkeley: University of California Press, 1995), pp. 123-4.
[6] Olivares and Boyce, *Tras el espejo*, pp. 496-7.

would bring us full circle to the poem we first considered, in which Christ calls Luisa "little dove," the established symbol of the Holy Spirit, which is of course theologically the love that binds God the Father and the Son, as well as the love uniting God to Creation.[7] But to burn with the Spirit is not to *be* the Spirit, as becoming a dove might subversively suggest. Yet these symbols are exquisitely ambiguous: for the dove is not only an image of the Spirit but of Christ himself, and the turtledove in particular, like the Phoenix, is also a symbol of renewal.[8] According to the *Physiologus*, Christ is the "flame-colored dove" of the Song, whose eyes the Bride compares to doves, saying, "My beloved is fair and ruddy."[9] The *Physiologus* further affirms that doves dwelling in the tree Peridexion, the tree of life, are symbols of Christ: the dragon or serpent fears the tree where doves dwell.[10]

But it is not unprecedented or audacious for Luisa to refer to herself with the same image used for both Christ and the Holy Spirit. Many of the early symbols are of course elaborated in the mystical traditions that precede and shape Luisa's era. It is said that when St. Polycarp (*circa* AD 156) was stabbed by his executioner with a dagger, a dove emerged from the wound.[11] But long before this, a sublime passage from the Song of Songs 2:10, "Surge . . . columba mea," includes the terms *amica, columba,* and *formosa*—"friend," "dove," and "beautiful." St. Bernard, in his 57th Sermon on the Song, regards these as three aspects of the soul. The soul as "friend" is the role of Martha:[12] preaching, advising, serving; the soul as "dove" weeps and prays for forgiveness of sins, as does Lazarus; and finally the soul as "beautiful" is Mary, clothed in "the beauty of heavenly contemplation."[13] The soul, however, in whom all three aspects come together is deemed perfect, and in his 23rd Sermon, Bernard has told us that the "perfect dove" of Song 6:8 is the Bride of Christ.[14] Given

---

[7] Ladner, *God*, pp. 33-4.

[8] A beautiful modern avatar can be found in a recent work of Japanese Catholic novelist Shusaku Endo, where he has Otsu, a young Japanese seminarian, speak of the power of grace to transmute sin: ". . . God, like a magician, can turn any situation to the best advantage. Even our weaknesses and our sins. . . . A magician puts a wretched sparrow in a box, closes the lid, and then with a wave of his hands opens the lid again. The sparrow in the box has been changed into a pure-white dove and comes flying out. . . . I didn't change myself. I was transformed by the conjurings of God." Shusaku Endo, *Deep River*, trans. Van C. Gessel (New York: New Directions, 1994), p. 63.

[9] Song of Songs 5:10, 12.

[10] Ladner, *God*, p. 34.

[11] J. Stevenson, ed., *A New Eusebius* (London: SPCK, 1968), p. 23.

[12] Luke 10:39-40.

[13] Kilian Walsh and Irene M. Edmonds, trans., *Bernard of Clairvaux: On the Song of Songs,* 4 vols. Kalamazoo, Michigan: Cistercian Publications, 1971-1980), 57:9-11, vol. 3, pp. 103-6.

[14] ". . . no maiden, or concubine, or even queen, may gain access to the mystery of that bedroom which the Bridegroom reserves solely for her who is his dove, beautiful, perfect,

the combination of the soul as dove, the perfect embrace, and the sacral bed, we can safely conclude that Luisa aligns with this Bernardine interpretation, whether or not she is directly influenced by it, as we know her to have been by Fray Luis de Granada, St. John Climacus, and others.[15]

But there can be no doubt that the poems reflect the two pillars of her spiritual and mystical life—the Passion and the Eucharist, those two most bodily mysteries. From early youth the Passion was the favored object of her mental prayer and meditation, and she mentions in particular that she never missed taking communion on the feast of Corpus Christi.[16] In Madrid, at the age of 26, she withdrew from her family and the court where she had been a lady in waiting, to fulfill her yearning to imitate Christ; of the paths that offered themselves to her, she felt she must follow only that one where could be found "the footsteps of Christ our Lord."[17] Despite spells of spiritual aridity, her practice of prayer and meditation upon images of Christ resulted in her feeling in the depth of her soul "a terrible love" and a desire "to follow his rough road unto death."[18] Wounded by the arrow of his love, she longs to embrace his poverty and humiliation, those treasures in which he lies wrapped up.[19] For many months, she experienced during interior prayer the grace of encountering in the depths of her soul "a most delicate and sovereign presence of the Incarnate Word"; there she embraces him and finds her heart both enlarged and illumined.[20] Sometimes, after communion, the torments of his Passion would appear to her, such as one Friday in February of 1599, when she had a vision of the open wounds of his head and of his pierced hands; when her soul clings to his agonized body, the joys of eternal life, of which she had been reading, seemed to her altogether bereft of delight, and she deemed a torment all that was not sharing in the Passion: ". . . and I should choose, for my sole and supreme glory, to see myself transformed into that sovereign Person . . . my soul raised up on his cross and run through with those very nails and thorns." Yet his suffering does not cause her anguish; rather it confers "a gently

---

and unique." Walsh and Edmonds, *Song*, vol. 2, p. 35. This is echoed in Gilbert of Hoyland, for whom the Bride has the "eyes of a dove"; see Lawrence C. Braceland, S.J., trans., *Gilbert of Hoyland: Sermons on the Song of Songs* (Kalamazoo: Cistercian Publications, 1979), pp. 274-6. See also Bernard McGinn, *The Presence of God* (New York: Crossroads, 1994), pp. 184-5, 189.

[15] Camilo María Abad, S.J., *Una misionera española en la Inglaterra del siglo XVII: Luisa de Carvajal y Mendoza (1566-1614)* (Comillas, Santander: Universidad Pontificia, 1966), p. 32.

[16] Abad, *Una misionera*, pp. 34-5.

[17] Abad, *Una misionera*, p. 82.

[18] Abad, *Una misionera*, p. 82.

[19] Abad, *Una misionera*, p. 89.

[20] Abad, *Una misionera*, p. 100.

penetrating love." His close embrace alone can satisfy her, and there can be no other heaven than suffering his torments.[21]

This is the "locura de la cruz," the folly of the Cross, of which Ignatius of Loyola speaks, echoing St. Paul.[22] Although she never became a nun, Luisa's association with the Jesuits was intimate: the house where she lived in Madrid belonged to the Order, her vows of poverty, obedience, perfection, and martyrdom were presented to the Rector of the Jesuit Imperial College, and her entire period in England during the persecution was spent in association with the Jesuits there.[23] When we consider Jesuit spiritual practice and theology, it becomes clear that Luisa's skill as a poet, a maker of images, accords perfectly with Jesuit orientation. Her focus on dramatic details is not limited to the Crucifixion: in the *redondilla* "¡No encubras, Silva, tu gloria!"[24] she gives us a loving description of Jesus' appearance; his eyes rob diamonds of their splendor (vv. 54-6), the sun receives its very light from the glints of his chestnut hair (vv. 57-60), his brows are rainbows of peace following the Deluge (vv. 65-8). The appeal to the senses intensifies as she takes us into his "eternal interior" (v. 111), the source of life that is given for all on the Cross: again, we are told, "he opened, for me to enter, a door I *saw* slashed in his right side" (vv. 118-20); at the *sound* of his voice, her soul dissolves (vv. 125-8); he takes her by the *hand* and enters into her garden (vv. 133-6), where the flowers of her soul spill forth a "*scent* transcendent" (vv. 137-40, 169-70), and nearly barren trees bear fruit (vv. 161-4), making her desert a heaven (vv. 171-2) (my emphases). Every sense is appealed to: this is at once consummate baroque poetry and a reflection of Jesuit meditational practice.

Ignatius's spirituality is deeply trinitarian,[25] yet the *Spiritual Exercises* evince an unsurpassed devotion to the Incarnation as revelation: through the mediation of the human-divine Christ, the world is drawn back to God; the center of that mediation is the Eucharist, the active presence of Christ in bread and wine. But the wider sphere—to borrow Jill Raitt's metaphor—includes not

---

[21] *Escrito* 15, quoted in Abad, *Una misionera*, pp. 100-101.

[22] *Examen* preceding *Constitutions*, chapter 4, number 44, cited in Abad, *Una misionera*, p. 70.

[23] See Abad, *Una misionera*, pp. 71, 376-81 and 185 ff.; see also Anne J. Cruz, "Luisa de Carvajal y Mendoza y su conexión jesuita," *Actas-Irvine '92: Asociación Internacional de Hispanistas* (Irvine: University of California Press, 1994), pp. 97-104.

[24] Olivares and Boyce, *Tras el espejo*, pp. 503-8.

[25] See Harvey D. Egan, S.J., "Ignatius of Loyola: Mystic at the Heart of the Trinity, Mystic at the Heart of Jesus Christ," in Annice Callahan, R.S.C.J., ed., *Spiritualities of the Heart: Approaches to Personal Wholeness in Christian Trandition* (New York: Paulist Press, 1990), pp. 97-113; and Jill Raitt, "Saints and Sinners: Roman Catholic and Protestant Spirituality in the Sixteenth Century," pp. 457-63 in Jill Raitt, ed., *Christian Spirituality II: High Middle Ages and Reformation* (New York: Crossroad, 1987).

only Mary and the angels but all of creation.[26] The Christocentric life is the aim of the exercise of daily examination of self: to achieve an ever more perfect following of Christ, so that one becomes not only an object of redemption but also a mediator.[27] It is precisely through Jesus' *humanity* that Ignatius grasps his *divine* nature and through this the twofold nature of Christ that he glimpses the life of the Trinity.[28] Ignatius's fervent prayer was that Jesus make him "conform to the will of the Most Holy Trinity."[29] In her prose writings, Luisa uses images from the Apocalypse of the precious stones of the Heavenly Jerusalem to suggest that spiritual work is an alchemical transformation of the soul's will, through the crucible of tribulations, into perfect conformity with divine will, the fulfillment of which is the "treasure."[30]

The epiphanaic emphasis on the divine presence shining through the visible is a constant motif of Jesuit thought, including that of perhaps the greatest modern theologian, Hans Urs von Balthasar, who writes: "The incarnate Word is . . . the *universale concretum et personale*, God's universal truth and love in concrete form." And this concrete form reaches its fullest expression in the Cross: "To say Incarnation is to say Cross."[31] But this is not simply a modern or Tridentine innovation, for early Greek Fathers like Athanasius as well as for the West, "the final goal of the Incarnation is the Cross."[32] Rooted in the Gospel of John, it reflects the Johannine paradox: as God's supreme glory is expressed in serving his creatures and washing their feet, so, to quote John Saward, "in the hour of his humiliation and obedience unto death . . . the Redeemer-Son draws all creation to himself," and the glory of the Father's love is "supremely manifested in the human form of the Son broken and obedient unto death. . . . "[33] Incarnation is not so much the changing of God into man, but rather the taking up of humanity into God, as Luisa is drawn up into Christ; it thus reveals the innermost life of the Trinity, which is one of "absolute self-surrender" of the three persons to each other,[34] most perfectly and paradoxically articulating divine omnipotence: God's almightiness, Balthasar affirms, "blazes forth in the powerlessness of the incarnate and crucified Son."[35] This goes all the way back to Gregory of Nyssa: God's "capacity to descend to the lowliness of the human condition is a far

---

[26] Raitt, "Saints," p. 458.
[27] Raitt, "Saints," p. 460.
[28] Egan, "Ignatius," pp. 106-7.
[29] *Spiritual Diary*, number 80, quoted in Egan, "Ignatius," p. 106.
[30] *Escrito* 5:14-16, quoted in Abad, *Una misionera*, pp. 104-6.
[31] John Saward, *The Mystics of March: Hans Urs von Balthasar on the Incarnation and Easter* (London: Collins, 1990), pp. xix, 3.
[32] Saward, *Mysteries*, p. 4.
[33] Saward, *Mysteries*, pp. 6, 8; compare John 12:32.
[34] Saward, *Mysteries*, pp. 12, 14, 28-30.
[35] *Mysterius Paschale*, pp. 151 ff., quoted in Saward, *Mysteries*, p. 34.

greater proof of power than the miracles of an imposing and supernatural kind .... The humiliation of God shows the superabundance of his power...."[36]

Unfortunately, it is precisely the concrete focus on the Word Incarnate that has often led to the parody of Jesuit spiritual method as an image-bound, mechanical approach, at best "non-spiritual," and at worst an "anti-spiritual" obstacle to genuine mysticism.[37] This is rooted in the prejudice that real spirituality is somehow dematerialized, that it disdains or even shuns creation. But this is a Platonizing, Reformation perspective that runs counter to the tradition that Thomas Aquinas articulates with such lucid beauty: the true form of human being is not simply a spirit using a body; rather, human nature is essentially a mysterious conjunction or composite of spirit and flesh.[38] Ignatius's Christology is congruent: emphasizing the twofold, divine and human nature of Christ; as Harvey Egan puts it, "The Ignatian Christ is always the Son of the Virgin Mary according to the flesh and the Son of the eternal Father."[39]

This emphasizes and elaborates an ancient tradition, which finds perhaps its most radiant cultural expression in the Gothic cathedral, conceived by medieval theorists like William Durandus and Abbot Suger as a arhcitectonic allegory of the Heavenly City, which Apocalypse 21 identifies with Jesus' body.[40] This is a late medieval elaboration of an idea expressed a thousand years earlier: the cruciform plan of churches dates back to Old St. Peter's in Rome, in AD 326, and St. Ambrose's assertion that his cross plan for the Church of the Holy Apostles at Milan symbolized the victory of Christ and his Cross.[41] While the Gothic ribbed vaults coincide with increasing human anatomical investigation, the translucent windows symbolize Mary's virginity, intact even as the Light of the World has passed through her; moreover, Fingesten argues, the deeply splayed porches "certainly have [female] anatomical connotations."[42] When one enters a cathedral, then, one is entering at once the womb of the Virgin, the crucified body of Christ, and the Heavenly City. The cathedral is thus a *Vierge Ouvrante*, the popular thirteenth-fourteenth-century carved wooden image of Mary which opens to reveal Christ within.[43]

---

[36] *Ordo catechetica*, p. 24, quoted in Saward, *Mysteries*, p. 34.

[37] See Egan, "Ignatius," pp. 97, 109n.

[38] See *Summa contra gentiles*, trans. English Dominican Fathers (London: Burns, Oates, and Washbourne, 1923), II, 57, vol. 2, pp. 138-42; and *Summa theologiae* (London: Blackfriars, 1964-76), I, 75, 4.

[39] Egan, "Ignatius," p. 107.

[40] Peter Fingesten, *The Eclipse of Symbolism* (Columbia, South Carolina: University of South Carolina Press, 1970), pp. 68-9, 79-80, 85.

[41] Fingesten, *Eclipse*, p. 86.

[42] Fingesten, *Eclipse*, pp. 88, 91-2.

[43] Fingesten, *Eclipse*, p. 93.

For Luisa, the body of Mary is also of great significance: in the *romance* "Mirando está a su Señor,"[44] Christ's flesh is a "holy vestment" woven of love within the immaculate Rose (vv. 113-18); and in a Christmas villancico,[45] she writes that it is "within the holy Mother" that the Father's divine Word is able to take on human flesh, thereby "opening the path" to lost humanity (vv. 29-35). Seen in this light, Luisa's work offers a vast perspective: bodies within bodies, worlds within worlds.

We ought to take seriously the suggestion in Sarah Beckwith's recent work, *Christ's Body*, of the need to bring the incarnate aspect of Christ "back from its exile,"[46] a problem exemplified in idealizing views like Johann Huizinga's notion that the late medieval tendency to embodiment is part of a decadent epoch's "tendency to reduce the infinite to the finite," a sign of the "deterioration of the faith."[47] Yet Beckwith's work itself suffers not only from a Marxist sociological slant which *a priori* denies genuine transcendence, while divinizing historical process.[48] When Beckwith defines the Body of Christ as a "contested social arena . . . where social identity was negotiated,"[49] and as the "locus and substance of historically momentous transference of, and struggle over, sacrality . . . where catholicity and protestantism . . . struggle for cultural capital,"[50] I can hardly think it is the body of the incarnate Logos that has been returned from exile. Her work also suffers from narrow, false historicizing: speaking of Christ's body as a ladder in Hugh of St. Victor, as though this idea were a late medieval phenomenon, while ignoring the explicit image of Christ as Jacob's ladder in John 1:51.[51] Moreover, she views mysticism not in terms of paradox, but as "conflict and . . . contradiction," and asserts a "dichotomy" between apophatic and kataphatic mysticism,[52] where in fact they are clearly complementary, their relation one of dynamic tension.[53]

Luisa de Carvajal's work needs to be seen in light of her particular moment, yet not as imprisoned by that moment. We must be wary of Beckwith's

---

[44] Olivares and Boyce, *Tras el espejo*, p. 520.

[45] Olivares and Boyce, *Tras el espejo*, pp. 529-30.

[46] Sarah Beckwith, *Christ's Body: Identity, Culture, and Society in Late Medieval Writings* (London: Routledge, 1993), p. 27.

[47] Johan Huizinga, *The Waning of the Middle Ages* (New York: Doubleday, 1954), pp. 155, 166; see Beckwith, *Christ's Body*, p. 17.

[48] See Beckwith, *Christ's Body*, pp. 125, n31, 120, n8, 129, n55.

[49] Beckwith, *Christ's Body*, pp. 26, 23.

[50] Beckwith, *Christ's Body*, p. 117.

[51] Beckwith, *Christ's Body*, p. 57.

[52] Beckwith, *Christ's Body*, p. 20.

[53] A. H. Armstrong, "Apophatic-Kataphatic Tensions in Religious Thought from the Third to the Sixth Century A.D.," pp. 12-21 in F. X. Martin, O.S.A., and J. A. Richmond, eds, *From Augustine to Eriugena: Essays of Neoplatonism and Christianity in Honor of John O'Meara* (Washington, DC: Catholic University of America Press, 1991).

facile dismissal of universality,⁵⁴ reflecting the fashionable postmodern prejudice that assumes the incommensurability of cultures and periods, an assumption demolished by such careful recent critiques as those of Leonard Angel and Ashok Gangadean.⁵⁵

Here I can only hint at the parallels with Luisa's "corporeal spirituality" in other traditions: in the Hindu *Rig-Veda*, incarnation and sacrifice are central themes; the whole world originates though the self-sacrifice of the original cosmic man, Purusha, the sun being born from his eye, the earth from his feet.⁵⁶ In both the *Mahabharata* and the *Bhaghavata Purana*, we find the story of the sage Markandeya, who wanders through the vast watery waste at the end of time, only to find wrapped in the leaf of a banyan tree the infant Krishna, who invites Markandeya into his mouth for rest; there the sage discovers the "universe . . . entire."⁵⁷ Or in the Buddhist tradition, where the *Lotus Sutra* indicates that Buddha is revealed in the Three Bodies: "the historical buddha (Sakyamuni), the cosmic or universal buddha, and the buddha of bliss."⁵⁸ Indeed, in Shingon Buddhism, with its emphasis on the Sun Sutra (*Mahavairocana Sutra* or *Dainichikyo*), the entire cosmos is understood as an emanation of the Sun Buddha, Vairocana (Dainichi).⁵⁹ Some hold that "All bodies are the Buddha body," that "your body . . . is all bodies,"⁶⁰ and that indeed one who is enlightened understands that "The whole universe in the ten directions is his whole body,"⁶¹ and initiates regularly recite, "I take refuge in the Buddha. . ." or "I find my home in the Buddha."⁶² In the theology of the Taoist tradition, we are told that the body of Lao Tzu, the Old Master and Immortal Child, "is the image and model of the entire universe," and that when he died "his body was transformed into a landscape," which is the source of life.⁶³ Jewish mysticism is particularly important here, both for its propinquity

---

⁵⁴ Beckwith, *Christ's Body*, pp. 7, 9, 13.

⁵⁵ See Leonard Angel, *Enlightenment East and West* (Albany, New York: State University of New York Press, 1994), esp. pp. 24-35; and Ashok Gangadean, *Meditative Reason: Toward Universal Grammar* (New York: Peter Lang, 1993), esp. pp. xi, xx, 246-60.

⁵⁶ *Rig-Veda* 10:90; see John B. Noss and David S. Noss, *Man's Religions*, 7th ed. (New York: Macmillan, 1984), pp. 76-7.

⁵⁷ See J. A. B. van Buitenen, ed. and trans., *Mahabharata*, 3 vols. (Chicago: University of Chicago Press, 1973-8), vol. 2, pp. 589-90; and A. C. Bhaktivedanta, Swami, Pabhupada, and Hridayananda dasa Goswami Acaryadeva, trans., *Srimad Bhagavatam* (Los Angeles: Bhaktivedanta Book Trust, 1984), vol. 12.2, pp. 58-77.

⁵⁸ See H. Byron Earhart, *Japanese Religion: Unity and Diversity*, 3rd ed. (Belmont, California: Wadsworth, 1982), p. 96.

⁵⁹ Earhart, *Japanese Religion*, p. 80.

⁶⁰ Robert Aitken, "The Body of the Buddha," *Parabola* 10 (1985): 26-7.

⁶¹ J. L. Walker, "Wordgates," *Parabola* 22 (1997): 69.

⁶² Aitken, "Body," p. 30; see also Noss and Noss, *Man's Religions*, p. 112.

⁶³ Kristofer Schipper, *The Taoist Body*, trans. Karen C. Duval (Berkeley: Univeristy of California Press, 1993), pp. 114, 116.

to Christianity and for its emphasis on the transcendent otherness of God, while still insisting on immanence and even a kind of mystical embodiment: the *Shi'ur Qomah* tradition predating the Kabbalah spoke of the hidden yet scintillating body of God.[64] The twentieth-century Kabbalist Abraham Isaac Kook (d. 1935) taught that all existence is the body of God.[65] In classic Kabbalah, the ten sephirot or aspects of God constitute the divine archetype of the original human nature, created in God's image. And at the very center of the sephirotic body or tree is *Tif'eret*, Beauty, which balances Love and Power, and is at once white and red, the very subject of the verse of the Song of Songs, "My beloved is white and ruddy" (5:10): body of God, body of Jesus, body of the dove.[66]

It is only within these wider dimensions that we can take the full measure of Luisa de Carvajal's particular crucifixion piety, which focuses on the crucified body as the locus of divine beauty, love, and power, in an ecstasy of utter self-surrender and union. She is unmistakably a poet of the world as well as a poet of the Word Incarnate, "through whom all things were made."[67]

---

[64] See Gershom Scholem, *Major Trends in Jewish Mysticism* (New York: Schocken, 1961), pp. 63-7, 113; Martin Samuel Cohen, *The Shi'ur Qomah: Liturgy and Theurgy in Pre-Kabbalistic Jewish Mysticism* (Lanham, Maryland: University Press of America, 1983), pp. 197-216; and Daniel Matt, *The Essential Kabbalah: The Heart of Jewish Mysticism* (San Francisco: Harper, 1995), pp. 4, 74-5.

[65] Matt, *Kabbalah*, p. 16.

[66] Compare Song of Songs 4:1, 5:12.

[67] John 1:3.

10 Cecilia de Nacimiento: Mystic in the Tradition of John of the Cross

Evelyn Toft

Although little-known to students of Spanish mysticism, Cecilia del Nacimiento, Discalced Carmelite of the early seventeenth century, merits recognition as an outstanding representative of the Carmelite mystical tradition epitomized by Juan de la Cruz and Teresa de Jesús. Cecilia gives very articulate and original testimony to the experience of intimate union with the Divine Spouse. An accomplished poet and prose writer, her work demonstrates an intellectual clarity and fullness of heart reminiscent of Juan de la Cruz. Cecilia's work demonstrates that Juan's legacy flourished among the second generation of Discalced Carmelite women.

Who Was Cecilia del Nacimiento?

Born in 1570, Cecilia was the second youngest child of Cecilia Morillas and Bachiller Antonio Sobrino, Secretary of the University of Valladolid.[1] Cecilia was not a typical woman of late sixteenth- and early seventeenth-century Spain. She studied literature, grammar, philosophy, rhetoric, and Sacred Scripture with her siblings under the tutelage of her mother (35-6). Her mother was so learned that her university professor sons sought her advice on theological and philosophical questions (7).

Cecilia and her sister, María, entered the Discalced Carmelite convent of Valladolid in 1587, five years after the death of Teresa de Jesús and four years before the death of Juan de la Cruz (7). Cecilia quickly assumed positions of leadership in her community. She served as mistress of novices after her full profession. In 1600 she was chosen prioress of the convent in Calahorra (8).

---

[1] José María Díaz Cerón, *Obras completas de Cecilia del Nacimiento* (Madrid: Editorial de Espiritualidad, 1971), 7, p. 34. Page references in this article are to this text. Gerardo de San Juan de la Cruz points out that Cecilia was not the youngest child, but the second youngest. He corrects Díaz Cerón's sources. See Gerardo de San Juan de la Cruz, *Obras del místico doctor, San Juan de la Cruz*, vol. 3 (Toledo, 1914), p. 341.

She returned to Valladolid in 1612. After serving her community in various capacities, Cecilia died in 1646 (9-10).

Her contemplative experiences caused suspicions in some quarters. When Tomás de Jesús, Cecilia's spiritual director for many years, fell out of favor with the Discalced Carmelite leadership, Cecilia was dismissed from the priorship at Calahorra. She returned to Valladolid and was ordered not to discuss her spiritual life with anyone. Her writings were scrutinized for evidence of heretical thinking. In the end she was vindicated and her writings were found to be free of error (9-10).

Cecilia's Writings

In addition to a number of essays and two commentaries on "Liras de la transformación del alma en Dios," Cecilia wrote almost one hundred poems. She wrote sonnets *a lo divino*. Some poems complained about her sufferings for love, while others celebrate the joys of intimacy with the Divine Spouse. She wrote sonnets, "liras," a ballad, and other poems in honor of Teresa (597, 611, 691, 692, 694, 708, 714). She composed "glosas" on the refrain "Vivo sin vivir en mí" in Teresa's honor (714-16). She also created a drama in verse based on the Song of Songs to be used on the occasion of religious profession (639-53). Many of her poems are occasional verse, written to be used in the celebrations of her community.

Cecilia's writing activity occurred in two different periods of her life, separated by almost thirty years (30). To the first period belong the first of her two commentaries on "Liras de la transformación del alma en Dios," composed in 1603. In this earlier period Cecilia also wrote the short treatise, "Tratado de la unión del alma en Dios" (1602). It describes how God touches the beloved in increasingly more sublime and deeper ways, filling her with expanded joy and fulfillment (269-71). She describes in great detail how the experience of union with God changes as it deepens, transforming the beloved in the Divine Lover (272-88).

Toward the end of her life (1629-43), in addition to the second commentary on "Liras de transformación del alma en Dios," Cecilia wrote two accounts of favors received in prayer, "Primera relación de mercedes" (1629) and "Segunda relación de mercedes" (1633). In the "Primera relación" she relates different kinds of spiritual experiences, including foreknowledge of events within her Order, and special insight into passages of Sacred Scripture. Cecilia also describes her more notable contemplative experiences. She also reports on her correspondence with her brother, Antonio Sobrino (309-20). Their detailed discussions of contemplative experience indicate that they both had a deep and wide knowledge of the Church's mystical tradition (315-17).

The "Segunda relación de mercedes" (1633), much like the "Primera relación," reports visions and insights into Scripture occurring after deep experiences of contemplation. Cecilia also describes her growing experience of the measureless riches to be found in the vast immensity of God's being (333). She makes one reference to Juan de la Cruz's *Llama de amor viva*, "Calor y luz dan junto a su querido," to suggest something of the gifts of contemplative union with God (332).

She also wrote essays on two passages from the Song of Songs, "My beloved is mine and I am his" (Song 2:16) in 1634 and "I adjure you, daughters of Jerusalem, by the gazelles and hinds of the field. Do not arouse, do not stir up love before its own time" in 1637 (Song 3:5). Cecilia remarks in her commentary on the first passage that God does not fail to give God's self totally to those who lose themselves completely and surrender themselves fully out of their ardent love. (344). Echoing Juan de la Cruz's commentary on his *Cántico espiritual*[2] (C32,6 and 8), she notes that God makes the Beloved beautiful so that God can take delight in contemplating her. The beloved's words penetrate to the core of God's being "penetran a este Amado en sus entrañas divinas" (346). The beloved is wounded by God and God by the beloved (347), echoing again Juan's *Cántico espiritual* (C35,7).

The bridal mysticism of the first essay also dominates the second one. In the second passage the Divine Lover asks others, "the daughters of Jerusalem," not to disturb the divine sleep of the beloved. This sleep is actually a profound vigilance in which the beloved attends to the Divine Lover and receives innumerable gifts beyond description (362). The beloved's union with the Divine Lover becomes so solidly established that the beloved's awareness is never removed from the Divine Lover even in the deepest natural sleep (369).

Although Arenal and Schlau conclude that Cecilia's writing reflects "mainstream patriarchal values" in as much as it deals with "mystical theology" and does not limit itself to "popular, female — marginalized traditions,"[3] they also observe that she was able to describe mystical experience more clearly and comprehensively than most of the male theologians of her time.[4] The Discalced Carmelite scholar, Emeterio de Jesús María also asserted that Cecilia explained "con maestría doctoral los puntos más delicados, difíciles y profundos de la

---

[2] The edition of Juan de la Cruz used is Matías del Niño Jesús and Lucinio Ruano, *Vida y obras de San Juan de la Cruz* (Madrid: Biblioteca de Autores Cristianos, 1972). References to his poetry give an abbreviation followed by a line number. Quotations from San Juan de la Cruz are taken from Kieran Kavanaugh and Otilio Rodríguez, trans., *The Collected Works of Saint John of the Cross* (Washington, DC: ICS Publications, 1991).

[3] Electa Arenal and Stacey Schlau, *Untold Sisters: Hispanic Nuns in Their Own Works* (Albuquerque: University of New Mexico Press, 1989), p. 137.

[4] Arenal and Schlau, *Untold Sisters*, p. 143.

Teología Mística."[5] She was an accomplished writer on spirituality, in spite of the fact that she had not benefitted from formal academic training in theology, in part because she had access to the same texts as did the male clerics and academics. Unlike many women of her day, including Teresa de Jesús, Cecilia was proficient in Greek and Latin. Although books on scripture and spirituality written in the vernacular had been banned since 1559, since Cecilia could read books on mystical theology written in Latin, she could access their doctrine and their specialized vocabulary.[6] She was in a position to interpret her mystical experience in light of the teaching of texts that had come to be under almost complete clerical control.[7]

Counter Reformation Spain was quite hostile to theological writings authored by women. In an environment antagonistic to women's religious authority, Cecilia managed to produce an impressive body of work in prose and poetry. Teresa de Jesús was one of Cecilia's models in this. She was the only woman writer of theological texts to be published in Counter Reformation Spain.[8] Not only did Teresa write about theological topics, she had exercised considerable religious authority as the genius behind the Carmelite reform. During Cecilia's lifetime, Teresa went from "a controversial and suspect figure" to "a sacrosanct object of devotion and national celebration."[9] Teresa's beatification and canonization provided some protection for Cecilia's writing activity.[10]

In sharp contrast to the attitude of much of the Counter Reformation Church, Juan de la Cruz affirmed the spiritual aspirations of women. His prose commentaries, when not expressly written for women, were all composed in response to the interest expressed by women.[11] Juan defended the interests of Discalced Carmelite women before the governing board of the friars at the end

---

[5] Emeterio de Jesús María,"La Madre Cecilia del Nacimiento," *El Monte Carmelo* 47 (1946): 154.

[6] Anyone interested in a life of prayer who could not read Latin was at a considerable disadvantage in Counter Reformation Spain. Once books on spirituality written in the vernacular were banned by the Inquisition, lay readers were cut off from the texts and vocabulary they needed to describe their experience in orthodox terms. This situation impacted women especially, making them vulnerable to accusations of heresy if they described their prayer experiences with the wrong language. Cecilia's training in Latin made it possible for her to dare to write about mystical prayer experiences. For a discussion of the problems confronting women because of censorship, see Gillian T. W. Ahlgren, *Teresa of Ávila and the Politics of Sanctity* (Ithaca, New York: Cornell University Press, 1996), pp. 15-21.

[7] Ahlgren, *Teresa*, p. 19.

[8] Ahlgren, *Teresa*, p. 18.

[9] Arenal and Schlau, *Untold Sisters*, p. 138.

[10] Arenal and Schlau, *Untold Sisters*, p. 138.

[11] Matía and Ruano, *Vida y obras*, pp. 250-1. Subsequent references to this text are in parentheses.

of his life (306-11).[12] The smear campaign, mounted by the leadership of the Discalced Friars against Juan in the last months of his life, targeted nuns who were close to him, resulting in the destruction of many of his letters and sayings (320-22).[13] Cecilia's writings demonstrate that Juan's teaching survived among Discalced Carmelite women in the early seventeenth century. Her poetry and essays were inspired by Juan's poetry and prose commentaries.

Liras de la transformación del alma en Dios

The composition of "Liras de la transformación del alma en Dios" clearly is indebted to Juan de la Cruz's poem, "Noche oscura." Although José María Díaz Cerón, editor of her *Obras completas* and author of a study of her mysticism, insists that Juan's writings did not exert a literary influence on Cecilia (734); many Discalced Carmelite scholars disagree with him.[14] Silverio de Santa Teresa finds Cecilia's writings permeated with Juan's spirit.[15] Among literary scholars, Luce López Baralt finds that Cecilia's liras clearly recall the liras of "Noche oscura."[16] Gerardo de San Juan de la Cruz included Cecilia's first "Tratado de la transformación del alma en Dios" in his edition of Juan's complete works because of its marked similarity in expository method and teaching with Juan's writings.[17]

There is no question that Cecilia was familiar with Juan's writings. She directly quotes him in the "Segunda relación de mercedes"[18] and in her essay on the passage from the Song of Songs, "My beloved is mine and I am his" (Song 2:16) (346). Although the first edition of Juan's works was not published until 1618, manuscript copies of his prose commentaries dating from the sixteenth century at the latest are still in the possession of the Carmelite convent of Valladolid (728).

Even a cursory comparison of the two poems reveals Cecilia's indebtedness to Juan de la Cruz. Many phrases from "Noche oscura" appear in "Liras de la transformación del alma en Dios." Furthermore, when she does not directly borrow Juan's language, she conveys a similar notion in her own words.

---

[12] See Richard P. Hardy, *Search for Nothing: The Life of John of the Cross* (New York: Crossroad, 1982), p. 103.

[13] Hardy, *Search*, pp. 105-6.

[14] According to Emeterio de Jesús María in his summary of the question of Juan's influence on Cecilia, almost all Discalced Carmelite authors claimed that at least some influence exists. See *Monte Carmelo*, 47 (1946), 155-8.

[15] Silverio de Santa Teresa, *Historia del Carmen Descalzo en España, Portugal Y América*, vol. 9 (Burgos: El Monte Carmelo, 1940), p. 904.

[16] Luce López Baralt, *San Juan de la Cruz y el Islam* (Mexico City: El Colegio de Mexico, 1985), p. 105.

[17] Gerardo de San Juan de la Cruz, *Obras*, p. 344.

[18] Díaz Cerón, *Obras*, pp. 332, 334.

In the first stanza of Cecilia's "Liras" she talks of a "niebla oscura" ("dark and shadowy cloud"), whereas Juan sets the stage for his poem by referring to a "noche oscura" ("dark night").[19] While Cecilia says that the soul left "sin vista de otra cosa" ("with nothing else in sight"), in Juan's poem the speaker says, "salí sin ser notada" ("I went out unseen"). In Cecilia's poem the soul "de amor está inflamada" ("with burning love inflamed") (stanza 2), while in Juan's poem the speaker describes herself as "en amores inflamada" ("fired with love's urgent longings") (stanza 1). Cecilia echoes again Juan's phrase, "salí sin ser notada" in her third stanza: "se sale sin ser vista / de nadie, ni notada" (the soul departs unseen, / unnoticed by anyone"). She repeats again that the soul is "dél inflamada" (stanza 3), again echoing the phrase in the first stanza of "Noche oscura."

Cecilia's reference to "su secreto centro" ("heaven's secret heart") in the fourth stanza parallels Juan's image of "mi pecho florido" ("my flowering breast") (stanza 6). In Cecilia's poem the soul searches for her Divine Lover "con la fuerza de amor toda encendida" ("with all the force of love with which she burns") (stanza 5), while in Juan's poem the speaker searches for her Lover without any other guide than "la que en el corazón ardía" ("than the one that burned in my heart") (stanza 3). The persona in Cecilia's poem finds "las potencias suspendidas" ("her powers overcome by greater force") (stanza 6). When the speaker unites with her lover in "Noche oscura," her experience through the senses is suspended: "todos mis sentidos suspendía" ("suspending all my senses") (stanza 7). In Cecilia's poem this experience comes by ascending "por escalera" ("by ladder") (stanza 7), while in Juan's poem the beloved ascends "por secreta escala" ("by the secret ladder") (stanza 2). In both poems the protagonists ascend in security: "segura" (Cecilia, stanza 7; Juan, stanza 2). In Cecilia's poem the persona experiences the Divine Lover, "estando sosegada" ("now stilled") (stanza 8). In Juan's poem the speaker leaves to begin searching for her lover, "estando ya mi casa sosegada" ("my house being now all stilled") (stanzas 1, 2).

Cecilia twice alludes to a breeze in her description of the encounter of the soul with the Divine Lover: " mueve un aire muy blando / que todo lo interior va regalando" ("an air both sweet and mild, / caressing sweetly all that is within.") (stanza 9) and "vienen las blandas olas de aqueste aire sereno" ("the gentle waves of that serene breeze come") (stanza 14). Juan's poetic persona

---

[19] The English translation of Juan's "Noche oscura" is taken from the Kavanaugh and Rodríguez translation in *The Collected Works of St. John of the Cross*. *Untold Sisters* by Arenal and Schlau includes Amanda Powell's translation of Cecilia's "Canciones de la Unión y Transformación del alma en Dios por la niebla Divina de pura contemplación," a version of her "Liras" (183-4). Many of the stanzas of the two poems are identical. I use Powell's translation when possible. When the quote from the "Liras" is not found in the "Canciones," I supply my own translation.

also notes the presence of breezes during her encounter with her lover, "el ventalle de cedros aire daba" ("in a breeze from the fanning cedars") (stanza 6). She also feels "El aire de la almena" ("the breeze blew from the turret") (stanza 7).

The reference to "noche serena" ("tranquil night") in Cecilia's poem (stanza 10) is paralleled by the reference to "noche dichosa" ("glad night") in Juan's poem (stanza 3). While the beloved in Cecilia's poem seeks her Divine Lover "con deseos saliόndole al encuentro" ("with desire she sets forth to meet him") (stanza 10), the speaker in "Noche oscura" left seeking her lover "con ansias" ("with urgent longings") (stanza 1). In "Liras" love directs the beloved to the Divine Spouse, "El amor la encamina . . . sin otra doctrina, camina muy segura" ("Love guides her on her way, / . . . unerring, she finds the way") (stanza 11). Juan's narrator proceeds "A escuras y segura" ("In darkness and secure") (stanza 2). She searches "sin otra luz y guía, / sino la que en el corazón ardía ("with no other light or guide / than the one that burned in my heart.") (stanza 3). Cecilia's poem further elaborates what Juan means by "sin otra luz y guía" by declaring "sin que haya entendimiento ni memoria" ("without understanding or memory") (stanza 12).

The similarities in structure and language between stanza 13 in Cecilia's "Liras" and stanza 5 of Juan's "Noche oscura" are readily apparent. There is the same exuberant exclamation at the consummation of union. The night joins the beloved to her Lover in both poems. The union transforms the beloved into her Lover. In both poems these stanzas are followed by comparable references to the lovers being completely alone together. In Cecilia's poem the beloved enjoys the Divine Lover, "gozando dél a solas," ("enjoying him in solitude") in a "prado ameno" ("pleasant meadow") protected by a wall (stanza 14). In "Noche oscura" the lovers together enjoy "mi pecho florido / que entero para él sólo se guardaba" ("Upon my flowering breast / which I kept wholly for him alone,") (stanza 6). The beloved in Cecilia's poem finds herself "de sí toda enajenada" ("completely forgetful of herself") (stanza 15). Juan's poem suggests a similar experience: "todos mis sentidos suspendía" ("suspending all my senses") (stanza 7).

In Cecilia's "Liras" the beloved is "robada" or ravaged, and it is in that sense that she is "de sí toda enajenada" (stanza 15). In "Noche oscura" the narrator reports that she lost herself, forgot herself: "olvidéme . . . dejéme, / dejando mi cuidado/ entre las azucenas olvidado" ("I abandoned and forgot myself / . . . leaving my cares/ forgotten among the lilies.") (stanza 8). The surrender of self in the encounter is explicit in the last lines of Cecilia's poem: "con darse por vencida/ pierde su ser y en Él es convertida" ("when she is overcome, / herself dissolves and is transformed in Him.") (stanza 16). These lines also recall the declaration of "Noche oscura": "amada en el amado transformada" that the beloved is transformed into her Lover (stanza 5).

As can be seen from this comparison of the two poems the principal themes of "Noche oscura" are found in Cecilia's "Liras." The poetic persona leaves, ascends, searching for her Lover in darkness, guided only by the love that burns in her heart. She finds him, unites with him. They are completely alone together in a safe and secret place where a gentle breeze blows. She surrenders herself and loses herself completely. The encounter transforms the beloved into her Lover.

There are also important differences in these two poems. Cecilia does not employ the sustained lyricism of "Noche oscura." The lyricism of the "Liras" is interrupted by explanatory passages and references to doctrine, a feature absolutely absent in Juan's poem. She identifies the "niebla oscura" to be a divine light, "una luz divina" (stanza 1). Cecilia remarks that the beloved sees nothing because knowledge has been both transcended and attained, "trascendida y alcanzada" (stanza 2). She ascends to her secret center, the "empíreo Cielo" (stanza 4). Cecilia explains that the beloved is still because her understanding is blind, her passions are in check, and her faculties are suspended: "su entender ya ciego, / las pasiones rendidas, / . . .las potencias suspendidas" (stanza 6). She also explains that Christ's mysteries served as the path for the encounter with the Divine Spouse sought by the beloved (stanza 7). The beloved enjoys "el Verbo Eterno" ("the Eternal Word") whose "espíritu divino mueve un aire muy blando / que todo lo interior va regalando" ("Holy Spirit breathes / an air both sweet and mild") (stanza 9). Juan never identifies the "Amado" for whom the "amada" searches. Cecilia notes that love is the only doctrine that guides the beloved in her search for God's beauty (stanza 11). Understanding and memory are not involved (stanza 12). Juan's poem only alludes to "la luz . . . que en el corazón ardía" ("with no other light or guide / than the one that burned in my heart") (stanza 3). Cecilia is careful to note in her poem that the beloved experiences her Divine Spouse only to the extent possible in this life (stanza 12). Cecilia added a final stanza written by her brother, Antonio Sobrino, at his request. It takes pains to point out that the poem in no way suggests that a creature can lose its creaturely status when united and transformed in God (stanza 17).

Cecilia incorporates important notions found in Juan's prose commentaries into the body of her poem. Cecilia's observation in the first stanza of the "Liras" that the dark cloud experienced by the beloved is divine light is an important theme of Book II of the *Subida*.[20] Cecilia echoes Juan's teaching on faith when she observes that the dark cloud has blinded the beloved in that knowledge has been both transcended and realized. According to Juan, faith blinds the intellect. It is the dark night and the dark cloud that give light to the

---

[20] Chapters 8 and 9 of Book II of the *Subida* focus on the darkness of contemplation as divine light and stresses that the contemplative must unite with the divine darkness.

soul (S2,3,4 and 5).[21] Cecilia's reference to the suspension of the faculties in stanza 6 recalls Juan's discussion in the *Subida* about how faith, hope and charity empty and darken the understanding, memory and will of the soul so that they can be united with God (S2,6,6). Cecilia's reference to the soul's secret center, its inner heaven (stanza 4), reflect Juan's call to hide within one's deepest center to find the dwelling place of the Divine Spouse (C1). When Cecilia asserts that love alone guides the beloved to her Divine Spouse, she calls to mind Juan's focus on love's central role in the movement of the soul toward God. Juan asserts, "el alma por amor se resuelve en nada, nada sabiendo sino amor" ("the soul, through love, is brought to nothing, knowing nothing save love") (C1,18). Juan devotes several chapters in Book II of *Noche oscura* to how love brings the beloved to union with God (N2,11 - N2, 20). She reaffirms these fundamental notions found in Juan's commentaries in her treatise on the "Liras."

Tratado de la transformación del alma en Dios

As noted above, Cecilia wrote her first treatise on the "Liras" at the behest of her spiritual director, Tomás de Jesús. Cecilia follows the procedure Juan employed in commenting his poems: she comments her poem stanza by stanza and verse by verse. Cecilia focuses almost exclusively on contemplative experience itself, as did Juan in *Cántico espiritual* and *Llama de amor viva*. Cecilia does talk about the purification and suffering that accompanies contemplative experience, particularly in her discussion of stanza 3, but these topics do not play a very prominent role in her commentary.

The commentary opens with a description of the basic features of contemplative experience. Once the person is emptied of all things, a divine darkness covers the profound abyss of the person's capacity ("la cubre una tiniebla divina los profundos abismos de su capacidad, en la inmensidad de Dios") (83).[22] Through this darkness the contemplative "recibe comunicación del mismo Dios en su misma sustancia" ("receives communication from God's very self in her very substance") (84). For Cecilia, darkness is a fundamental feature of contemplative experience; "no hay ver, sino gozar en oscuro al mismo que tiene consigo, sin saber ni entender cómo" (There is no sight, only the enjoyment in darkness of the very one with whom one is, without knowing or understanding how") (112). Contemplation is experienced as darkness "por el exceso de la luz divina que ciega el entendimiento humano" ("because of the excess of divine light that blinds human understanding") (129). The darkness of

---

[21] The following abbreviations are used to refer to Juan's commentaries: S = *Subida del Monte Carmelo*, N = *Noche oscura*, C = *Cántico espiritual*, L = *Llama de amor viva*. The numbers refer to the book, chapter and verse respectively.

[22] I prepared the translations of Cecilia's "Tratado."

contemplation gives the contemplative more power to control her passions (131).

In contemplative prayer, God drowns the beloved in the immensity of divine being ("la ahoga en la inmensidad de su Ser") (100). Cecilia observes: "el perderse es ganarse" ("to lose oneself is to gain oneself") (133). She notes: "cuanto más se sume en esta muerte y vida divina, tanto con mayor fuerza tiene las cosas de este Señor y vive en El" ("the more one unites with this divine death and divine life, the greater the power with which one has the things of the Lord and the greater the force with which one lives in Him") (139). Contemplatives learn to "soltarse en la inmensidad de Dios" ("throw themselves into the immensity of God") (117) and in so doing they discover "este lugar inmenso que tienen en sí mismos y en El mismo" ("this immense place that they have within themselves and within Him (120).

Cecilia also discusses the contemplative's transformation in God. As God's light is a divine fire, it consumes the soul and infuses it with divine properties (85). God's light is God's gaze:

> Con su gloria la hermosea, con su hermosura la purifica, con su limpieza la clarifica y resplandece con su claridad rayos y resplandores divinos; la alumbra con su luz, la hace verdadera en su verdad, hácela toda amor en su amor, la santifica en su santidad y hace graciosa en su gracia divina, hécela Dios por la participación y unión con su Deidad, y se cumple bien lo del Salmo que dice: "Son dioses e hijos del Altísimo."

> With divine glory God beautifies her, with beauty God purifies her, through polishing God brightens her. She glows with God's clarity, and radiates divine rays. God enlightens her with his light, makes her true in his truth, makes her full of love in his love. God sanctifies her in his holiness and makes her full of grace in his divine grace. God makes her God through participation and union with Divinity. Thus is fulfilled the psalm which says: "You are gods and children of the Most High" (Psalm 82,6). (92)

Through the contemplative experience of God's pure and simple being, God bestows "inmensas riquezas, tesoros y secretos divinos, estando el alma vuelta y reducida en nada" ("great riches, divine treasures and secrets, while the soul is reduced to nothing") (128).

Beginning with stanza 6, Cecilia's "Tratado" relates the full flowering of contemplative experience. She discusses the divine means by which the contemplative gains knowledge of God's divinity through the human Word, which is Christ (138-9). The presence of her Divine Lover is the only good that can satisfy the longings of the beloved:

> Goza con esta divina posesión . . . le comunica al alma una manera de inmensidad que antes no tenía, recibiéndola de Dios, o por mejor decir, recibiéndola en Sí, siendo transformada en El, que la llena aquel inmenso vacío que sólo El puede satisfacer.
>
> She takes joy in this divine possession . . . a kind of immensity never before experienced is granted to the soul. She receives it from God, or better said, she receives it within his being, having already been transformed in Him who fills that immense void in her which only He can satisfy. (141)

Deeper contemplative experience moves her to greater service of others (142). She is always moving within God and for God, while possessing a sublime inner peace (143). The substance of her soul is so deified that she no longer gives any thought to discomforts that affect the more superficial levels of her being (147). The Divine Lover unites himself more fully with her (150) and fills her with his beauty and holiness (151).

The union of the two lovers expands and deepens until no further development is possible in earthly life (158). The Divine Spouse reveals himself immensely in an immense and limitless place which he himself is: "se le muestra con inmensidad en un lugar inmenso y sin límite, que es en El mismo" (153). In this contemplative state of infinite expansion, God places the beloved in a limitless dimension:

> Le pone Dios los pies en un lugar espacioso, en un divino cielo, pues El es el Creador del cielo, en donde se extiende, ensancha y camina inmensamente, y sin necesidad de otro camino, porque en esta latitud inmensa camina el alma excediendo a todos los demás caminos, que ésos quedan atrás y como acabados de andar . . . y cuanto más camina las (inmensidades) descubre de nuevo infinitamente mayores.
>
> God sets her feet in a spacious place, in a divine heaven (After all, He is the Creator of heaven.) where she extends and stretches herself and walks with immensity and without need for any other path. In this immense latitude the soul walks, exceeding all known paths, for those are left behind as if they had all already been walked. As she walks more, she discovers more immensities which are infinitely greater. (154)

The beloved lives in an unbreakable unity with her Divine Spouse, in spiritual marriage (161). She praises the night that makes the union possible:

> Más clara eres que el cristal para el alma, pues en ti se le dio (aunque encubierto), del modo que se le ha de dar en la eternidad; mas con admiración grande de cuanto bien y claridad le comunicas en esta vida,

> juntándola consigo el que es esencialmente luz, haciendo el efecto que hace esta luz esencial en ella, pues de ella recibe toda la que tiene, y ella la juntó consigo para hacerla luz; así le dice: Oh clara encubierta, oscura y clara manifestación de la Divinidad del Esposo.

> For the soul you are clearer than cristal, for in you was he given (although concealed), in the way in which he will be given in eternity. Even so the soul is greatly astounded at the clarity and extent to which you do make him known in this life, uniting the soul to the one who is essentially light, causing the effect that this essential light makes in her. For from the night she receives all the light that she has, and the night united her to itself in order to transform her into light. Therefore, she says: Oh hidden clarity, dark and clear manifestation of the Divinity of the Spouse. (160)

There is no part of her that does not belong to her Divine Spouse (166). Even the humblest created thing is bathed in divine glory. She observes:

> Y así parece que de aquel golpe de gloria que recibe de Dios en su centro, se deriva y extiende hasta coger lo más bajo; y así todo lo que mira le parece bañado de luz de gloria y Divinidad.

> It seems that that blow of glory she receives from God in her center, drifts and extends until it includes the lowest thing; so that all the she sees seems to be bathed in the light of divine glory. (168)

While remaining a creature she is transformed into her creator (171). This occurs because in dying to herself she expands to receive the very immensity of God.

> Mas éste es el altísimo misterio y bien de las criaturas racionales que, siendo tan pequeñas y tan nada en respecto de Dios, las levante El en SÍ para que verdaderamente gocen de El mismo. Y cuanto más esta nada se aniquila a sí misma, tanto más habilidad tiene para que se extienda su capacidad en la inmensidad de Dios, porque está en esta nada sin detenerse en cosa limitada.

> This is the highest mystery and benefit granted to rational creatures, that, being so small and of such nothingness with respect to God, that God should raise them up in Himself so that they can truly possess Him. The more that this nothingness annihilates herself, the greater her ability to extend her capacity in the immensity of God, because she is immersed in this nothingness without lingering in something limited. (173)

The rending of a transparent veil at death, will allow her to experience God with complete clarity (176). In eternal life she will receive from the Lord of her soul "tantos bienes y efectos divinos, que es imposible poderse decir ni dar a entender" ("so many divine goods and favors that it is impossible to be able to express them nor make them understood") (176).

Cecilia's "Tratado" reiterates many themes found in Juan's commentaries. One has the impression that she had his commentary on the "Cántico espiritual" before her while writing it. Her language often echoes his.

Not surprisingly, given the dependence of Cecilia's "Liras" on Juan's "Noche oscura," the themes of divine darkness and light are as central to Cecilia's discussion of spiritual development as they are to Juan's. Cecilia understands the darkness of God in many of the same ways that Juan does. The contemplative is in darkness when she has been completely emptied:

> Habiendo acabado por echar de sí todas las afecciones y apetitos, vencido y rendido todas las pasiones, borrado de sí todas las imágenes y formas que la podían estorbar . . . así de esta suerte dispuesta, luego la cubre una tiniebla divina los profundos abismos de su capacidad.
>
> Having thrown off all affections and appetites, having conquered all passions, having erased all images and forms that could impede her . . . thus disposed, a divine darkness covers the profound abysses of her capacity. (83)

Juan points out that through the negation of anything that one can understand, enjoy or imagine, it becomes possible to "unirse con la tiniebla" ("be united with the darkness") because "debajo de ella está Dios escondido" ("it is joined with God under this cloud") (S2,9,4;S2,9,1). Juan and Cecilia both understand divine darkness to be in reality divine light. It is experienced as darkness because it exceeds human capacity. Cecilia says: "es por el exceso de la luz divina, que ciega el entendimiento humano" ("human understanding is blinded by the excess of divine light") (129). Juan explains: "Como Dios es tiniebla para nuestro entendimiento, así ella también ciega y deslumbra nuestro entendimiento." ("and just as God is darkness to our intellect, so faith dazzles and blinds us.") (S2,9,1).

For Juan, the practice of the virtue of faith leads the contemplative to union with God. The darkness of faith guides the beloved to her innermost center where her Divine Lover resides (S2,4,2). Book II of the *Subida* deals primarily with the indispensable role of faith in the reception of contemplative experience. Faith leads the beloved's attention away from limited images, concepts and feelings, characteristic of the practice of meditation, toward "una noticia amorosa general, no distinta ni particular como antes" ("a general loving knowledge . . . neither distinct nor particular, as was the previous knowledge") (S2,14,2), characteristic of contemplative experience. Cecilia also insists on the necessity of proceeding in prayer by faith if contemplative experience is to dawn (124, 159).

Both Juan and Cecilia understand contemplation to be the infusion of God's being into the human person. Juan defines it as the pure and simple wisdom of God which transcends specific and particular forms of knowledge (S2,16,7). Contemplation bestows "la sustancia de los secretos" which is "el mismo Dios" ("The substance of the secrets is God himself.") (C1,10). Cecilia defines it as "comunicación del mismo Dios" ("communication of God's self") which is "sobre toda inteligencia y noticia particular" ("above all particular forms of knowledge") (84, 85). She states: "es de la misma sustancia de Dios" ("it is of the very substance of God") (85).

Juan stresses that the beloved can best control her passions and grow in virtue through the experience of contemplation. The supreme delight of contemplation effortlessly detaches the beloved from inappropriate desires (L3,51). Cecilia asserts the same: "Cuanto más el alma se allegare a este divino bien, tanto más fuerza tendrá contra sus pasiones" ("The more the soul approaches this divine good, the more strength she will have to fight her passions.") (131). She further observes: "Vale más una hora de verdadera y pura contemplación para esto y salir con ello con perfección, que muchas diligencias nuestras." ("For this purpose one hour of authentic and pure contemplation, perfectly realized, is worth more than many efforts on our part.") (131). She echoes Juan's position. For him one powerful experience of contemplation "basta . . . para quitar al alma de una vez todas las imperfecciones que ella no había podido quitar en toda la vida." ("would be sufficient . . . to remove definitively all the imperfections that the soul would have been unable to eradicate throughout its entire life.") (S2,26,6).

Juan describes spiritual development as a progressively greater participation in the being of God. Contemplation fills the beloved with divine virtue (S2,26,6). It makes her "engrandecida, honrada y hermoseada" (C33,7). It clothes her with delight and bathes her in inestimable glory (C17,7). Cecilia also understands spiritual development in terms of a progressive deification much as does Juan. God infuses divine brilliance into the beloved, giving her life, strength, beauty, holiness and glory (151, 158).

When Cecilia describes the deification of the soul in terms of spiritual marriage in stanzas 13 through 16, she echoes Juan's discussions of spiritual marriage in the *Cántico espiritual*. Juan notes that in spiritual marriage "se hace tal junta de las dos naturalezas y tal comunicación de la divina a la humana, que, no mudando alguna de ellas su ser, cada una parece Dios." ("The union wrought between the two natures and the communication of the divine to the human in this state is such that even though neither changes its being, both appear to be God.") (C22,5).

Everything she does is divine: "En este estado no puede el alma hacer actos; que el Espíritu Santo los hace todos y la mueve a ellos." ("In this state the soul cannot make acts because the Holy Spirit makes them all and moves it toward them.") (L1,4). In full transformation the beloved possesses all that God possesses through participation:

> De donde las almas esos mismos bienes poseen por participación que El por naturaleza; por lo cual verdaderamente son dioses por participación, iguales y compañeros suyos de Dios. (C39,6)
>
> Accordingly, souls possess the same goods by participation that the Son possesses by nature. As a result they are truly gods by participation, equals and companions of God.

Cecilia also understands spiritual marriage to unite two natures in one spirit (161). The beloved is transformed in God without losing her own nature (171). Earlier in her commentary, she describes contemplation as "una participación de la misma esencia de Dios . . . y hace que sea en El otra El." ("participation in the very essence of God. It transforms her within Him to be another 'Him'") (100). The beloved is transformed to the point that a clearer communication of God's being is not possible in this life (159). God has completely stolen her; all her soul's operations are divine (166). In spiritual marriage the union of the beloved with her Spouse cannot be broken as she is completely transformed in God (161).

Juan and Cecilia both use the symbol of the garden, taken from "The Song of Songs" (5,1) to describe spiritual marriage. For Cecilia God's immensity is like a meadow and God's goods are like the flowers that fill it. A breeze which bespeaks of eternity moves through the meadow. It causes a delicate dizziness, filling her with a taste of divine, eternal life: "Como una sauvísima marea que suavemente anda por toda ella y la penetra con este gusto y sentir de vida divina y eterna" (164). This breeze brings the touch of the Holy Spirit which makes her lose all awareness of external things (165). Through all of this the beloved is protected from all possible disturbance by a wall established by the power of her Divine Spouse (164).

Juan observes that after the beloved has been the spouse of the Son of God for some time, God takes her to his garden full of flowers ("huerto florido") to consummate the union (C22,5). The fruits and flowers of the garden signify the delights that God has waiting for her there. In this state the beloved finds "mucha más abundancia y henchimiento De Dios, y más segura y estable paz, y más perfecta suavidad sin comparación" ("a much great abundance and fullness of God, a more secure and stable peace, and an incomparably more perfect delight") (C22,5). Elsewhere Juan explains "el silbo de los aires amorosos" ("the whistling of love-stirring breezes" as God touching the substance of the soul:

> Así como el toque del aire se gusta en el sentido del tacto y el silbo del mismo aire con el oído, así tambión el toque de las virtudes del Amado se sienten y gozan con el tacto de esta alma, que es en la sustancia de ella, y la inteligencia de las tales virtudes de Dios se sienten en el oído del alma, que es el entendimiento.
>
> As the feeling of the breeze delights the sense of touch, and its whistling the sense of hearing, so the feeling of the Beloved's attributes are felt and enjoyed by the soul's power of touch, which is in its substance, and the knowledge of these attributes is experienced in its hearing, which in the intellect. (C14-15,13)

In Conclusion

These parallels between Cecilia's "Liras" and her "Tratado" and Juan's "Noche oscura" and his prose commentaries suggest that Cecilia was greatly indebtedness to Juan. Teresa de Jesús certainly inspired her as well. Cecilia refers to her several times in the "Tratado" (105, 112, 118, 135, 143). Teresa's influence is yet to be explored. The work of Tomás de Jesús and Cecilia's brother, Antonio Sobrino, constitute two other possible sources of influence that need to be examined as well. Tomás de Jesús, author of several treatises on prayer and mysticism, was her spiritual director for many years. Her brother, Antonio Sobrino, also wrote on prayer and mysticism. Cecilia and he corresponded frequently about their experiences in prayer.

It is hoped that this essay contributes to its readers appreciation for Cecilia del Nacimiento's work. She is an accomplished author of spiritual texts that offer precious descriptions of spiritual and mystical experience. Her work indicates that Juan's teaching was kept alive among Discalced Carmelite women into the seventeenth century. Although Juan de la Cruz's works were an important source for her texts, Cecilia's testimony about the human experience of God as Divine Lover is clear and compelling. As yet her writings have not received the attention they deserve. I hope more scholars will explore it and bring it to the attention of students of the Christian mystical tradition.

11 Inside My Body Is the Body of God:
Margaret Mary Alacoque and the Tradition of Embodied Mysticism

Wendy M. Wright

On December 27, 1673, the feast of John the Evangelist, Margaret Mary Alacoque, a young professed religious of the Visitation convent in Paray-le-Monial, France, while praying before the Blessed Sacrament, was initiated into loving intimacy with Christ through the experience of an exchange of hearts. She narrated the incident in this manner:

> Once when I was before the blessed sacrament, (I had found a little space of time, though the work I had been given left me little), I was suddenly completely surrounded by the divine presence. It was so intense I lost my sense of who and where I was. I abandoned myself to the Spirit, yielding my heart to the power of his love. He made me rest for a long time on his divine breast where he showed me the marvels of his love and the unspeakable secrets of his sacred heart that had always been hidden before. He opened them to me there for the first time, in such a real and tangible way. Even though I am always afraid of deceiving myself about what I say happens inside me, I could not doubt what was happening because of the effects that the grace produced in me. This is what seemed to me to happen:
>
> He said to me "My divine heart is so impassioned with love for humanity, and for you especially, it cannot contain the flames of its burning charity inside. It must spread them through you, and show itself to humanity so they may be enriched by the precious treasures that I share with you, treasures which have all the sanctifying and saving graces needed to draw them back from the abyss of destruction. I have chosen you as an abyss of unworthiness and ignorance to accomplish this great work so that everything will be done by me."
>
> Afterwards, he asked for my heart. I begged him to take it and he did, placing it in his own adorable heart. He let me see it there like a little atom consumed in a burning furnace. Then he returned it to me

as a burning heart-shaped flame, and placed it where it had been, saying, "Here is a precious token of my love, my beloved. This will enclose a tiny spark of living flame within your side. It will serve as your heart and consume you until your last moment. Its intensity will be so unyielding that you will be unable to find relief, except briefly by bleeding. I will mark it so with the blood of my cross that it will bring you more humiliation and suffering than comfort. That is why I want you to ask for it in all simplicity, so that you can practice what is asked of you and be given the joy of shedding your blood on the cross of humiliation. And to prove that the grace I have just given is not imaginary and is the foundation of all the others I intend to give you, the pain in your side will always remain, even though I have closed the wound. If up until now you have only been called my slave, I now give you the name "Beloved Disciple of My Sacred Heart."[1]

This account of the exchange of hearts with Jesus, the embodied God, that Margaret Mary Alacoque narrated in her Autobiography sets the stage for a discussion of what might aptly be termed the tradition of "embodied mysticism" within Christianity. I will attempt to identify that tradition, and situate the devotion to the Sacred Heart and Margaret-Mary's account of the exchange of hearts within that tradition.

The Embodied God

The Christian religion has a long and venerable tradition of imaging the divine in bodily form. At the core of this tradition, of course, is the theological assertion of the incarnation—that God became human. Parallel to this theological teaching runs the long-standing practice of lavishly depicting the embodied God—as a baby in the manger, being baptised in the Jordan and, most especially, suffering and dying upon the cross. This practice is not simply literary or artistic. It is performative as well. Within the contemplative/ meditative streams of Christian life that might well be termed "embodied mysticism." Devotees have not only gazed upon God's embodiment, they have entered that body in prayer and explored it. Especially have they enjoyed an intimacy with the body's apertures, the wounds, and with the divine heart revealed by entry into those wounds. Furthermore, Christian practitioners have affirmed that the divine body can be manifest in their own bodies. They can

---

[1] *Vie et Oeuvres de Sainte Marguerite-Marie*, presentation du Professeur R. Darricau, (Paris-Fribourg: Editions St. Paul, 1991), pp. 82-4. Margaret Mary recorded several versions of this incident. This is the one found in her autobiography. On the various versions see E. Glotin, "'Un jour de saint Jean l'Evangéliste': les differentes récits d'une même apparition" R. Darricau and B. Peyrous, eds, *Sainte Marguerite-Marie et le message de Paray-Le-Monial* (Paris: Editions Desclée, 1993), pp. 291-322.

become the wounded body. The wounds, indeed the heart of God itself, can take fleshy form in them once more.

Margaret Mary's experienced "exchange of hearts" did not take place in a vacuum. It occurred within a rich and historically conditioned symbolic context. As a devout Roman Catholic of late seventeenth-century France, she was steeped in modes of prayer that encouraged a radical participation with the suffering of Jesus. The crucifixion, since the church's inception, had been the paradox upon which believers had dwelt to ascertain ultimate meaning. But in the medieval era Christians desired more and more to conform their lives to the crucified in a manner that can be described as literal affective participation.[2] Certainly, the martyrs of previous centuries had died to become part of the victory over death ushered in by the Christ event, and the desert ascetics and monastics had undertaken a life of ascetic martyrdom in conformity with Christ. But a Francis of Assisi, with his guerilla theatre sensibilities, "acting out" the Christ event in his own flesh, took imitation of Christ to extraordinary lengths. His imitation was more than interior transformation of character, more than a disciplining of the passions, more than the adoption of a counter-cultural lifestyle. It was a theatrical embodiment, an enfleshing of God revealed as the poor, crucified Christ. This Christian spirituality of the high Middle Ages has been described as highly affective, somatic and participatory.[3] And so it was. It was also increasingly personal and narrative in character. The Christ story was explored not simply as historical fact or theological truth or metaphor but as an unfolding drama to which the collective Christian imagination supplied vivid theatrical details. Spiritual followers of Christ lived into this dramatic scenerio. Francis was only one example. And his reception of the stigmata, his personal somatic realization of the wounds of his beloved Lord, was a logical outcome of a life given over to the absorption and expression of the truths of the crucified one.

Scholars have noted that this affective, somatic spirituality was, Francis notwithstanding, primarily a woman's spirituality.[4] The annals of the spiritual tradition from this period are full of striking female figures who embodied, "acted out", or were joined in union to the person of the crucified Lord. The

---

[2] Ewert Cousins, in his "The Humanity and Passion of Christ" in *Christian Spirituality II: High Middle Ages and Reformation*, ed. Jill Raitt, Vol. 17 of *World Spirituality* (New York: Crossroads, 1987), pp. 375-91 refers to this type of spirituality as the "mysticism of the historic moment."

[3] Carolyn Walker Bynum, "The Female Body and Religious Practice in the Later Middle Ages," *Zone 3: Fragments for a History of the Human Body*, (New York: Cambridge University Press, 1989), pp. 160-219.

[4] See Carolyn Walker Bynum, *Holy Feast, Holy Fast: The Religious Significance of Food to Medieval Women* (Berkeley: University of California Press, 1987); and Carolyn Walker Bynum, "Religious Women in the Later Middle Ages," pp. 121-69 Raitt, *Christian Spirituality*.

motifs and lived expressions of this embodiment were varied—stigmata, mystical marriages, intensely affective emotions and cruciform illnesses.

Beyond the medieval era, this tradition of passionate, somatic identification survived in womens' religious communities. The vivid experience of bodily and mental anguish became more and more constitutive of the unitive event. Suffering, particularly as a sacrificial victim, became a primary category through which knowledge and intimacy with God was cultivated.[5] Moreover, the suffering participant became part of the redemptive movement unleashed in the Christ event. The sufferer became an alter-Christus whose own pain was efficacious. Suffering was redemptive for both self and others. By the seventeenth century, the spirituality often discovered in cloistered women's communities was of this sort. Margaret Mary Alacoque may be viewed as a direct descendent of this tradition.[6]

The Heart of God

Interwoven with this spirituality of the suffering body was the image of God's sacred heart. Seen in retrospect, the cumulative prayer of the Christian community, through its centuries long gazing upon the crucified body, i.e. its "reading" of the text of that body, moved more and more inward and, finally entering the body, discovered the definitive text—the heart. For the heart was known to be the core of the person, the central integrating and energizing principle from which thought, feeling and action flow. To know the heart was thus to know the foundational truth of the person. To know the heart of Jesus was to become intimate with the ultimate mystery of God.

The reading of the body-text which yielded the ultimate mystery of the heart had begun in the patristic era with an allegorical reading of the pierced side and the ecclesial fountain of life that issued from it. In the early medieval era, the community probed the wounds and arrived finally at the heart where the depth of divine love was discernable. The side-wound especially became an object of cultic devotion. It became the symbol par excellence of the intimate loving relationship between creator and creatures. The sacrifice on the Cross more and more came to be understood as an expression of profound love so that the devotee in praying to the wounds, particularly the side-wound which was conceptualized as the entryway to the heart, experienced Love itself. The

---

[5] Jacques Le Brun, "Institution et le corps, lieux de la mémoire: d'après les biographies spirituelles feminines aux XVII siècle", in *Corps écrit et l'image*, pp. 111-12.

[6] S. Ringborn, "Devotional Images and Imaginative Devotions: Notes on the Place of Art in Late Medieval Piety," *Gazette des Beaux-Arts*, 6th Series, 73 (1969): 159-70; Jeffrey F. Hamburger, "The Use of Images in the Pastoral Care of Nuns: The Case of Henry Suso and the Dominicans," *Art Bulletin*, 71 (1989): 20-46; and Jeffrey F. Hamburger, "The Visual and the Visionary: The Image in Late Medieval Monastic Devotions," *Viator* 20 (1989): 161-82.

flowing fountain issuing from the side wound was both eucharistic and baptismal.

The mystical tradition of the high Middle Ages entered even more boldly into the heart, and in its intensely personal, affective, somatic style, sought identification with that heart. Through the lens of the Song of Songs the medieval world gave articulation to a love affair between the heart of Jesus and the heart of the mystic spouse. The one who desired union would drink from the opened side, seek intimacy inside the refuge of the wound, and be incorporated into God's body through the bleeding portal portal.

Devotion to the wounds and the heart was associated with the great names of the Cistercian renewal, with the Benedictines, the mendicant orders and the Carthusians. By the thirteenth century women in the circle of the Rhineland Cistercian monastery of Helfta, like Gertrude the Great and Mechtilde of Hackborn, were recording visions of Christ appearing to reveal his Heart. Fourteenth century members of the extended Dominican family, like Henry Suso and Catherine of Siena, gave eloquent theological and mystical expression to their attraction to the Lord's wounded body.[7] With the dawn of the modern era, the loving, virtuous heart had become a model for emulation and the interior transformation of the human heart. By the seventeenth century, the Catholic community was deep within the body, enraptured by the varied rich messages it "read" on Jesus' heart.

One variant of this enraptured gaze was the visionary tradition of the "exchange of hearts." Within the stream of female visionary history there are a number of recorded instances of such an "exchange of hearts" taking place. Dorothy of Montau, Lutgard of Trond, Catherine of Siena, Catherine de Ricci and Jeanne Deleloe are numbered in this group.[8] The details of each of these visionary and/or mystical experiences differs according to the prevailing spirituality of the era, region, and individual visionary. But all of these accounts point to an experience of radical experiential participation in the Christ event as it is focused on the heart of the crucified and the experience of loving conformity to or union with his suffering life. This participation is understood to be not only personally edifying but to be initiated by God for a greater good. God, as it were, continues the redemptive work encoded in the body of the crucified through the bodies of the women visionaries, the very core of whose beings—the heart—has been replaced or inhabited or regenerated by the heart

---

[7] On this rich and complex era see Josef Stierli, "Devotion to the Sacred Heart From the End of the Patristic Times Down to Saint Margaret Mary," pp. 55-108 in Josef Stierli, ed., *Heart of the Saviour*, trans. Paul Andrews S.J. (Freiberg: Herder and Co., 1957); Walter Baier, "Key Issues in Medieval Sacred Heart Piety," pp. 81-99 in Leo Scheffczyk, ed., *Faith in Christ and the Worship of Christ*, trans. Graham Harrison (San Francisco: St. Ignatius Press, 1986).

[8] "Coeurs (changement des, echange des)" in *Dictionnaire de spiritualité ascetique et mystique*, Vol. II, col.1046-51.

of God. Margaret Mary's experience is certainly shaped by this ongoing tradition.

The devotional and visual environment in which the Visitandine lived encouraged her in this spirituality. A dense tapestry of religious symbols and practices functioned together almost alchemically to transmute the Visitandine's ideational, affective, volitional and somatic reality. She was surrounded by iconographic representations of God's heart in the form of devotional images and jewelry, she was heir to a narrative devotional tradition that provided previous examples of the exchange of divine and human hearts, she was trained in ascetic disciplines that created the conditions for the radical interior and exterior transmutation to occur and she was schooled in a prayer tradition designed to encourage imitation, in fact to produce literal embodied participation with the suffering Jesus.[9]

In a focused way, the Salesian spiritual tradition of which Margaret Mary was a part was saturated with verbal and visual symbolism that could encourage such participation. Her religious community, the Visitation, had been co-founded by Francis de Sales (hence the term Salesian) and Jane de Chantal at the dawn of the seventeenth century. Although formal devotion to the heart of Jesus as it was promulgated after the apparitions that Margaret Mary received was not a part of early Visitation practice, nevertheless the language of "heart to heart" intimacy with God and neighbor was prominant in that tradition.[10] The Salesian world was a world of interconnected hearts—the hearts of God and humankind bridged by the crucified heart of Jesus. Indeed, in the writings of founder de Sales are found exhortations to those who pray to take on, as it were, the heart of God.

> Our Lord wants His side to be open for several reasons. The first is so that so that we might see that the thoughts of His heart are thoughts of love and affection for us, His beloved children and creatures created in the divine image and likeness, in order that we might see how He wishes to give us graces and blessings and even His heart itself, as He did saint Catherine of Siena. I admire the incomparable grace by which He exchanged hearts with her; for previously she had prayed in this manner: 'Lord, I commend my heart to you ' but later she said, 'Lord, I commend our heart to you' in the sense that the heart of God was her heart. Certainly, devout souls should not have any heart but His, no

---

[9] See especially the first essays by A. Brix, H. Bordes, J.-M. Lemaire, H. L'Honore and J. Arragain in R. Darricau and B. Peyrous, eds, *Sainte Marguerite-Marie et le Message de Paray-le-Monial* (Paris: Desclée, 1993).

[10] Compare Wendy M. Wright, "'That is What It Is Made For:' The Image of the Heart in the Spirituality of Francis de Sales and Jane de Chantal," pp. 143-58 in Annice Callahan, R.S.C.J., ed., *Spiritualities of the Heart* (New York: Paulist Press, 1990).

will but His, no other affections or desires than His, in short, they must be completely in Him.[11]

Taking On the Heart of Jesus

Margaret Mary's account of the exchange reads as a rite of initiation. It takes place on December 27th, the feast of John the Evangelist, the beloved disciple long considered to be the archtypal contemplative, the one who rests upon the breast of Jesus (i.e. on his heart) and is intimate with divine love. She is before the blessed sacrament, the sacramental body of God. At that powerful transparent time and place, the encounter with divinity is prepared. The Visitandine feels "surrounded by presence" and yields herself, adopting the position of the beloved disciple as she leans on Jesus' breast. Some sort of showing then takes place. The hidden "secrets" of the divine heart are revealed. It is unclear whether Margaret Mary visually perceives these events outside herself or whether they occur interiorly although they appear to her to be "real." But it is clear that a somatic effect occurs. She claims that the "effects" took the form of an intense and enduring pain in her side.

She describes Jesus, the embodied God, his heart on flame with love of humankind so much that the flames cannot be contained. This, the Visitandine knows, is the heart that died for love, that suffered ultimate agony in desire to redeem humankind. This Jesus then asks for her heart and, as she consents, it becomes consumed in those spreading flames. When it is given back to her, it is altered. Now it too is a flame that consumes and must be spread. Now she holds within her own body the very heart of God. She suffers as He suffered. She redeems as He redeemed. She quite literally experiences pain in her flesh as He did. The love of God has become incarnated in her. Her new identity is complete and confirmed by her new Name which echoes John the evangelist's name. Jesus calls her "the beloved disciple of My Sacred Heart."

Embodied Mysticism

Such an occurrence can accurately be described as "embodied mysticism." There is a tendency in cross-cultural analyses of mysticism as well as in highly regarded treatments of Christian mysticism to distinguish between the "visionary" and the "mystical." Mysticism has been described as the non-conceptual, "unmediated," direct consciousness of the presence of divinity.[12] But must all direct experience of presence be seemingly non-conceptual and

---

[11] *Oeuvres de Saint François de Sales, Edition Complète* (Annecy: Monastère de la Visitation, 1892-1964), t. IX, 80.

[12] See Bernard McGinn, *The Foundations of Mysticism: Origins to the Fifth Century* (New York: Crossroad, 1991), general introduction, pp. xi-xx.

unmediated? Margaret Mary's account makes the claim that she experienced God's presence directly. As she underwent the removal of her own heart and its replacement by the divine heart she declared that she had become an extension of God's own body. Her consciousness of God's presence was located within her own physicality, specifically within the heart. Furthermore, that consciousness was manifested in somatic form. While the crucial distinction (for Christianity) between Creator and created was maintained in the exchange, nevertheless an intimate participation in divine life which was radically transformative took place.

Christianity is a religion that concerns itself with the embodied meeting of heaven and earth. Pivotal concepts such as the incarnation, the resurrection of the body, and the communion of saints (which bridges heaven and earth as well as time and eternity), continue to direct attention to the divine-human intersection—the body. Embodied matter matters in the Christian vision of things. The tradition claims: God comes to us as a body, we go to God as bodies; in embodiment God becomes human and human becomes divine. There are certainly strains of Christian thought, and hence mysticism, which locate the divine presence in an intuitive, non-conceptual apprehension. There is, in other words, an "apophatic" tradition. But I would suggest that the apophatic tendency is also discovered in "embodied mysticism." It is not simply that Christianity contains cataphatic and apophatic insights. It is not a simple choice between knowing and unknowing, seeing and not seeing, revelation and the night of obscurity. In embodied mysticism there is a variant type of "unknowing." This is accomplished somatically, especially in the embodied experience of loss, pain, poverty, suffering, and dying. The embodied mystical tradition is not foreign to the apophatic insight but it explores that insight through bodies: the mystics' and God's.

Embodied mysticism takes seriously the divine disclosure of the cross, a disclosure which is an invitation into unknowing, paradox, abandonment, and ultimately, absence. For centuries, Christian practitioners have continued to affirm performatively this sort of embodied unknowing. Their martyred, mortified, and suffering bodies have become over and over again the meeting place of heaven and earth. The heart especially has been the ultimate place of encounter—both God's heart and the human heart. In the mystical exchange of hearts we have a recorded instance of a profound, direct consciousness of the presence of God. Margaret Mary perceived God's most intimate embodied life, the heart, within her. Her union was complete. She had been transformed. The embodied God had become embodied in her.

12 Making Use of the Holy Office: Exploring the Contexts and Concepts of Sor Juana's References to the Inquisition in the *Respuesta a Sor Filotea*

Amanda Powell

Introduction

In a prose work frequently referred to simply as the "*Respuesta*" or *Answer [to Sor Filotea de la Cruz]*, the seventeenth-century Mexican (or more properly, New Spanish) poet, playwright, and woman-of-letters Sor Juana Inés de la Cruz (1651?-1695) makes strangely amusing references to the Holy Office of the Inquisition.[1] Boldly, she exploits contemporary cultural meanings of the

---

[1] An earlier version of this essay was presented at the Congreso Internacional "Sor Juana y su mundo," Universidad del Claustro de Sor Juana, Mexico, D.F., November 1995. I thank numerous colleagues for their assistance with both contexts and concepts presented here; especially Asunción Lavrin, who generously shared details of her recent research on nuns and Inquisitorial cases in New Spain, as well as Mary Giles, Kathleen A. Myers, and Dianne Dugaw. When I began the considerations reported here, the scholarly picture of Sor Juana's final years was quite different—both murkier, and simpler. Since then, important investigations have clarified, if not settled, certain questions to which I could then propose only speculative solutions. A complete review of these re-evaluations is not to the purpose here, but it is important to note that "the past" is never less fixed than in a consideration of "today's" Sor Juana, whose final years have been changing, as it were, before our eyes. Rarely does a major writer of 300 years past produce "new" texts, but that in effect is what has happened in the canon of writings by Sor Juana. Since 1980, three previously unknown or disputed texts have been firmly attributed to her. These are: Sor Juana's letter to her confessor, Antonio Núñez de Miranda, known as the "*Carta de Monterrey* (Mexico)" since its discovery there in 1980; first published as *Autodefensa espiritual de Sor Juana* (Monterrey: Universidad de Nuevo León, 1981). *Enigmas ofrecidos a la casa del placer* (discovered in 1968 but republished and validated, Mexico D. F.: El Colegio de México, 1994). "*Carta de Sor Serafina de Cristo*" (facsimile edition, Toluca, Mexico: Instituto Mexiquense de Cultura, 1996). In addition to this broadening of the Sor Juana corpus, recent research has revealed

Inquisition in order to build a defense of her own doctrinal orthodoxy, while establishing the God-given nature of the pursuit of "humane" letters for which she has been criticized by Church authorities. Explicitly, the Inquisition figures in Sor Juana's *Answer* as a feared source of *ruido* ["trouble"] or disturbance that has kept her from pursuing sacred letters. A closer look, however, shows these references functioning to quite different effect: they underscore her implicit immunity from Inquisitional persecution. Establishing her orthodoxy, her citing of the Holy Office serves to justify the many areas of her activities subject to dispute and possible censure: theological disquisition and the writing of profane verses, as well as the study in both sacred and secular letters that allowed her to attain notable accomplishments in these areas. That Sor Juana is bold enough to use the much-feared Inquisition to her own ends underscores her courage and her resourceful uses of language; at the same time, it confirms other scholars' recent demonstrations that the Holy Office did not in fact pose the most immediate threat to Sor Juana's hard-won intellectual autonomy.

A close reading of Sor Juana's remarks and a review of available historical data, in conjunction with the record given by other nuns' writings, suggest that we tend to assign greater importance to the Holy Office as a regulating, let alone threatening, force in the lives of New World women religious than it merits. On a daily basis and in most cases, other institutions exercised more direct control over the lives and writings of nuns in the period, including Sor Juana. This control was, especially, experienced from the authorities closest at hand: the confessor and his superiors, as historian Elías Trabulse's findings confirm and as other scholars have indicated.[2]

The Inquisition functioned not only against but in some instances *for* religious women of the early modern period, and Sor Juana made careful, rhetorical use of its presence. The institution most fearful in our later view—with its torture and burnings—was the one she cited to defend herself against difficulties close at hand, from her immediate superiors. "Model nuns"—those brides of Christ dedicated to devotional rather than intellectual pursuits and thus "unlike Sor Juana" (as Asunción Lavrin puts it)[3]—far from regarding the Holy Office as a threat or an opponent, were likely to see it as forwarding their projects of preservation of Catholic orthodoxy and

---

several documents that illuminate mysteries that have generated debate among *sorjuanistas* for decades, especially regarding the poet's final years and her supposed "renunciation" of writing and intellectual activity.

[2] Trabulse's recent, major discoveries are cited below. On the role of the confessor, see also Kathleen A. Myers, "The Addressee Determines the Discourse: The Role of the Confessor in the Spiritual Autobiography of Madre María de San Joseph (1656-1719)," *Bulletin of Hispanic Studies* 69:1 (1992): 39-47.

[3] Asunción Lavrin, "Unlike Sor Juana? The Model Nun in the Religious Literature of Colonial Mexico," in Stephanie Merrim, ed., *Feminist Perspectives on Sor Juana Inés de la Cruz* (Detroit: Wayne State University Press, 1991), pp. 61-85.

evangelization of the "true faith." They and the Inquisition were pitted against the common enemy of heresy. In the *Answer*, Sor Juana is at pains to position and, often, contrast herself with regard to those nuns, as she posits herself as a subject possessing, and defending, the right to secular study within the religious world.[4] Yet historically and culturally, she and they navigated the same currents in the deep waters of social and ecclesiastical hierarchy in the midcolonial viceregency. Certainly Sor Juana, with her intellectual vocation, is in no way to be taken as "representative" of nuns generally. Yet members of religious life, including nuns, who saw themselves as participating on the same side as Church institutions in the contest for salvation could in a sense "use" the Holy Office to confirm their own orthodoxy.

Sor Juana's references to the Holy Office of the Inquisition have been read uironically by some critics in their examination of the relationships to, and interrogations of, power that Sor Juana's texts construct.[5] In fact, little in Sor Juana's work can be appreciated at face value. No writer is more conscious than Sor Juana, especially in the elaborate *Answer*, of exploiting the rhetorical means at her command, as she navigates between women's supposed duty to "holy ignorance," with the silence that imposes, and her own claims to authority. Rosa Perelmuter's essay on the rhetorical structure of the *Answer*[6] pierced earlier readings of the document as a "transparent" rendering of Sor Juana's reflections on her intellectual development and aims. The poet's

---

[4] On textual parallels between Sor Juana's *Answer* and nuns' *lives* of the period, see Kathleen A. Myers, "Sor Juana's *Respuesta*: Rewriting the *Vitae*," *Revista Canadiense de Estudios Hispánicos* 14 (1990): 459-72.

[5] In *Plotting Women: Gender and Representation in Mexico*, Jean Franco says, "the Inquisition did not need to burn in order to be feared. Sor Juana's writing shows that the Holy Office was a powerful deterrent whose procedures were so well known among the population that they induced a kind of self-censorship" (p. 58). Franco's chapter 3, "The Power of the Spider Woman: The Deluded Woman and the Inquisition" dicusses one considerably later (early 19th-century) case of an *ilusa* and her trial by the Holy Office. Octavio Paz, *Sor Juana or The Traps of Faith*, trans. Margaret Sayers Peden (Cambridge, Massachusetts: Harvard University Press, 1988), cites Sor Juana's "fear of the Inquisition," p. 259, as well as her (more general) fear of coming into "conflict with the Church," p. 272. Yet while Paz perceptively offered complex background for such situations as the nun's involvement in the conflicts between bishops Fernández de Santa Cruz and Aguiar y Seijas—thus anticipating more recent findings like Trabulse's on the specific role played by the archbishop in the eventual silencing of Sor Juana—Paz never goes into detail regarding the background of Inquisition trials of religious women. Important aspects of the scholarly discussion of Sor Juana's relationship to the Holy Office are discussed in Ricardo Camarena's recent essay, "'Ruido con el Santo Oficio': Sor Juana y la censura inquisitorial," in Margarita Peña, ed., *Cuadernos de Sor Juana* (Mexico City: UNAM, 1995), pp. 283-306.

[6] Rosa Perelmuter, "La estructura retórica de la *Respuesta a Sor Filotea*", *Hispanic Review* 51 (1983): 147-58.

language is actually most highly figured where she seems most plain-spoken.[7] Of these references to the Holy Office, Marie-Cécile Bénassy-Berling observes, "Various passages in the *Respuesta* prove that Sor Juana felt no fear as she wrote it. She would not have spoken of her fear of the Inquisition if such a fear were truly felt in earnest."[8] Striking, indeed, is the ironic tone of the first three remarks, verging almost on the flippant. Sor Juana's argument does not assert her innocence against the Holy Office; rather, she uses the Inquisition in her own defense. The Tribunal serves her as a force assuring, first, her own right to study, speak, and write in the way she does; and second, her orthodoxy. Here we see the at once creative and calculated genius of Sor Juana; though it is very much her own, it is nevertheless a genius with contextual roots.

The Inquisition of New Spain, as in Spain, was an institution that operated through open and secret processes of intimidation, interrogation, and torture, as well as the elaborate public performance of terrifying spectacles of humiliation and execution, in its attempt to "safeguard" orthodoxy among the populace. In what follows, I do not wish to suggest that the Inquisition was not a threat, either to Sor Juana or to the population at large, but that Sor Juana did not perceive the Holy Office as a direct menace in her own case. The Inquisition existed as a generally foreboding and threatening presence that effectively produced an ambiance of regulation and hierarchy that affected anyone in the culture—especially, one would assume, so bold and independent a thinker as Sor Juana. However, it is precisely as this kind of presence that Sor Juana enlists the Holy Office in the *Answer*: she carefully positions herself in relation to it as a defense that simultaneously buttresses her orthodoxy, underscores the fact that she is not under suspicion (even in a suspicious context), and probably maneuvers to avert such trouble. That is, Sor Juana positions herself *vis à vis* the Holy Office, carefully defining and delimiting its presence. This strategy is effective precisely because the institution is so generally feared and genuinely threatening.

The *Answer* has long been considered key to Sor Juana's manner of self-representation, both as member of a religious order (a Jeronymite) and as a scholar, and to expression of her conviction regarding the essential unity of

---

[7] See, in addition to Perelmuter, Josefina Ludmer, "Tretas del debil" (published in English as "Tricks of the Weak," in Merrim, ed., *Feminist Perspectives on Sor Juana*), which speaks of "at least three texts" comprising Sor Juana's letter, "[t]hree zones in constant contradiction, three significant registers that transform the meaning of the utterances" (in Merrim, *Perspectives*, p. 88). See also *The Answer/La Respuesta*, ed. Arenal and Powell, "Sor Juana's Art and Argument," pp. 19-25.

[8] [*Varios pasages de la Respuesta nos prueban que Sor Juana no tiene miedo cuando la escribe. No hablaría de su temor a la Inquisición si éste fuera realmente serio . . .*] Marie-Cécile Bénassy-Berling, "Más sobre la conversión de Sor Juana," *Nueva Revista de Filología Hispana* XXXII (1983): 464.

sacred letters and secular learning, and women's right to education.[9] The text was written in March of 1691, an address to the pseudonymous "Sor [Sister] Filotea [or Philo-thea, Lover-of-God] de la Cruz [of the Cross]," nominally a "sister" religious, but in fact—as Sor Juana knew well—Manuel Fernández de Santa Cruz, the Bishop of Puebla, a religious center in New Spain second only in importance to Mexico City, where Sor Juana's own Convento de San Jerónimo was located.

A complex background of epistolary exchange stands behind the *Answer*. The bishop, a friend of Sor Juana's, had put into print a *"Crisis de un Sermón* or "Critique of a Sermon" that Sor Juana had composed, explicitly disputing central points in an earlier sermon by the renowned Portuguese Jesuit, Antonio Vieira. In publishing the critique, Fernández de Santa Cruz titled it the *"Carta Atenagórica"* or "Athenagoric Letter" (1690).[10] The object of criticism, Vieira's *"Sermón del Mandato"* ["Maundy Thursday Sermon"], had insisted that Christ's greatest *fineza*, or act of love, to humankind lay in bidding human beings to love one another rather than reserving all human love for himself.[11] Sor Juana's refutation, citing Doctors of the Church and theological sources, concluded with her own, daring proposition: that Christ's greatest *fineza* consisted of withholding his *finezas* from us; it would be easier for God, being God, to shower us with love than to leave us to find our own way by our own devices. Elías Trabulse has pointed out that Sor Juana was thus arguing forcibly for her own intellectual freedom and also countering her powerful ex-confessor, Antonio Núñez de Miranda, who had recently published a description of the Eucharist as Christ's greatest act of love.[12] In speaking against Núñez de Miranda, she was opposing not only one influential and highly placed cleric (indeed, he served as *calificador* or censor for the Inquisition) but an entire community of the political and ecclesiastical elite of Mexico; Núñez

---

[9] Juana Inés de la Cruz, "Respuesta de la poetisa a la muy ilustre Sor Filotea de la Cruz," *Obras completas*, IV, ed. Alberto Salceda (Mexico: Fondo de Cultura Económica, 1954; Instituto Mexiquense de Cultura, 1994), pp. 440-75 [henceforth referred to as *OC*]; see also *The Answer/La Respuesta*, ed. and trans. Electa Arenal and Amanda Powell (New York: The Feminist Press), especially Introduction, pp. 1-37.

[10] *"Carta Atenagórica", OC* IV, pp. 412-39. The letter from "Sor Filotea" appears in Appendix I, *OC*, pp. 694-7. The careful composition of the letter and its sophisticated argumentation indicate that Sor Juana did intend it to be published.

[11] *"Sermón del Padre Antonio Vieira en la Capilla Real. Año 1650,"* Appendix II, *OC*, pp. 673-94.

[12] Eléas Trabulse, *Los años finales de Sor Juana: una interpretación* (Mexico, D.F.: Condumex, 1995) and *La memoria transfigurada: Tres imágenes históricas de Sor Juana* (Mexico, D.F.: Universidad del Claustro de Sor Juana, 1996). Sor Juana had resoundingly dismissed Núñez as her confessor in the letter discovered in Monterrey, Mexico (Tapia Méndez, 1980); published in English as Appendix, "Sor Juana: Witness for the Prosecution," in Octavio Paz, *Sor Juana*, trans. Margaret Sayers Peden (Cambridge, Mass.: Harvard University Press, 1988), pp. 491-502.

headed the *Congregación de la Purísima*, a devotional group dedicated to the Immaculate Conception and to the principle of frequent communion, which was perceived as being slighted by Sor Juana's arguments. Among the members of the Congregation were, for example, the current viceroy of New Spain. Thus, Sor Juana was jeopardizing the political support that had counterbalanced her precarious vulnerability, in religious life, to disapproving Church authorities. Trabulse emphasizes the political error Sor Juana committed by affronting such a group.[13] In them, political and ecclesiastical power merged; she was in need of their good favor, not their displeasure.

In 1690 and 1691, however, Sor Juana was enjoying the height of a remarkable literary productivity. Her continued confidence is shown in the daring tone of another recently discovered document, the bitingly ironic "Letter from Sor Serafina" (February, 1691; discovered in 1995) in which Sor Juana declares that the true target of her "Athenagoric Letter," which ostensibly aimed at Vieira, was in fact her ex-confessor, Núñez.[14] This assurance is evident, though more subtly displayed, in the subsequent *Answer to Sor Filotea*. Sor Juana wrote this answer in response to the prefatory letter that Fernández de Santa Cruz, signing as "Sor Filotea" or "Sister Lover-of-God," attached to his publication of the "Athenagoric Letter." In it, he praised Sor Juana and her erudition; but at the same time, he chided her for devoting her time almost exclusively to secular rather than sacred studies.[15]

Fernández de Santa Cruz's praise of Sor Juana's abilities did not offset the risk which she incurred by venturing so thoroughly into theological disputation—and she knew it. Women were not supposed to "do theology." Both Spanish and colonial religious women's texts in the period, while voluminous, were almost exclusively devotional in nature or written in the genres of the *Vida* (life-story) or the *cuenta de conciencia*, a day-to-day detailing of the inner life; most of these were done under order of obedience to a confessor, to allow scrutiny of details of a nun's reported spiritual experience. Rarely were these writings markedly literary. While a knowledge of Scripture, liturgy, homiletic discourse, and major points of doctrine is often reflected in these writings, explicit theological inquiry *per se* was considered the province only of university-trained men. Sor Juana's display of her capacity for such argumentation demonstrated her dismissal of sanctions against "ignorant" and "irrational" women's participation in the field, at a time when women were

---

[13] *[(A)l refutar la tesis de Nuñéz, sor Juana cuestionó la Regla 18 de la Congregación de la Purísima sobre sa coomunión frecuente. . . . Al hacer eso Sor Juana cometió un error político grave ya que la Congregación de la Purísima agrupaba a personajes importantes de la Nueva España . . ."]* Trabulse, *Memoria transfigurada*, p. 21.

[14] "*Carta de Sor Serafina de Cristo*," *op. cit.*

[15] Filotea de la Cruz [*sic*, Manuel Fernández de Santa Cruz], "Carta de Sor Filotea de la Cruz" in *OC* IV, pp. 694-7.

considered ignorant by definition.[16] Already under ecclesiastical scrutiny and meeting with displeasure for her secular verses, she had now produced sacred writing of the wrong kind—neither properly womanly nor correctly doctrinaire.[17]

At the moment of writing her *Answer to Sor Filotea* in March of 1691, condemning ecclesiastical powers were offset, in Sor Juana's life, by protection and patronage received from the other pole of the early modern Hispanic ruling order—the crown, or in the colonies, the viceregency. Her protectors were powerful aristocratic figures, connected to the highest state and ecclesiastical powers in Madrid; they had proven able to shelter the accomplished nun, unusually celebrated outside her convent for secular love poems and verse dramas as well as religious verse, from adverse consequences to her varied activities. Directly after the period of Sor Juana's boldest literary production, however, a shift occurred in the delicate political balance that for years had made possible her relative autonomy within the thick wall of the Convento de San Jerónimo; for Sor Juana, the consequences were tragic. Her most significant supporters had returned to Spain, or had fallen out of favor, when she would most need their protection. The powerful forces opposed to Sor Juana's brilliant cultural production lost no time in moving against her.

As Trabulse has recently revealed, a special *proceso* or tribunal was initiated against Sor Juana from the office of the Archbishop, the highest ecclesiastical power in New Spain and the superior having direct authority over nuns in her convent; the secret procedure could be used against members of religious orders for a number of reasons, including failure to fulfill thoroughly

---

[16] See Antonio Alatorre, "*La carta de Sor Juana al Padre Núñez,*" *Nueva Revista de Filología Hispánica* 35 (1987), p. 644. Cited in María Agueda Méndez, "La prohibición y la conveniencia: Antonio Núñez de Miranda y la Inquisición Novohispana," in *Sor Juana & Vieira: Trescientos Años Después*, ed. K. Josu Bijuesca and Pablo A.J. Brescia (Santa Barbara, California: *TINTA*, Department of Spanish and Portuguese, 1998).

[17] There is a conspicuous absence of reference to the Inquisition in writings by other religious women of the period. The Mexican visionary and mystical writer Madre María de San José, a contemporary of Sor Juana, in more than 2,000 manuscript pages that abound in references to anxiety about the outcome of scrutiny of her writings by her superiors, never names the Inquisition as a possible threat. She does report being told, by the five confessors for whom she wrote while in the convent, what she should and should not write. She also speaks of the burning of certain of her writings, imposed not by the Inquisition but by the circle of confessors and their superiors—not an isolated case among religious women, both in Spain and the New World. This loss of personal control over literary production, however, forms an integral part of the vows of obedience and enclosure taken by nuns on their entrance into the convent. (See Kathleen A. Myers and Amanda Powell, *A Wild Country Out in the Garden: The Spiritual Journals of a Colonial Mexican Nun*, Bloomington: Indiana University Press, forthcoming).

their religious vows, especially that of obedience.[18] Sor Juana's opponents, including the archbishop and other highly placed ecclesiastics, among them members of the Inquisition, were thus able to censure a nun they found troublesome, yet avoid the scandal of a necessarily public Inquisitorial denunciation and trial that would have drawn the attention and protests of Sor Juana's now international supporters. The findings of the episcopal procedure against her required Sor Juana to divest herself of all her books and papers, as part of an obligatory "renewal of the vows of the faith." The terms and requirements of this procedure are followed in several documents in Sor Juana's hand that had previously been taken, by some scholars, to confirm a saintly religious "conversion" at the end of her life, accompanied by a willing sacrifice of studies and literary pursuits.[19]

However, in her *Answer* to the fictional Sor Filotea we read the words of a woman who has completed an extraordinary decade of literary productivity, at the height of her own powers and confidence; there, uncensored and still declaring her freedom from outer coercion, Sor Juana insists on the intrinsic unity of intellectual powers, rightly employed, with an appreciation of creation and its Creator. The obligatory statements of the later documents of rededication and renunciation are undercut by the freedom of utterance in the *Answer*. Moreover, the mute testimony of an inventory of personal belongings taken at Sor Juana's death (also recently brought to light) shows an impressive quantity of books (180) and papers in her possession, as she was working to reassemble the rich personal library that she had been forced to cede to the archbishop.[20] The confidence of the *Answer* thus stayed with the poet-scholar to her last days.

Sor Juana's three direct references to and one oblique mention of the menacing presence of the Holy Office of the Inquisition, in the *Answer*, make a carefully plotted and dynamic argument of self-defense against possible accusations of heresy. However, these references were long taken at face value, as indicating that institution as the threat against which Sor Juana had to protect herself as both her theological forays and her secular publications drew unfavorable Church attention. But the real danger lay elsewhere (and Sor Juana

---

[18] Trabulse, "Los años finales de Sor Juana," pp. 29-31; *Memoria transfigurada*, pp. 24-6.

[19] The Diego Calleja biography, (published in Juana Inés de la Cruz, *Fama y obras póstumas* (Madrid: Imprenta de Manuel Ruíz de Murga, 1700), first proposed this interpretation, which has been supported and contested by many scholars. See, for example, Trabulse, *Memoria transfigurada*, pp. 10-11.

[20] Trabulse cites the "*Libro General de Inventarios de los objetos que cada celda de las monjas tiene*," recorded by Nazario López de la Vega, the chaplain of the Convento de San Jerónimo, and copied in a document dated July 17, 1843, for the Conde de Cortina; uncovered by the historian Teresa Yturbide Castelló in 1995. See Trabulse, *Años finales*, pp. 36-7.

was less secure from it than she must have thought). It is curious, then, that Sor Juana brings to the foreground an organization of ecclesiastical inquiry and punishment which to us may represent the worst abuses of religious power, but which in fact was unlikely to threaten her. In her oft-noted but little-examined remarks, Sor Juana used the Inquisition to her own ends. What attitude on Sor Juana's part towards the Holy Office do these statements suggest? What sort of presence was the Inquisition for the poet, as she wrote her intellectual self-defense?[21] To answer the first of these questions, I briefly review key contextual elements that mark the historical and cultural backdrop to her statements about the Inquisition, focusing on studies of women and the Holy Office in Mexico and recent reassessments of the Tribunal.[22] Second, to review how and to what effect Sor Juana speaks of the Inquisition in these four passages, I analyze her rhetorical strategies in making these references.

Historical and Cultural Backdrop

The Inquisition operated in New Spain in three distinct organizational phases, from its formal establishment in 1569 until its dissolution in 1820. In both the colonial setting as in Spain, the overt purpose of the Holy Office was the defense of Spanish-Catholic belief, observance, and culture against individuals with heretical views and those lacking respect for religious principles.[23] However, recent interpretations find the Holy Office primarily expressive of social rather than strictly religious attitudes: "insularity, exclusivisim, xenophobia, even racial attitudes, were more important factors than religion in developing the climate of intolerance that prevailed from the fifteenth century to the 1800s."[24]

---

[21] These questions may be considered as reflections, respectively, of the two spheres outlined by Mabel Moraía as Sor Juana's authorial "marginalidad" and the ecclesiastical hierarchy's "orden dogmático"; see "Orden dogmático y marginalidad en la *Carta de Monterrey* de Sor Juana Inés de la Cruz," *Hispanic Review* 58 (1990): 205-25.

[22] Sources on the Holy Office in Spain and New Spain include historical, ethnohistorical, and anthropological studies. See, for example, Solange Alberro, *La actividad del Santo Oficio de la Inquisición en la Nueva España, 1571-1700* (Mexico City: Fondo de Cultura Económica, 1988); Angel Alcalá et al., eds, *Inquisición española y mentalidad inquisitorial* (Barcelona, Ariel, 1984); Ruth Behar, "Sex and Sin, Witchcraft and the Devil in Late-Colonial Mexico," *American Ethnologiest* 14 (1987): 34-54; Mary Elizabeth Perry and Anne J. Cruz, eds, *Cultural Encounters: The Impact of the Inquisition in Spain and the New World* (Berkeley: University of California Press, 1991); and essential studies by Richard Greenleaf, Alvaro Huerga, and Asunción Lavrin, cited below.

[23] Greenleaf, *The Mexican Inquisition of the Sixteenth Century* (Albuquerque: University of New Mexico, 1969), p. 1.

[24] Greenleaf, "Historiography of the Mexican Inquisition," in Perry and Cruz, *Cultural Encounters*, p. 271.

To assess Sor Juana's relative vulnerability to or immunity from Inquisitional condemnation, it is important to distinguish between laypeople and religious when considering both the Holy Office's treatment of individuals and contemporary attitudes towards the Inquisition. The laity received different, essentially more severe treatment from the Holy Office than did members of religious orders. This distinction is particularly true with regard to women.[25] Generally, lay women came under more scrutiny and suspicion than female members of religious orders, because of the potential of the former to foment "luteranismo" or Protestant influence in communities.[26] Already "in the fold," nuns had to be quite overtly heretical before they roused Inquisitorial suspicion.[27] Scrutiny and correction would first, and usually finally, come from the individual confessors. When a nun reported having unusual, potentially supernatural experiences—whether these were considered likely to be divine in origin or to be doctrinally suspicious—she could be asked by her confessor to document them in written form. Were her writings to arouse either interest or doubt, they would be examined not only by her spiritual director, but by the confessor of her confessor, and quite likely by an entire circle of priests known to one another through professional circles, without necessarily involving the Inquisition.[28] This describes the kind of circle, at the highest levels of New

---

[25] There are numerous reasons for this difficulty. First, there is a shortage of sources regarding male or female religious in relation to the Inquisition; many existing studies deal principally with secular men and women rather than those in religious life. Also, much work has been anecdotal rather than analytical, presenting the more spectacular cases investigated and tried by the Holy Office; quantitative approaches are still applied only to shorter time periods and limited sites. Finally, where women are discussed there are not always clear delineations of their lay or religious status. Therefore, to date, it is difficult to make a general summary on the situation of religious women—whether professed nuns, "third-order" members, or *beatas*—with regard to the Inquisition in Mexico; several obstacles arise regarding limitations in available historical sources. Studies that do discuss religious women do not often categorize data so as to make possible complex distinctions between professed members of religious orders and *beatas* or holy women living outside a convent setting, "*ilusas*" or (allegedly) deluded women, and third-order women. However, available studies do allow clarification, if not resolution, of the presence the Inquisition may have had for nuns in convents in the 17th century.

[26] See chapter 1, "Little Women: Counter-Reformation Misogyny," in Alison Weber, *Teresa of Ávila and the Rhetoric of Femininity* (Princeton: Princeton University Press, 1990), pp. 17-41.

[27] See for example the case of Agustina de Santa Clara, in Puebla, Mexico, who was involved with Illuminist [*alumbrado*] circles, reportedly had a love affair with a priest, and made false claims to holiness. In Alvaro Huerga, *Historia de los alumbrados*, III, *Los alumbrados de Hispanoamerica (1570-1605)* (Madrid: Fundación Universitaria Española, Seminario Cisneros, 1986), pp. 683-1.

[28] See, for example, the case of the Mexican María de San José, Augustinian Recollect, presented in Myers and Powell, *Wild Country*.

Spanish ecclesiastical authority, that in fact closed in upon Sor Juana—not for doctrinally suspicious beliefs or writings, but for insufficient obedience.

The self-denunciations that characterize religious women's appearances before the Inquisition underscore the important role of the confessor (who would have prompted such revelations) as a regulatory figure for nuns; such self-accusations are very different from Sor Juana's self-defense. Within the "family" of the Church, as within society at large, the Inquisition took issues of faith very seriously in its attempt to maintain an orthodoxy clear of all superstition. However, inquisitors did not deal in the same way with religious who might be promoting deviations *within* orthodoxy, as they did with what they saw as outright heresy in the case of "Judaizers" or Protestants. As the cases examined by Alvaro Huerga make clear, Inquisitors were alert, too, to the complex and sensitive process applied to "discernment of spirits" in assessing false from true visionaries.[29] Asunción Lavrin notes that religious people committed different transgressions and received different (though not always more lenient) treatment than did laypeople who came under investigation. Lavrin further points out that the majority of religious brought before the Inquisition were men, primarily priests charged with sexual solicitation of female penitents in the confessional; while most women appeared for blasphemy, and it appears that a majority of these accused themselves. Inquisition records indicate that such voluntary confessions were frequently, but not always, prompted by the individual woman's confessor.[30]

A statistical overview gives perspective on the judicial activities of the Holy Office in seventeenth-century Mexico. Solange Alberro analyzes all 11,441 Inquisition records from 1571-1700, covering the period of greatest activity for the institution: from its inception as an autonomously governed Tribunal, through its burnings of condemned Jews and Protestants in the 1680s, to the beginning of its very long decline. With the exception of blasphemy, as mentioned above, these categories of offenses mostly did not involve nuns.[31]

---

[29] Huerga, *Historia*.

[30] For information on this topic, drawn from her extensive and as yet unpublished archival research, I am grateful to Asunción Lavrin (private conversations, 1994 and 1995).

[31] Unfortunately, in this important study figures for women are not separated by religious and lay categories in ways that would most assist analysis of convent experience. According to Alberro, of the denunciations examined in Inquisitional archives for New Spain (not all of which came to trial), 49 per cent were for "religious crimes" (such as blasphemy, impersonating a priest, simony, etc.); 20 per cent for "sexual crimes" (mostly bigamy and solicitations by priests); 11 per cent for heresies, mostly Judaism and Protestantism (not surprisingly, there were many more cases in this category occurred Spain); 9.5 per cent for witchcraft; 8 per cent for miscellaneous civil crimes; at the end of the list were 0.7 per cent for idolatry; and 0.4 per cent for "tendencies" such as Erasmianism. Solange Alberro, *La actividad del Santo Oficio de la Inquisición en la Nueva España, 1571-1700* (Mexico, D.F.: Instituto Nacional de Antropología e Historia, 1981), p. 260; quoted by Ruth Behar in "Sex and Sin, Witchcraft and the Devil in Late-Colonial Mexico," *American Ethnologist* 14:1

For the entire period of the late sixteenth to late eighteenth century, few religious women in convents actually faced the Inquisition—especially when processes resulting from self-denunciations are discounted. While the Inquisition continued throughout much of the seventeenth century to be concerned about "false holy women, false miracles, and distortions of worship and doctrine,"[32] it nonetheless brought professed nuns to trial relatively rarely. Asunción Lavrin reports finding at most between fifteen and twenty cases stemming from third-party denunciations, the majority late in the eighteenth century rather than in the seventeenth. Among the trials of religious women that are documented in the archives, most were heard either because of self-denunciation, when they expressed doubts about their own experience of inner, spiritual life in regard to dogma, or because of their reports of visions into which the Inquisition wished to inquire. Moreover, these infrequent cases do not apply to the experience of Sor Juana in the moment of writing her *Answer*; rather than self-denunciation, she is intent on self-defense: defense of her ideas as expressed in the *Carta Atenagórica*, and defense of the study that led her to those ideas.

Perhaps a majority of this "pre-secular" society—and certainly a preponderance of those in religious life—would have subscribed to and defended the purposes of the Holy Office, even while they would fervently have preferred never to appear before it. Sor Juana writes from and for this world and its premises, even when she is challenging the latter, rather than from the assumptions with which our later period may approach the topic of the Holy Office. In attempting to understand the actions and effects of the Inquisition in New Spanish writings, public life, and "mentalities," Richard Greenleaf offers this perspective: in the colonial period, about 95 percent of the entire population never had any contact with the Holy Office. Of the 5 per cent that did, the great majority (5/6 of these persons) never came to trial because of insufficient evidence. Of the 1/6 who were tried, about 2 per cent were convicted and one-half of one per cent executed.[33] That number was clearly sufficient to evoke fear of a dread possibility, however remote, as the explicit sense of Sor Juana's references reflects. At the same time, her playful tone in

---

(1987): 51 n. 3; Behar's citation of Alberro's figures varies somewhat from the latter's book. In comparison with Spain: For sixteenth- and seventeenth-century Castile, 43 per cent heresies (Jews, Moors, "Lutherans"); 40 per cent religious crimes; 7 per cent sexual crimes; less than 5 per cent for witchcraft and superstition. Gustav Henningsen, "El banco de datos del Santo Oficio: Las relaciones de causas de la Inquisición Española (1550-1700)." *Boletín de la Real Academia de la Historia* 174 (1977): 547-70.

[32] [*las falsas beatas, los falsos milagros, y la deformación del culto y del dogma*] Lavrin, "Unlike Sor Juana," p. 30.

[33] Greenleaf, "Historiography," pp. 269-70. (In the same period, punishment by the civil arm of law was grisly enough to make up for any perceived "benignity" on the part of the Inquisition—but that is another story.)

these remarks makes clear that she knew she was an unlikely target for the Tribunal.

As we shall see, Sor Juana's first two allusions to the Holy Office speak with declared fear of its powers of textual scrutiny and censorship. The Inquisition in New Spain focused its activities particularly on surveillance and prohibition regarding importation and publication of manuscripts, books and printed materials. These tasks of surveillance and approbation or censorship statistically outweighed other inquisitorial functions.[34]

Anthropologist Ruth Behar's concept of the "interiorization" of Inquisitional priorities is useful for an examination of the confessor's role as "filter" for the Tribunal, although her work treats primarily lay women whose experiences differed significantly from those of women in convents. When hearing cases of witchcraft and devil-pacts among women of the eighteenth-century "*gente vil*" or "base folk" (that is, people of indigenous, African, or mixed race, and poor whites), inquisitors "treated [such cases] as a religious problem that could be resolved through confession and absolution" rather than bringing these infractions to trial or greater punishment.[35] Behar attributes the high number of self-denunciations made by such women to an "interiorization of inquisitorial ideas . . . a self-censoring process especially prevalent among women that began with a prohibited act and ended with a desire for reintegration into the Church."[36] These self-denunciations, Behar notes, were frequently prompted by the confessor. A variant interpretation of Behar's perhaps anachronistically psychological concept of "the interiorization of inquisitorial ideas" might see the role the Inquisition played *for* (and not only against) these religious women as offering another form for the fulfillment of belief in the efficacy of confession and penance for salvation. That is, both data and case records suggest that the Tribunal functioned as an extension of the confessional. This would be especially true for nuns, who often had close and formative relationships (whether predominantly positive or negative) with their confessors.

Results of the second heresy trial initiated against a nun in Mexico (1568) illuminate Sor Juana's apparently confident declarations, in the *Answer*, regarding matters of faith and doctrine. Elena de la Cruz of the Convent of the Immaculate Conception was questioned about highly articulate theological views that she had expressed before witnesses, regarding such pointed

---

[34] "In New Spain, expurgation and emendation rather than outright prohibition usually resulted from this inspection." Irving Leonard, *Baroque Times in Old Mexico*, p. 104. On the situation in Spain, see also Angel Alcalá et al., eds, *The Spanish Inquisition and the Inquisitorial Mind* (Boulder, Colorado: Social Science Monographs, 1987); especially, Virgilio Pinto, "Censorship: A System of Control and an Instrument of Action," pp. 303-20, and Angel Alcalá, "Inquisitorial Control of Humanists and Writers," pp. 321-60.

[35] Behar, "Sex and Sin," p. 34.

[36] Behar, "Sex and Sin." p. 36.

questions as the powers of the papacy and the decrees of Trent.[37] (Much fault for her heretical ideas was placed on her reading of banned books by Fray Luis de Granada, prior to entering the convent.) She was imprisoned, defended by two family-appointed lawyers during a lengthy trial, and finally admitted her error. After the ordeal (and institutional expense) of such treatment, followed by her admission of guilt, her sentence may strike us as surprisingly light: she had to stand in the choir of the convent with a penitential candle during Mass, publicly abjure her error, repeat penitential psalms, and fast on three Fridays. Such punishments were typically meted out to those in religious life who confessed erroneous belief. Elena's case exemplifies, again, that even for learned nuns making unusual incursions into the male precincts of theological discourse, the Inquisition *per se* did not pose a life-or-death threat.

I Want No Trouble with the Holy Office / No Quiero Ruido con el Santo Oficio

Towards the end of paragraph 5 of her *Answer* to Filotea, Sor Juana twice summons up the specter of the Inquisition in its role as source of censorship and surveillance. The institution first appears as an inhibiting presence that censures and *castiga* ["punishes"] heresy in written works. At the first mention of the Holy Office, the "fear" Sor Juana expresses with regard to the proposal that she more thoroughly dedicate herself to "sacred letters" would seem not only to apply to but to base itself in a fear of the Inquisition and, specifically, its power to excommunicate the accused:

> Then how should I dare take these [sacred letters] up in my unworthy hands, when sex, and age, above all our customs oppose it? And thus I confess that often this very fear has snatched the pen from my hand and has made the subject matter retreat back toward that intellect from which it wished to flow; an impediment I did not stumble across with profane subjects, for a heresy against art is not punished by the Holy Office but rather by wits with their laughter and critics with their censure. And this, "just or unjust, is not not be feared," for one is still permitted to take Communion and hear Mass, so that it troubles me little if at all. For in such matters, according to the judgment of the very ones who slander me, I have no obligation to know how nor the skill to hit the mark, and thus if I miss it is neither sin nor discredit....
> [*Answer*, pp. 45, 47][38]

---

[37] Richard E. Greenleaf, *The Mexican Inquisition*, (Albuquerque: University of New Mexico Press, 1969), pp. 134-7.

[38] [*Pues ¿cómo me atreviera yo a tomarlo en mis indignas manos, repugnándolo el sexo, la edad y sobre todo las costumbres? Y así confieso que muchas veces este temor me ha quitado la pluma de la mano y ha hecho retroceder los asuntos hacia el mismo*

The rather pert humor of this reference to the Holy Office and possible excommunication marks an argument that she herself will subsequently undermine, further on. Here, however, she declares that her secular or "profane" activity is safer than "sacred" subjects, because the former does not jeopardize her right to "take Communion and hear Mass." Nonetheless, as in the other three references, Sor Juana cites her "fear" in order to prove her "reverence." Ultimately, through irony, she uses the power of the Inquisition in order to solidify her own defense, through the close argumentation that follows. While Sor Juana first insists on her unsuitability for the study of holy matters, this humility is soon strategically deployed, to exonerate her on two counts. First, she states that men privileged with university education had long been restricted in their access to certain sacred texts in their youth; here she cites the Doctor of the Church and eponymous leader of her Jeronymite order as source of the prohibition. "Even learned men" studying with such masters as Jerome were restricted from studying biblical texts such as Genesis or the Song of Songs until after the age of thirty, lest they be misled by obscurity or apparent sensuality in the text. Therefore she—young, female and self-taught—cannot be faulted for failing to undertake such studies: she has no such "obligation"; they are not appropriate to her. Sor Juana has asked, "How could I dare take them in my unworthy hands, when sex, age, and above all our customs" oppose it? Here is the second, and deeper, strategic use of her argument of "unsuitability": it is "above all, *customs*" that oppose her study of sacred matters. A primary purpose of the *Answer* is to show that "custom" does not equate to "correct interpretation" of Scripture or doctrine—especially such time-worn "custom" as what she will show to be the misapplied, as well as misogynist Pauline prohibition. This second strategy contradicts and undoes the first, in Sor Juana's characteristic, and deeply ironic, doubling of argumentation: presenting herself explicitly as unworthy, she makes use of the authority of the Inquisition to point out that it is *not* ecclesiastical power that interferes with her creative and "profane" activities. Social "custom" is not holy law; Sor Juana will establish that the study of sacred matters is in fact appropriate to her—and her text, with its rich biblical allusions, makes clear that she has been conducting such study all along.

Some lines earlier in the passage before us, Sor Juana has presented "Sor Filotea" with a "confession":

---

entendimiento de quien querían brotar; el cual inconveniente no topaba en los asuntos profanos, pues una herejía contra el arte no la castiga el Santo Oficio, sino los discretos con risa y los críticos con censura; y ésta, iusta vel iniusta, timenda non est, pues deja comulgar y oír misa, por lo cual me da poco o ningún cuidado; porque, según la misma decisión de los que lo calumnian, ni tengo obligación para saber ni aptitud para acertar; luego, si lo yerro, ni es culpa ni es descrédito. . . .] OC IV, 443-4:151-65.

> And to speak more specifically, I confess, with all the candor due to you and with the truth and frankness that are always at once natural and customary for me, that my having written little on sacred matters has sprung from no dislike, nor lack of application, but rather from a surfeit of awe and reverence toward those sacred letters, which I know myself to be so incapable of understanding and which I am so unworthy of handling... [*Answer*, p. 45][39]

And a bit further on, as we have seen, she again confesses:

> And thus I confess that often this very fear has snatched the pen from my hand and has made the subject matter retreat back toward that intellect from which it wished to flow... [*Answer*, p. 45]

Rhetorically, the verb "I confess [*confieso*]" marks her situation as vulnerable, that of an inferior speaking to an addressee of greater authority, whether in the confessional or the civil or ecclesiastical court; it also marks the content of the passage as an admission of guilt. As is so often the case in Sor Juana's ironically "double-voiced" utterance,[40] however, the actual content does not bear out the rhetorical expectation that has been constructed for us by the author. These "confessions" admit that the "fear and reverence due" to sacred matters have stopped her in the very act of writing on holy things (which therefore is revealed to be the pursuit she would have preferred, over "profane" writing, as Octavio Paz notes of this "ambiguous" paragraph).[41] No such obstacle was encountered with secular writings—that is, with "art" rather than theology, for "a heresy against art is not punished by the Holy Office" but by the scoffing of "wits" and the censure of "critics," whose displeasure cannot result in the harsh penalties of excommunication. Writing on profane subjects, then, is safer; it is also, by clever extension of the very arguments used against her, doctrinally neutral. Here she is following the first strategy of humility that I outlined above: presenting her unfitness, to show how higher authority supports her activities. By this reasoning, the opinion of "those who slander" her secular writings removes the possibility of either "sin" or "discredit" ("ni culpa ni descrédito" p. 444) on her part, because she is neither obliged (by her religious state) nor suited (by her sex) to do such writing. Thus the very "slander [*calumnia*] of her detractors is turned to her defense; again, the Holy Office,

---

[39] [*Y hablando con más especialidad os confieso, con la ingenuidad que ante vos es debida... que el no haber escrito mucho de asuntos sagrados no ha sido dasafición... sino sobra de temor y reverencia debida a aquellas Sagradas Letras...*] OC IV, 443:128-34.

[40] See Emilie Bergmann, "Sor Juana Inés de la Cruz: Dreaming in a Double Voice" in Seminar on Feminism and Culture in Latin America, eds, *Women, Culture, and Politics in Latin America* (Berkeley: University of California Press, 1984), pp. 151-72.

[41] Octavio Paz, *Sor Juana Inés de la Cruz*, trans. Margaret Sayers Peden (Cambridge, Massachusetts: Harvard University Press, 1988), p. 416.

which does not rule against artistically heterodox creations, is presented as tacitly approving her incursions in literary spheres. The "cheeky" nature of this reference to the Inquisition marks an argument which she herself aims to undo, further on, in a closely argued process. The following examples show how this first, relatively neutral presentation of the Holy Office is turned more actively to the advantage of Sor Juana's argument as she defends not only her profane writings, but her studious and intellectual pursuits.

To do so, her text continues to make strategic use of the dread power of the Holy Office. The second mention of the Inquisition follows only 15 lines further on, in the same paragraph 5. Sor Juana slips into colloquiality here, putting on the voice of a simple, uneducated *mujercilla* ["little woman"], much as did Teresa of Ávila, also strategically and more extensively, in her mystical writings and chronicles one century earlier.[42] Here Sor Juana claims to cite herself, moving (as did the more typical writing nuns) from orality into writing by quoting from conversation to give her own "usual reply to those who urge [her] to write, especially if it is on a sacred subject":

> Do I have any understanding, any studies, any texts, or any preparation for that, except some four profundities of a superficial scholar? They can leave such things to those who understand them; as for me, I want no trouble with the Holy Office, for I am but ignorant, and tremble lest I say some proposition that sounds wrong or twist the true meaning of a passage. I do not study in order to write, nor far less in order to teach (which would be boundless arrogance in me), but simply to see whether by studying I may become less ignorant. . . [*Answer*, p. 47, translation modified][43]

Sor Juana's lexicon departs from her customary usage and becomes markedly informal with the phrase *no quiero ruido* ["I want no trouble"]: this shift toward colloquiality alerts us to her ironic intent here and in the following, "for I'm just ignorant and tremble, lest I say some proposition that sounds wrong or twist the true meaning of a passage" [*que soy ignorante y tiemblo de decir alguna*

---

[42] See especially Weber, *Teresa of Ávila and the Rhetoric of Femininity*; also Georgina Sabat de Rivers, "Autobiografías: Santa Teresa y Sor Juana" in *Estudios de literatura hispanoamericana: Sor Juana Inés de la Cruz y otros poetas del barroco* (Barcelona: Promociones y Publicaciones Universitarias, 1992), pp. 225-39. Sor Juana's three references to Teresa in the *Answer* show her high consciousness, and use, of St. Teresa as a model.

[43] [*¿Qué entendimiento tengo yo, qué estudio, qué materiales, ni qué noticias para eso, sino cuatro bachillerías superficiales? Dejen eso para quien lo entienda, que yo no quiero ruido con el Santo Oficio, que soy ignorante y tiemblo de decir alguna proposición malsonante o torcer la genuina inteligencia de agún lugar. Yo no estudio para escribir, ni menos para enseñar (que fuera en mí desmedida soberbia), sino sólo por ver si con estudiar ignoro menos. . . .*] *OC* IV, 444:174-82.

proposición malsonante o torcer la genuina inteligencia de algún lugar].[44] Whether placed in high or low register, Sor Juana's diction is deliberately chosen. The entire learned content of her *Answer* militates against a transparent reading of this *soy ignorante* ["for I'm just ignorant"]; Sor Juana is unlikely to "tremble" over this particular possibility.[45] Most of all, the brief final sentence in this paragraph, which stands out as uncharacteristically straightforward ("This is my answer, and these are my feelings" [*Así lo respondo y así lo siento*]), serves to tip the informed reader to Sor Juana's ironic intent: beware, when our highly baroque author appears to be this direct. Obliquity constantly infuses this curvilinear text. What does this "not-saying" say? Here, Sor Juana slips evasively into the "ignorant little woman's" voice to underscore, by contrast, the evident extent of both her learning and the reasoning power with which it is deployed, in the numerous allusions that serve to strengthen her closely argued self-defense.

A double irony in these lines directs the reader, first, to contrast Sor Juana's discursive dexterity with the typical writings of "ignorant women," and next, to compare the writing nun with her most immediately acclaimed, and approved, conventual forebear, Saint Teresa of Ávila. To this end, the "popular" tone is important: Sor Juana here steps into the voice of the "humble little nun" [*monjita*] to introduce the "narrative of her inclination" that will follow in the next twenty-some paragraphs. As Kathleen Myers has shown, Sor Juana's *Respuesta* makes extensive and effective use of the conventional *vida* form, replacing the model nuns' holy vocation with her own "wicked" [*negra*] (but God-given) "inclination" to study.[46] Teresa of Ávila skillfully used the complex and conscious "rhetoric of femininity," delineated by Alison Weber, to position herself authoritatively in the polemical debate between "learned men" [*letrados*] and spiritual or "experienced" men [*espirituales* or *experimentados*]. The former claimed the greater worth of spirituality "grounded in a firm understanding of dogma"; the latter, the superiority of "knowledge gained through direct religious experience and prayer."[47]

Not only does Sor Juana set forth her "inclination" in terms and narrative patterns drawn from the "vida de monjas" genre; but she most

---

[44] My translation here is changed from that published in the *Answer*, to reflect more thoroughly this colloquiality.

[45] As Sabat de Rivers points out: "Teresa is a visionary, while Juana is pure intellect. In her *Life*, the saint hides her knowledge; in the *Answer*, knowledge pours in torrents from the New World nun [*Teresa es una visionaria, Juana es puro intelecto. En la Vida, la santa esconde su saber; en la Respuesta sale el saber a borbotones de la monja novomundista*]. "Autobiografías." pp. 229-31.

[46] Myers, "Rewriting."

[47] Jodi Bilinkoff, *The Ávila of Santa Teresa* (Ithaca, New York: Cornell University Press, 1989), p. 142; see pp. 142-4 for discussion of this topic related to Teresa's writings and the saint's "troubles with the Inquisition."

ironically presents and exonerates what we would call her "intellectuality" [*intelectualidad*] with arguments that resonate with the "spirituality" [*espiritualidad*] of Teresa and other defenders of the *experimentados*. The "experience" Sor Juana claims is not that of supernatural "visions, voices, raptures, and the 'quiet' experience of God through recollection and mental prayer" that, in Teresa, provoked the suspicion of theologically educated *letrados*.[48] Sor Juana's experience is rather that of a "compulsion" to learn. The irony is this: by echoing the debate between "*letrados*" and *experimentados* and by "vocalizing" her own position in language reminiscent of the writings of humble model nuns, Sor Juana uses the learning of learned men against themselves and in favor of her own learning. To do so, she calls implicitly and explicitly on Teresa, who earlier exploited the culturally limiting view of women (as having access to the divine only through feeling and not through reason) to assert an authority that male theologians could not attain.[49] Again, she makes use of the Inquisition to support this move: because, for all its vigilance, it has not subjected her to its scrutiny, she has not erred. Sor Juana calls up, by allusion, the course by which the highly suspect nature of Teresian spirituality in the sixteenth century had by the seventeenth—when channeled into dozens of nuns' spiritual narratives, duly overseen by the women's confessors—become strong and literally sanctified precedent. In her day, Teresa was literally avoiding the Inquisition, which was a constant threat; indeed, the *Book of her Life* was impounded after its writing, but by Sor Juana's day had become the single most important textual model for "model nuns."

Sor Juana's prosopopoeic "disguise" as a "humble little nun" here casts her as a Teresian rhetorician: she claims humility and obedience in order to assert her authority in the matters of which she will speak. She uses the form of the sanctified, Teresian tradition of life-narratives to defend her untraditional content: she shows this authority to come from direct experience and divine gift: she studies the world when she cannot get books; God made her that way. The tone and lexicon of the voice itself remind her readers of the nun of Ávila, who, canonized in 1622 (that is, 69 years before Sor Juana's writing of the *Answer*) was certainly beyond reproach. Sor Juana places herself not among the "*espirituales*" in the content of her own experience, but with Teresa in her conscious adaptation of available discourse—a discourse that, by the time of the colonial viceregency, had come to be a recognizable commonplace, used by numerous nuns who wrote under order of obedience. Like Teresa, Sor Juana is a highly learned woman who knows how to adapt her extensive knowledge to the language of the uneducated "little woman" in order to speak with authority and against misogynistic attack. The implicit citing of Teresa joins three

---

[48] Bilinkoff, *Ávila*, p. 143.

[49] See Weber, *Rhetoric of Femininity*; Bilinkoff, *Ávila*; and Gillian Ahlgren, *Teresa of Ávila and the Politics of Sanctity* (Ithaca, New York: Cornell University Press, 1996).

explicit references to the saint in the *Answer*[50] in developing the second, deeper level of Sor Juana's "strategic humility." Again, custom is the target: it is misguided custom—not doctrine, or ability—that prevents women from being allowed to study and write: Teresa, and the approval of her writings by the Inquisition, are proof of this.

About halfway through the *Answer*, Sor Juana makes a third reference to the dreaded Tribunal, again in the context of the conventional, and conventual, genre of the *Vita* or spiritual life-story written by nuns. Nuns' *Lives* from the medieval tradition typically delineated the early and irresistible nature of the devotion that gave rise to a vocation for the religious life of the individual woman—the autobiographical or biographical subject—in her childhood.[51] Sor Juana shows that her culturally unbecoming "inclination" to booklearning and to the making of verses proceeds from a source beyond herself. (It is not her fault; God made her that way.) However, various objections, including jealousy of her abilities and accomplishments, have caused some to want to prohibit her "studious endeavors." She says:

> Once they achieved this, with a very saintly and simple mother superior who believed that study was an affair for the Inquisition and ordered that I should not read. I obeyed her (for the three months or so that her authority over us lasted) in that I did not pick up a book . . . [*Answer*, p. 73][52]

Yet Sor Juana's "inclination" proved intractable (as was characteristic, generically, of nuns' and holy women's vocations in their life narratives), and she tirelessly "studied" the book of the world, until this "simple" [*cándida*] Mother Superior was replaced.

This explicit naming of the Holy Office appears in paragraph 26. The intervening paragraphs 7 through 25 present material that vigorously develops the assertion of the author's "compulsive" need—and what will eventually be presented as her right—to study. Sor Juana gives her account of the irresistible "inclination" to letters from childhood and early life, (pars. 7-10) until she entered the convent with the aim of learning enough in all fields to make possible an adequate approach to Theology (par. 11); she outlines her manner of study and the obstacles to it caused by lack of instruction and interruption

---

[50] These three references to Teresa are found in paragraph 20 (*OC* IV, p. 453) and in paragraph 39 (p. 467, and p. 468) of the *Respuesta a Sor Filotea*.

[51] Asunción Lavrin, "La vida femenina como experiencia religiosa: biografía y hagiografía en Hispanoamérica colonial," *Colonial Latin American Review* 2 (1993): 25-51.

[52] [*Una vez lo consiguieron con una prelada muy santa y muy cándida que creyó que el estudio era cosa de Inquisición y me mando que no estudiase. Yo la obedecí (unos tres meses que duró el poder ella mandar) en cuanto a no tomar libro* . . .], *OC* IV, 458:734-41.

(12-15). She especially details the disturbance and oppression occasioned for her by the envy of others (16-25). She compares herself to Christ in the "fires of persecution" and "crucible of torture [*fuego de la persecución . . . crisol del tormento*]" caused her, like him, by others' jealousy of talents (that, in her case, she had no hand in choosing). This has gone to "such an extreme," she says, that "some have even sought to prohibit me from study [*que han llegado a solicitar que se me prohiba el estudio*]" (458:765).

Clearly, we are to place Sor Juana's tormentors with those of Christ himself. This casts an especially unflattering light on the "very holy and very simple Mother Superior" in this passage, undermining her credibility even before she is introduced. Sor Juana swiftly demolishes any lingering credence that might be given to this superior with the parenthetical remark about the brevity of her tenure in office. She links the adjectives "holy [*santa*]" and "simple [*cándida*]" (including the sense of *cándido* given by the *Diccionario de la Real Academia Española* as "uninformed [*poco advertido*]") to describe this woman distrustful of study: the Mother Superior is the very voice of ignorant custom, which is enforced blindly and against reason. This uninformed perspective automatically, and incorrectly, associates "learning" with punishment by the Holy Office, Sor Juana implies. This "*cándida*" superior is the opposite of the knowingly "simple" Teresa (and embodies the very mentality that led Teresa to adopt her complexly "simple" rhetorical stance in self-defense, as Weber shows).

Sor Juana's reference recalls Teresa's well-known dismay at increasing censorship in the latter half of the sixteenth century; the newly established Index of Prohibited Books eliminated many of the spiritual works written in or translated into the vernacular that Teresa had found most helpful in developing her practices of mental prayer. God responded to her distress by saying, "I shall give you a living book."[53] When Sor Juana is denied access to books, she "studies" the world around her; the loss is similar to the saint's, though Sor Juana's solution is characteristically rational, rather than mystical. Here she is concluding her proof of the compulsive—and thus compulsory—or "necessary" (460:837) nature of her inclination. This Mother Superior is mentioned at a hinge-moment, as Sor Juana moves toward initiating her list of "exemplars [*exemplares*]" (460:846), that is, classical, Biblical, and historical women in whom intelligence and learning are united with moral rectitude, leadership, probity, or saintliness. Here she can abandon the stance of humility, for she is not speaking of herself but of admired models, in the medieval-early modern tradition of the *querelle des femmes*. As Sor Juana makes clear, these are the women to hold up in positions of leadership, not the "very holy and very

---

[53] Teresa, *Book of Her Life* [*La vida*], 26:6.

simple" (quickly removed from office, presumably because she had not served suitably).

A fourth reference does not mention the Holy Office by name. Sor Juana challenges the (anonymous) critic of her "*Carta Atenagórica*" to denounce her officially, if her writing has fallen outside the bounds of orthodoxy:

> If it is heretical, as the critic says, why does he not denounce it? Thus he would find revenge and I contentment, for I more greatly value, as I ought, the name of Catholic and obedient daughter of my Holy Mother Church than any praise that might befall me as a scholar. [*Answer*, p. 93]⁵⁴

Explicitly, a humble Sor Juana submits herself to correction, which she welcomes as assuring her orthodox and "obedient" status rather than her renown for learning. Yet implicitly, her rhetorical question ("Why does he not denounce it?") asserts her confidence in her own orthodoxy and in approval by Church officials. She asks this, affirming that she can indeed receive renown for learning and at the same time retain her good "name as a Catholic and obedient daughter" under the ecclesiastical hierarchy.

Here (at the conclusion of paragraph 39), Sor Juana will make explicit her "answer" to the Pauline prohibition.⁵⁵ She delineates the type of "teaching" that is permitted by precedent established and sanctified by the Church itself: "that which is permissible to women—to teach by writing" [*lo que es lícito a las mujeres, que es enseñar escribiendo*]—like St. Teresa, María de Agreda, María de la Antigua, and others. Sor Juana now arrives at the crux of her defense of her earlier *Carta Atenagórica*: "If it is heretical, as the critic says, why does he not denounce it?" [*Si es, como dice el censor, herética, ¿por qué no la delata?*] Adherence to custom—not to doctrine—has led to the criticisms and attacks against her theological document. Here Sor Juana most clearly asserts her assurance of immunity from prosecution on the basis of heresy. The scrupulous adherence of the Inquisition to dogmatic correctness has found no fault with her writing; she challenges her detractor to denounce her, because she is sure her orthodoxy will be upheld. Sor Juana thus rhetorically makes use of the Inquisition to support her position—that is, to position herself against her critics. This stance is made the stronger by the fear of the Holy Office that she

---

⁵⁴ [*Si es, como dice el censor, herética [la Carta Atenagórica], ¿por qué no la delata? y con eso él quedará vengado y yo contenta, que aprecio, como debo, más el nombre de católica y de obediente hija de mi Santa Madre Iglesia, que todos los aplausos de docta.*] *OC* IV, 469:1183-7.

⁵⁵ Nina M. Scott, "Sor Juana Inés de la Cruz: 'Let Your Women Keep Silent in the Churches...'," *Women's Studies International Forum* 8 (1985): 511-19.

expressed at the outset of the *Answer*: as frightening as the institution is, she is willing to stand before it, and stands to gain in the process.

The *Answer* defines and defends an epistemological "space" in which it might be possible to mend the polarized divisions between theological knowledge ("the Queen of the Sciences" [*la Reina de las Ciencias*]) and humanistic learning ("the ancillary sciences" [*las (ciencias) ancilas*] [447:316-17]), as well as between men and women ("learned older women [*ancianas sabias*]" [465:1051]) who undertake such studies. Explicitly, Sor Juana's text (with its rhetorics of humility and obedience) does not challenge, and indeed reinscribes, the hierarchical relationship between fields of knowledge, between men and women. However, her lexical choices, narrative strategies, and play of concepts, such as those we have seen regarding the Inquisition, infuse the text with energy and purpose—that is, with effects—that extend beyond this explicit reinforcement of the "status quo ante." Particularly, the use of the voice of the "*mujercilla*" and of the paradoxically assertive Teresaian "rhetoric of femininity" permit Sor Juana to speak of the Inquisition in ways that back up her own position. Sor Juana thus makes use of the institution's function of defining legitimacy, as well as heresy.

Not only rhetorically, but in her lived experience, the poet made use of strategies similar to those employed by Teresa to avoid conflict with authority, including the Inquisition. Alliances both nuns formed with friends in high places aristocratically and politically—assured protection that made possible the writings that were challenging to the status quo.[56] However, there were also important contextual differences between Hispanism's two most prominent writing nuns—"worldly" differences, of their historical and social environments that shaped their experience with regard to the Inquisition. Teresa lived and recorded her mystical experiences in the conflictive second half of the sixteenth century, when the Inquisition was increasing and consolidating its forces for the eradication of heresy. We have seen that emphases and forms of inquisitorial censure were notably different in Sor Juana's context, especially for religious women, who were rarely brought before the Inquisition.

Like much else in her writing, the boldness of Sor Juana's reference to the Holy Office makes her "unlike the model nun." Current well-founded interest, within our disciplines, in readings and representations of "resistance" to dominant cultural, religious and political structures of power can make it difficult to identify and assess the relationships of individuals and groups

---

[56] Aristocratic supporters of Teresa included Luisa de la Cerda (daughter of the Duque de Medinaceli), the Marquesa de Villena, the Duquesa de Escalona, the bishop Alvaro Hurtado de Mendoza (also a member of nobility), and King Felipe II. See Weber, *Rhetoric of Femininity*, p. 4.

committed to orthodoxy.[57] Nuns' texts of the period make clear that women were not always and everywhere opposed to individuals and systems holding authority over them; many women did find in the convent, as Asunción Lavrin says, "a place of their own and an environment in which to express themselves,"[58]—finding or making a place for themselves that allowed them to carry out work to which they were deeply committed. In historiographic terms, Sor Juana's citation of the Holy Office, considered contextually, suggests that religious women looked to the Inquisition to "defend the faith" from inner as well as outer error; in this tradition, and certain that she is free of false doctrine, Sor Juana "calls on" the Tribunal in her own self-defense. In an analysis of Sor Juana's discourse, her references to the Holy Office open further perspectives on her conscious and complex rhetorical strategies.

---

[57] See, for example, the study that begins, "Orthodoxy has been ill served by historians. . . . Colonial Mexican society and culture were an orthodox achievement." Michael Destephano, *Miracles and Monasticism in Mid-Colonial Puebla, 1600-1750: Charismatic Religion in a Conservative Society* (Unpublished dissertation, University of Florida, 1977).

[58] Lavrin, "Unlike Sor Juana," p. 27.

List of Contributors

Robert Boenig (Editor of the volume)
Professor of English and Religious Studies
Texas A&M University

Jane Ackerman
Chair, Department of Philosophy and Religion
University of Tulsa

Gillian T. W. Ahlgren
Department of Theology
Xavier Univeristy

Michael Bradburn-Ruster
Liberal Arts Division
Yavapai College

Joseph F. Chorpenning
Editorial Director
Saint Joseph's University Press
Saint Joseph's University, Philadelphia

Sister M. Clemente Davlin, O.P.
Dominican University
Department of English
River Forest, IL

Kathryn Hohlwein
Department of English
California State University, Sacramento

Amanda Powell
Department of Romance Languages
University of Oregon

Elizabeth Rhodes
Department of Romance Languages and Literatures
Boston College

Frank Tobin
Professor of German
University of Nevada, Reno

Evelyn Toft
Professor of Spanish
Fort Hays State University

Alison Weber
Chair, Department of Modern Languages
University of Virginia

Wendy M. Wright
Department of Theology
Creighton University

Index

Abad, Camilo María   162n, 163n, 164n
Abelard, Peter   41
Abraham   26
Acaryadeva, Hridayananda dasa Goswami   167n
Accardo, A. L.   104n
Adam   16n, 26, 27
Adam (Anglo-Norman play)   16n
Adso   9
Aelred of Rievaulx   48n
Aers, David   24n, 30n, 31n
Agreda, María de   214
Ahlgren, Gillian T. W.   56n, 57n, 58n, 61n, 63, 64n, 65n, 88n, 107, 108n, 138, 153n, 172n, 211n
Ahumada, Juana de   117-18
Aitken, Robert   167
Alacoque, Margaret Mary   185-93
Alatorre, Antonio   199n
Alberro, Solange   201n, 203
Alcalá, Angel   142n, 201n, 205n
Alcalde, María Palacios   142n
Alcántara, Pedro de   117-19, 122, 128, 129n
Alfaya, Javier   144n
Alford, John   26n
Ælfric   50
Alumbrados   141-58
Alvarez, Hernando   150
Alvarez, Rodrigo   153n
Álvarez, Baltasar   96n
Amboise, Frances d'   110n
Ambrose, St.   165
Amerindians   67-77
Ancrene Riwle, The   30
Andrés, Melquíades   86n, 142n
Andrews, Paul   189n
Angel, Leonard   167
Angela of Foligno   86, 96

Angeles, Ana de los   122, 124
Angels   13n
Antichrist   9, 19-22, 28, 146
Antigua, María de la   214
Antolín, Fortunato   130n
Apóstoles, Francisca de los   53, 63
Aquinas, Thomas   55, 165
Arenal, Electa   81n, 83n, 107, 108n, 109, 129, 130, 131n, 133n-135n, 171, 172n, 174n, 196n, 197n
Aristotle   41, 43, 45, 101
Armstrong, A. H.   166n
Arragain, J.   190n
Aston, T. H.   24n
Athanasius, St.   164
Atkinson, Clarissa   101n
Audett, Florestine   71n
Augustine   20, 92-5
Ave Maria   110
Ave stella matutina   110
Ávila, Juan de   85, 143
Ávila, Julian de   119, 122-3
Ayto, John   48n

Baier, Walter   189n
Baldwin, Anna   24n
Balthasar, Hans Urs   164
Balust, Luis Sala   85n, 143n, 153n
Báñez, Domingo   85, 117, 127
Baralt, Luce López   173
Barghahn, Barbara von   73n
Barone, Guila   83n
Barratt, Alexandra   48n
Barrientos, A.   132
Barry, Gabriel   110n, 112n, 113n
Bautista, Isabel   124
Bautista, María   109, 115, 119, 122-3, 125-8
Bayón, Balbino Velasco   110n, 113n

INDEX

Bazan, B.   41n
Beatas   141-58 *passim*
Becket, Thomas   50
Beckwith, Sarah   166, 167n
Bede   50
Behar, Ruth   201n, 203n, 204n, 205
Bell, Rudolph   59, 93, 101n
Beltrán, Clara López   72n
Bénassy-Berling, Marie-Cécile   196
Benedictine Order   189
Benediktbeuern play cycle   16, 20
Bennassar, Bartolomé   144n, 150n, 156n, 157n
Bennett, J. A. W.   23n, 34n, 35n
Benson, Larry D.   42n
Bergmann, Emilie   208n
Bergmann, Rolf   17n
Bernard, St.   29, 161
Bernardine of Siena   704
Bérulle, Pierre de   134-5
Bhaghavata Purana   167
Bhaktivedanta, A. C.   167n
Bible, the   23, 26, 27, 34, 48, 112n
Bijuesca, K. Josu   199n
Bilinkoff, Jodi   59, 83n, 84n, 107-8, 117, 118, 129, 137-8, 210n, 211n
Birgitta, St.   96
Blásquez, Jimena   118
Bloomfield, Morton   26, 28-9
Blumenfeld-Kosinski, Renate   59n
Boaga, Emanuele   112n, 113n, 115n
Boccaccio, Giovanni   37
Boenig, Robert   47n, 50n
Boethius of Dacia   41-52 *passim*
Bordes, H.   190n
Bostius, Arnold   113n
Bourquin, Guy   24n, 32
Boyce, Elizabeth   159n, 160n, 163n, 166n
Braceland, Lawrence C.   162n
Brescia, Pablo A. J.   199n
Brewer, Derek   45n
Brigettine Order   50
Brix, A.   190n
Brodzki, Celeste Schenck   82n
Brothers of the Common Life   69
Buddha   167
Buitenen, J. A. B. van   167n

Burkey, Blaine   70
Bynum, Caroline Walker   25, 36, 93, 104, 187n

Callahan, Annice   163n, 190n
Calleja, Diego   200n
Calvo, Thomas   72n
Camarena, Ricardo   195n
Camarero, Manuel   152n
Cánovas, Rodrigo   81n
Carmelite Order   60-11, 73, 83, 85, 107-39, 169-70, 173, 184
Carreño, Antonio   82-3n, 104n
Carroll, Eamon   115n
Carthusian Order   50, 189
Carvajal y Mendoza, Luisa   159-68
Castelló, Teresa Yturbide   200n
Catherine of Siena   53-65, 84, 96, 98, 100, 102-3, 189-90
Cepeda, Diego de   125n
Cerda, Doña Luisa de la   155n, 215n
Ceroke, Christian   113n
Cerón, José María Díaz   169n, 173
Chambers, E. K.   15n, 16n
Chamizo, Crisbobal   150
Chance, Jane   143
Chantal, Jane   73n, 190
Charles V   69
Charnon-Deutsch, Lou   82n
Chatman, Seymour   93n
Chaucer, Geoffrey   23, 30, 32, 41-52 *passim*
Chorpenning, Joseph F.   75n, 76n
Cirlot, J. E.   75n
Cisneros, Cardinal Francisco Jimenez de   53, 58, 86
Cistercian Order   189
Clare, St.   96, 99, 101-2, 110n
Clement VII, Pope   54
Climacus, St. John   162
Clopper, Lawrence   24n
Cloud of Unknowing, The   50-1
Coakley, John   55, 59n, 89n, 96n
Cohen, Martin Samuel   168n
Colish, Marcia L.   42
Colledge, Edmund   35n, 43n, 49n, 51n, 100n
Concha, Victor García de la   97n
Cooney, Adrian James   100

INDEX

Cotta, Augusta de Castro 112n
Court, Elisa Narin van 32n
Cousins, Ewert 187n
Covarrubias Sebastión de 85, 152
Covella, Francis 23n
Cruz, Anne J. 163n, 201n
Cruz, Elena de la 205-6
Cruz, María de la 122, 124
Cuadriello, Jaime 69n
Cuevas, Julión Zarco 147n
Cummins, Thomas 74n

Dante 25
Darricau, R. 186n, 190n
David 26
Dávila, Francisco 117
Dávila, Doña María 118
Davlin, M. Clemente 26n
Dawson, Christopher 30, 31n, 37
Daza, Gaspar 119, 123
Dedieu, Jean-Pierre 155n
Delany, Sheila 41-2, 45
Deleloe, Jeanne 189
Derrida, Jacques 50n
Destephano, Michael 216n
Devil 9-19, 62, 147, 155, 157, 205
Di Pasquale, P. 28n
Díaz, Mari 117, 129-30
Divarkar, Parmananda R. 67n
Dixon, Laurinda S. 102
Dominican Order 19, 50, 54, 189
Donaldson, E. Talbot 23n
Doria, Nicolás 133
Dorothy of Montau 189
Doze, Andrew 71n, 73n
Drama, medieval 9-22 *passim*
Dugaw, Dianne 193n
Dunning, T. P. 24n
Durandus, William 165
Duval, Karen C. 167n
Dyer, Christopher 24n, 30

Earhart, H. Byron 167n
Eboli, Princess of 88, 155n
Eckhardt, Meister 25, 49, 50n
Economou, George 23n
Edmonds, Irene M. 161-2n
Edwards, Robert R. 24n
Egan, Harvey D. 163n, 164n, 165

Egan, Keith 109
Ehlers, Benjamin A. 143n
El Saffar, Ruth A. 81n
Elder, E. Rozanne 25n
Elijah 19-22
Eliot, T. S. 52n
Emmerson, Richard K. 52n
Endo, Shusaku 161n
England, George 42n
Enoch 19-22
Enrique, Cardinal Prince 151-2, 155
Erasmus 160
Escalona, Duquesa de 215n
Espíritu Santo, Antonia del 109, 122-4, 127
Eve 16n, 26, 27

Farago, Claire 74n
Fawtier, Robert 54n
Fernández, James D. 81n, 93n
Fernández, Simeón Tomás 68n
Fernéndez-Sevilla, Julio 97n
Findeln, Paula 79n
Fingesten, Peter 165
Flor, Fernando R. de la 74n
Francis, St. 71, 99, 101, 187
Franciscan Order 29, 48n, 67-77 *passim*, 147
Franco, Jean 195n
Frank, Robert Worth, Jr. 37n
Frantzen, Allen 24n
Fuente, Alonso de la 141-58
Fuentes, Carlos 72n

Gabriel, the Angel 14
Gaffney, Wilbur 30
Gangadean, Ashok 167
Ganss, George E. 67n
Gante, Pedro de 69-71
Garcia, Maximiliano Herraíz 91n
García, Félix 84n
Gerloh or Reichersberg 15
Gersh, Stephen 49n
Gerson, Jean 69, 76-7
Gertrude, St. 96, 189
Gessel, Van C. 161n
Gilbert of Hoyland 162n

INDEX

Giles, Mary E.   34n, 35n, 40n, 54n, 58-9, 63-4n, 108, 142n, 143, 158, 193n
Gilmore, Leigh   105
Glascoe, Marion   24n
Glotin, E.   186n
Gomez, Ana   122
Goodridge, J. F.   23n
Gosman, Martin   81n
Granada, Luis de   143, 151, 162, 206
Greenleaf, Richard   201n, 204, 206n
Greenway, Diana   50n
Gregory, Brad S.   89n
Gregory of Nyssa, St.   164
Gregory XI, Pope   54
Gregory XV, Pope   69
Griado de Val, Manuel   83n
Grossi, Jean   115n
Guiera, Doña Catalina   118
Guilhem, Claire   144n, 151n, 156n

Haliczer, Stephen   144n, 157n
Hamberger, Jeffrey F.   188n
Hamilton, Alastair   142n
Hardy, Richard P.   173n
Harrad of Landsberg   15
Harris, Barbara J.   81n
Harrison, Graham   189n
Heffernan, Thomas J.   98n
Hell   18
Hendriks, Rudolf   115n
Henningsen, Gustav   156n, 204n
Herlihy, David   77n
Hermans, Hub   81n
Hernández, Francisca   142n
Hernéndez, Francisco Martín   85n
Herod   14, 16, 73
Herpoel, Sonja   81n, 82n, 97n
Herrera, Doña María de   118
Hessisches Weihnachtsspiel   17
Hewett-Smith, Kathleen   35
Hildegard of Bingen   25
Hilton, Walter   50
Hirsh, John C.   52n
Hodgson, Phyllis   50n, 51n
Holdsworth, Christopher   50n
Hort, Greta   28
Huerga, Alvaro   54n, 142n, 144n, 148n, 150n, 201n, 202n, 203

Hugh of St. Victor   166
Huizinga, Johann   166
Humez, Jean M.   81n
Hussey, S. S.   24n

Ignatius of Loyola   48n, 67n, 100n, 141n, 163-5
Innocent III, Pope   15
Inquisition, the   58, 60, 63, 88, 141-58, 172n, 193-216
Iparraguirre, Ignacio   96n
Irigaray, Luce   101n
Isabel, María   122

Jacob's Ladder   166
Jambeck, Thomas J.   46n, 52n
Jeffrey, David L.   48n
Jerome, St.   9, 102, 104, 207
Jeronymite Order   196, 207
Jesuit Order   48n, 117, 151, 163, 165
Jesus, Beatriz de   117
Jesús, Ana de   108, 126, 133, 139
Jesús, Isabel de   82n
Jesús, Matías del Niño   171n, 172n
Jesús, Tomás de   134-5, 170, 177, 184
Jesus   11, 14, 15, 17, 25, 26, 33-5, 76, 109, 153, 163-5, 186-8, 190-1
Jesús María, Juan de   88n
Jesús María, Emetrio de   171-2, 173n
Jochim of Fiore   20
John, St.   191
John of Salisbury   50
John of the Cross, St. (Juan de la Cruz)   88n, 133, 141n, 169-84
Jordanova, L. J.   80n
Joseph, St.   67-77, 94, 114
Juana Inés de la Cruz   73n, 193-216
Judas   31-2
Julian of Norwich   25, 35-6, 43, 50-2, 100

Kabbalah   168
Kagan, Richard   155n
Kamen, Henry   150n, 156
Kavanaugh, Kieran   72n, 73n, 80, 82, 81n 96n, 107n, 108n, 125n, 134n, 171n, 174n
Kearns, Conleth   55n, 60n
Kempe, Margery   86n, 101n

222

INDEX

Kennedy, E. D.   24n
Kieckhefer, Richard   29n
King, Archdale A.   110n
Kirk, Elizabeth   24n, 30n, 34n
Klaren, Peter F.   74n
Knipping, John B.   75n
Kook, Abraham Isaac   168
Krishna   167
Kuczynski, Michael P.   26

L'Honore, H.   190n
Lactantius   160
Ladner, Gerhart B.   160n, 161n
Langland, William   23-40
Lao Tzu   167
Lapa, mother of St. Catherine of Siena   98
Laredo, Bernardino de   67-77
Lavrin, Asunción   193n, 194, 201n, 203-4, 212n, 216
Lawlor, John   25n, 33n, 37
Lazarus   100, 161
Le Brun, Jacques   188n
Leclercq, Jean   25, 101n
Lemaire, J.-M.   190n
León, Lucrecia de   155n
León, Luis de   84, 89-90, 95
Leonard, Irving   205n
Lepow, Lauren   46n
Leturia, Pedro de   96n
Lilio, Martín de   99n, 101n, 102
Linke, Hansjürgen   15n, 16n, 21n
Liturgy   23, 27
Liubheid, Colm   48n, 49n
Llamas, Román   70n
Llorca, Bernardino   142n, 151n
López-Morillas, Frances M.   74n
Lora, José L. Sánchez   89, 141n
Lorenzo, brother of Teresa of Ávila   87
Lotus Sutra   167
Lovett, A. W.   155n
Lucifer   14, 16, 18-9
Ludmer, Josefina   196n
Luke, Gospel of   10, 11
Luscombe, David   50n
Lutgard of Trond   189
Luther, Martin   153
Lynch, Cyprian J.   70n

Machuca, María   88n
Macrobius   44-5
Macy, Gary   47n
Madre de Dios, Efrén de la   99n, 103n, 117, 118n-120n, 122n, 123n, 125n 127n, 129
Madre de Dios, Jerónimo Gracián de la   75n
Magdalene, Mary   61-2, 95
Magnificat   110
Mahabharata   167
Malatesta, Edward J.   67n
Maldonado, Felipe,   152n
Mâle, Émile   69, 75n
Man, Paul de   83n, 105n
Mann, Jill   30
Mannarelli, Maria Emma   72n
Manning, Stephen   24n
Mark, Gospel of   10, 11
Marotti, María Ornella   104n
Márquez, Antonio   142n
Martha, St.   161
Martin, F. X.   166n
Martínez, Enrique Llamas   93n, 153n
Martz, Louis   48n
Mary, Blessed Virgin   17, 67-70, 72-3, 77-6, 104, 109-16, 135, 137, 139, 164-5
Mary, St. (sister of St. Martha)   161
Mason, Mary   82n
Matt, Daniel   168n
Matter, E. Ann   96n
Matthew, Gospel of   10, 11
McAndrew, John   68n, 70n, 71n
McGinn, Bernard   49n, 162n, 191n
McNamara, Jo Ann K.   81n
McNeil, Maureen   80n
Mechthild von Hackeborn   86, 189
Mechthild von Magdeburg   9-22
Medina, Doña Elvira González de   118
Medinaceli, Duque de   215n
Meditations on the Life of Christ   70
Meeks, Wayne A.   47n
Méndez, María Agueda   199n
Mendoza, Bishop Álvaro de   87, 128, 215n
Mendoza, Pedro de Quintanilla y   86n
Merrim, Stephanie   194n, 196n
Metford, J. C. J.   75n

223

INDEX

Middleton, Anne 36-7
Migne 9n
Miller, Nancy K. 82n
Miranda, Antonio Núñez de 193n, 197-8
Moffat, Douglas 24n
Mohammed 153
Mojares, Resil B. 97n, 98n
Molina, Juan de 102n
Monter, E. William 155n
Montoya, Juan López de 147-9
Mooney, Catherine M. 96n
Moraía, Mabel 201n
Morán, Juan Antonio 69n
Morillas, Cecilia 169
Moses 26
Mulhall, M. 111n
Murtaugh, Daniel 24n
Muscatine, Charles 34
Myers, Kathleen 81n, 193n, 194n, 195n, 199n, 202n, 210

Nacimiento, Cecilia de 169-84
Nacimiento, María del 64, 169
Neoplatonism 49
Nepaulsingh, Colbert I. 97
Neumann, Bernd 15n, 16n
Neumann, Hans 9n
Noble, David F. 79-80n
Noss, David S. 167n
Noss, John B. 167n

Ocampo, María 125n
Ogilvy, J. D. A. 50n
Ojeda, José Carlos Carrillo 71
Olivares, Julián 159n, 160n, 163n, 166n
Olmedo, Daniel T. 69n
Onrubia, María Luisa García-Nieto 159n
Orellana, Juan de 117

Pabhupada, Swami 167n
Palmer, Martin E. 67n
Parker, Geoffrey 155n
Paul, St. 47, 48, 163, 207, 214
Paz, Octavio 195n, 197n, 208
Pearsall, Derek 24n, 30n
Peden, Margaret Sayers 195n, 197n

Peers, E. Allison 67n
Pelayo, Marcelino Menéndez 141-2
Peña, Antonio de la 53, 54n, 58-9
Peña, Margarita 195n
Pepler, Hilary 24, 26, 27, 28n, 29, 37
Perelmuter, Rosa 195, 196n
Perry, Mary Elizabeth 144n, 151n, 156, 201n
Peyrous, B. 186n, 190n
Philip II, King of Spain 143, 144n, 145n, 148, 152, 155, 158n, 215n
Phillips, Helen 24n
Pinto, Virgilio 205n
Play of Antichrist (*Ludus de Antichristo*) 21-2
Pollard, Alfred W. 42n
Pollard, William F. 50n
Polycarp, St. 161
Poutrin, Isabel 81n, 83n
Powell, Amanda 81n, 174n, 196n, 197n, 199n, 202n
Prádanos, Juan de 117
Pseudo-Dionysius 13n, 41-52
Purgatory 18

Quiroga, Don Gaspar 152, 155

Raitt, Jill 163, 164n, 187n
Raw, Barbara 24n
Raymond of Capua 53-65 *passim*, 84, 98n, 100n, 102, 104n
Réau, Louis 75n
Regina coeli 110
Ribadeneira, Pedro de 97n
Ribera, Francisco de 90, 95, 100n, 101n
Ribera, Juan de 143, 147n
Ricard, Robert 67n
Ricci, Catherine de 189
Richard of St. Victor 29
Richmond, J. A. 166n
Rig-Veda 167
Ringborn, S. 188n
Riquer, Martín de 85n
Rodríguez, Otilio 72n, 73n, 80n, 81n, 107n, 125n, 171n, 174n
Rojan, Cristóbal de 143
Rolle, Richard 29

INDEX

Roney, Lois   45n
Rorem, Paul   48n
Ros, Fidèle de   67n, 68n, 77n
Ross, Stephen   88n
Rossi, John Baptist   113n
Ruano, Lucinio   171n, 172n
Rubin, Miri   47n
Ruh, Kurt   16n
Rule of St. Albert   107, 111n
Russell, Jeffrey Burton   12n, 17n, 18n
Rutledge, Dom D.   28n

Sabat de Rivers, Georgina   72n 74n, 77n, 209n, 210n
Sacred Heart   185-93
Sage, Jack   75n
Saggi, Ludovico   112n
Saint-Saens, Alain   59n
Salazar, María de   124
Salceda, Alberto   197n
Sales, Francis de   73n, 190
Salve Regina   110-1
San Bartolomé, Ana de   108-9, 123, 128-37
San Bernardo, Leonor de   133
San Geronimo, Isabel de   60
San Jerónimo, Manuel de   88n
San Jerónimo, María de   122, 131
San Jose, María de   122, 124, 199n
San Juan, Ana de   122
San Juan de la Cruz, Gerardo de   122, 127, 169n, 173
San Pablo, Isabel de   122
Sanabría, José Rubén   69n, 71n
Sánchez, Hermenegildo Ramírez   71n
Sánchez, Gaspar   143-4
Sánchez, Magdalena S.   59n
Sánchez, Mari   145, 150-1
Sánchez, María Helena   157n
Santa Clara, Agustine de   202n
Santa Cruz, Fernández de   195n, 197-8
Santa María, Pedro de   150
Santa Teresa, Silverio de   64n, 115n, 173
Santo Domingo, Isabel de   109, 122, 128
Santo Domingo, Maria de   53, 58-9
Santos, Ursula de los   122-4
Sarracenus, John   50

Satan   14, 16, 18, 60, 146-7, 149, 151
Saward, John   164
Sayers, Jane   50n
Scheffczyk, Leo   189n
Schipper, Kristofer   167n
Schlau, Stacey   81n, 83n, 107, 108n, 109, 129, 130, 131n, 133n-135n, 171, 172n, 174n
Schmidt, Margot   10n
Schmidt, A. V. C.   23n, 24n, 35
Scholem, Gershom   168n
Scott, Karen   84
Scott, Nina M.   214n
Sebastión, King of Spain   152
Second Shepherds' Play, The   41-52
Seijas, Aguiar y   195n
Senebre, Ricardo   97n
Shakespeare, William   79
Shaprio, Meyer   77n
Shepherd, Geoffrey   24n, 30n
Siger of Brabant   41-52 *passim*
Simpson, James   25n, 34n
Sisters of Penance, the   56, 60
Sixtus IV, Pope   70
Skeat, W. W.   39n
Skeptical Fideism   41-52
Slade, Carol   82
Smet, Joachim   113n, 119n
Smith, Paul Julian   81n, 97n
Smith, Sidonie   105n
Sobrino, Antonio   170, 176, 184
Sobrino, Bachiller Antonio   169
Soreth, Jean   119n
St. Jacques, Raymond   25n
Stahl, William Harris   44n
Staley, Lynn   86n
Staring, Adrian   112n, 114
Starobinski, Jean   93n
Stearns, Mary   46n
Steggink, Otger   99n, 103n, 117, 119, 120n, 125n, 129
Stevens, Martin   46n
Stevenson, J.   161n
Stierli, Josef   189n
Stock, St. Simon   113
Suger, Abbot   165
Sullivan, John   109n
Suso, Henry   189
Szell, Timea   59n

INDEX

Tavormina, M. Teresa 25n, 27n, 28n, 29n, 33n, 337
Tax, Petrus 10, 18n
Tegernsee, Monastery of 21-2
Teresa of Ávila 53, 56n, 59-65, 67-8, 72, 75n, 79-106, 107-139, 141n, 152, 155n, 169-70, 172, 184, 209-11, 213-15
Tertullian 160
Tobin, Frank 10n, 11n, 12n, 13n, 17n, 18n
Tolosana, Carmelo Lisón 144n
Toscano, Sebastión 92
Trabulse, Elías 194, 195n, 197-9, 200n
Trent, Council of 84, 156n
Tugwel, Simon 25

Ulloa, Doña Guiomar 109, 116-19, 129
Urban VI, Pope 54

Valabek, Redemptus Maria 110n
Vasta, Edward 24n
Vaughan, Micéal 52n
Vega, Nazario López de la 200n
Vega, Pedro de la 97n, 99n
Velasco, Sherry Marie 81n
Vesach, Tomas de 54n
Vieira, Antonio 197-8
Villanueva, J. Pérez 157n
Villena, Marquesa de 215n

Visitationist Order 185-93
Vitoria, Diego de 58
Vollmann-Profe, Gisela 21n
Voragine, Jacobus de 97n

Waldron, R. 24n
Walker, J. L. 167n
Walsh, Kilian 161-2n
Walsh, James 35n, 43n, 51n, 100n
Walsh, Terrance 78n
Walthaus, Rina 97n
Watts, Pauline Moffitt 74n
Weber, Alison 80-81, 95, 105n, 107, 108n, 121-2, 138, 202n, 209n, 210, 211n, 213, 215n
Weckmann, Luis 74n
Weinstein, Donald 93, 101n
William of Ockham 41
Williamson, Amy R. 81n, 89
Williamson, Edwin 72n
Wilson, Christopher C. 73n, 76n
Wippel, John F. 41n, 45n
Witchcraft 156, 205
Wittig, J. S. 24n
Wright, A. D. 144n
Wright, John 21n
Wright, Wendy M. 190n

Young, Karl 15n

Zumárraga, Juan de 67, 75